D1712427

VOLUME 530 NOVEMBER 1993

THE ANNALS

of The American Academy of Political
and Social Science

RICHARD D. LAMBERT, *Editor*
ALAN W. HESTON, *Associate Editor*

INTERMINORITY AFFAIRS IN THE U.S.:
PLURALISM AT THE CROSSROADS

Special Editor of this Volume
PETER I. ROSE
Smith College
Northampton
Massachusetts

SAGE Periodicals Press *THOUSAND OAKS LONDON NEW DELHI*

THE ANNALS

© 1993 *by* The American Academy *of* Political *and* Social Science

Editorial Office: 3937 Chestnut Street, Philadelphia, PA 19104.

For information about membership* (individuals only) and subscriptions (institutions), address:

SAGE PUBLICATIONS, INC.
2455 Teller Road
Thousand Oaks, CA 91320

From India and South Asia, write to:
SAGE PUBLICATIONS INDIA Pvt. Ltd.
P.O. Box 4215
New Delhi 110 048
INDIA

From the UK, Europe, the Middle East and Africa, write to:
SAGE PUBLICATIONS LTD
6 Bonhill Street
London EC2A 4PU
UNITED KINGDOM

SAGE Production Staff: LINDA GRAY, LIANN LECH, and JANELLE LeMASTER
*Please note that members of The Academy receive THE ANNALS with their membership.
Library of Congress Catalog Card Number 92-62094
International Standard Serial Number ISSN 0002-7162
International Standard Book Number ISBN 0-8039-5112-4 (Vol. 530, 1993 paper)
International Standard Book Number ISBN 0-8039-5109-4 (Vol. 530, 1993 cloth)
Manufactured in the United States of America. First printing, November 1993.

The articles appearing in THE ANNALS are indexed in *Book Review Index, Public Affairs Information Service Bulletin, Social Sciences Index, Current Contents, General Periodicals Index, Academic Index, Pro-Views,* and *Combined Retrospective Index Sets.* They are also abstracted and indexed in *ABC Pol Sci, Historical Abstracts, Human Resources Abstracts, Social Sciences Citation Index, United States Political Science Documents, Social Work Research & Abstracts, Sage Urban Studies Abstracts, International Political Science Abstracts, America: History and Life, Sociological Abstracts, Managing Abstracts, Social Planning/Policy & Development Abstracts, Automatic Subject Citation Alert, Book Review Digest, Work Related Abstracts, Periodica Islamica,* and/or *Family Resources Database,* and are available on microfilm from University Microfilms, Ann Arbor, Michigan.

Information about membership rates, institutional subscriptions, and back issue prices may be found on the facing page.

Advertising. Current rates and specifications may be obtained by writing to THE ANNALS Advertising and Promotion Manager at the Thousand Oaks office (address above).

Claims. Claims for undelivered copies must be made no later than three months follow month of publication. The publisher will supply missing copies when losses have b sustained in transit and when the reserve stock will permit.

Change of Address. Six weeks' advance notice must be given when notifying of chan address to ensure proper identification. Please specify name of journal. Send address ch to: THE ANNALS, c/o Sage Publications, Inc., 2455 Teller Road, Thousand Oaks, CA

Origin and Purpose. The Academy was organized December 14, 1889, to promote the progress of political and social science, especially through publications and meetings. The Academy does not take sides in controverted questions, but seeks to gather and present reliable information to assist the public in forming an intelligent and accurate judgment.

Meetings. The Academy occasionally holds a meeting in the spring extending over two days.

Publications. THE ANNALS is the bimonthly publication of The Academy. Each issue contains articles on some prominent social or political problem, written at the invitation of the editors. Also, monographs are published from time to time, numbers of which are distributed to pertinent professional organizations. These volumes constitute important reference works on the topics with which they deal, and they are extensively cited by authorities throughout the United States and abroad. The papers presented at the meetings of The Academy are included in THE ANNALS.

Membership. Each member of The Academy receives THE ANNALS and may attend the meetings of The Academy. Membership is open only to individuals. Annual dues: $42.00 for the regular paperbound edition (clothbound, $60.00). Add $9.00 per year for membership outside the U.S.A. Members may also purchase single issues of THE ANNALS for $13.00 each (clothbound, $18.00). Add $2.00 for shipping and handling on all prepaid orders.

Subscriptions. THE ANNALS (ISSN 0002-7162) is published six times annually—in January, March, May, July, September, and November. Institutions may subscribe to THE ANNALS at the annual rate: $132.00 (clothbound, $156.00). California institutions: $141.57 paperbound, $167.31 clothbound. Add $9.00 per year for subscriptions outside the U.S.A. Institutional rates for single issues: $24.00 each (clothbound, $29.00). California institutions: $25.74 paperbound, $31.10 clothbound.

Second class postage paid at Thousand Oaks, California, and additional offices.

Single issues of THE ANNALS may be obtained by individuals who are not members of The Academy for $17.00 each (clothbound, $26.00). California residents: $18.23 paperbound, $27.89 clothbound. Add $2.00 for shipping and handling on all prepaid orders. Single issues of THE ANNALS have proven to be excellent supplementary texts for classroom use. Direct inquiries regarding adoptions to THE ANNALS c/o Sage Publications (address below).

All correspondence concerning membership in The Academy, dues renewals, inquiries about membership status, and/or purchase of single issues of THE ANNALS should be sent to THE ANNALS c/o Sage Publications, Inc., 2455 Teller Road, Thousand Oaks, CA 91320. Telephone: (805) 499-0721; FAX/Order line: (805) 499-0871. *Please note that orders under $30 must be prepaid.* Sage affiliates in London and India will assist institutional subscribers abroad with regard to orders, claims, and inquiries for both subscriptions and single issues.

Printed on recycled, acid-free paper

THE ANNALS

of The American Academy *of* Political *and* Social Science

RICHARD D. LAMBERT, *Editor*
ALAN W. HESTON, *Associate Editor*

--- **FORTHCOMING** ---

THE EUROPEAN COMMUNITY:
TO 1992 AND BEYOND
Special Editor: Pierre-Henri Laurent

Volume 531   January 1994

FOREIGN LANGUAGE POLICY:
AN AGENDA FOR CHANGE
Special Editor: Richard D. Lambert

Volume 532   March 1994

TRENDS IN U.S.-CARIBBEAN RELATIONS
Special Editor: Anthony P. Maingot

Volume 533   May 1994

See page 3 for information on Academy membership and
purchase of single volumes of **The Annals.**

CONTENTS

PREFACE . . . . *Peter I. Rose*   7

HISTORICAL ENCOUNTERS: INTERGROUP
   RELATIONS IN A "NATION OF NATIONS" . . . . *Ronald H. Bayor*   14

VOLUNTARY IMMIGRATION AND CONTINUING
   ENCOUNTERS BETWEEN BLACKS: THE
   POST-QUINCENTENARY CHALLENGE. . . . . . . *Roy Simón Bryce-Laporte*   28

THE TURBULENT FRIENDSHIP:
   BLACK-JEWISH RELATIONS
   IN THE 1990s . . . . *Milton D. Morris and Gary E. Rubin*   42

OLD MINORITIES, NEW IMMIGRANTS:
   ASPIRATIONS, HOPES, AND FEARS . . . . *Rita J. Simon*   61

THE NEW SECOND GENERATION:
   SEGMENTED ASSIMILATION
   AND ITS VARIANTS . . . . *Alejandro Portes and Min Zhou*   74

RIGHTS, RESOURCES, AND MEMBERSHIP:
   CIVIL RIGHTS MODELS IN FRANCE
   AND THE UNITED STATES . . . . *Jeremy Hein*   97

MULTICULTURALISM:
   BATTLEGROUND OR MEETING GROUND? . . . . *Ronald Takaki*   109

IS ASSIMILATION DEAD? . . . . *Nathan Glazer*   122

LIVING PROOF:
   IS HAWAII THE ANSWER? . . . . *Glen Grant and Dennis M. Ogawa*   137

RECRAFTING THE COMMON GOOD:
   IMMIGRATION AND COMMUNITY . . . . *Robert L. Bach*   155

AN AGENDA FOR TOMORROW: IMMIGRATION
   POLICY AND ETHNIC POLICIES . . . . *Lawrence H. Fuchs*   171

"OF EVERY HUE AND CASTE":
   RACE, IMMIGRATION, AND
   PERCEPTIONS OF PLURALISM . . . . *Peter I. Rose*   187

BOOK DEPARTMENT   203

INDEX   221

BOOK DEPARTMENT CONTENTS

INTERNATIONAL RELATIONS AND POLITICS

LeBLANC, LAWRENCE J. *The United States and
the Genocide Convention.* Eric Markusen 203

AFRICA, ASIA, AND LATIN AMERICA

GUHA, RAMACHANDRA. *The Unquiet Woods: Ecological
Change and Peasant Resistance in the Himalaya.* Renu Khator 204

HARRIS, RICHARD L. *Marxism, Socialism, and
Democracy in Latin America.* Sandor Halebsky 205

HAYNES, DOUGLAS E. *Rhetoric and Ritual in
Colonial India: The Shaping of a Public Culture in
Surat City, 1852-1928.* George H. Conklin 206

EUROPE

BLACK, CYRIL E., JOHNATHAN E. HELMREICH,
PAUL C. HELMREICH, CHARLES P. ISSAWI, and
A. JAMES McADAMS. *Rebirth: A History of
Europe since World War II.* Joe Amato 207

BREMENT, MARSHALL. *Reaching out to Moscow:
From Confrontation to Cooperation;*
KRIESBERG, LOUIS. *International Conflict Resolution:
The U.S.-USSR and Middle East Cases.* William J. Weida 207

HORNE, THOMAS A. *Property Rights and Poverty:
Political Argument in Britain, 1605-1834.* Roy L. Brooks 208

UNITED STATES

BOBBITT, PHILIP. *Constitutional Interpretation.* John B. Gates 210

COSTAIN, ANNE N. *Inviting Women's Rebellion: A Political Process
Interpretation of the Women's Movement.* Joan C. Tronto 210

PRATT, ROBERT A. *The Color of Their Skin: Education and
Race in Richmond, Virginia, 1954-1989.* Arnold A. Sio 211

SOCIOLOGY

REINHARZ, SHULAMIT. *Feminist Methods in Social Research.* M. F. Stuck 212

ECONOMICS

BEST, MICHAEL H. *The New Competition:
Institutions of Industrial Restructuring.* Joseph W. Weiss 213

ROSNER, DAVID and GERALD MARKOWITZ.
*Deadly Dust: Silicosis and the Politics of
Occupational Disease in Twentieth Century America;*
REICH, MICHAEL R. *Toxic Politics: Responding
to Chemical Disasters.* Graham K. Wilson 216

PREFACE

"America as a multicultural society" was the theme of a special issue of *The Annals* published in 1981. Edited by Milton M. Gordon, a sociologist well-known for his writings on assimilation, it was a comparative examination of the backgrounds, cultures, and characteristics of America's diverse peoples, with a principal focus on the largest ethnic groups and racial cohorts. While almost all of the articles addressed, in one way or another, the asymmetrical character of dominant-minority relations in this country and the ways various groups have sought to gain full equality, several focused primary attention on relations between minorities, including those long assumed to be allies.

In the 12 years since that issue of *The Annals* was published, the positive, upbeat, unifying concept of "multicultural"—long associated with the ideology of hyphen-connecting pluralism—underwent a significant sea change. With the mere addition of a brief suffix, it turned from a descriptive adjective into a controversial shibboleth subject to a variety of interpretations.

"Multiculturalism" became the rallying cry of a movement for group-based recognition for some who felt they had been too long relegated to the margins of society and to the footnotes of intellectual discourse. To others, not least certain old-fashioned liberal integrationists, the term came to be seen as representing a scary strategy that intentionally threatened to reverse the course of integration and tear apart the very fabric of society.

The fact is that the tensions that underlay the new semantic—and ideological—debate have long been a fundamental reality of life in the United States. From its inception, this country has been a nation of shifting coalitions of interest groups. Major interests often centered on the struggles of minorities trying to move into the mainstream and the resistance of those who felt threatened by the presence of the strangers in their midst. Periodically, smoldering embers of nativism were fanned afresh, making them central topics of public concern. There were flare-ups in the 1850s and the 1890s; in the period right after World War I, when the Ku Klux Klan was again on the rise; and in the 1930s. It happened again during the civil rights struggle of the 1950s and 1960s and, especially, in the early days of the Black Power and Black Consciousness movements that came in its wake. The militancy of African Americans and of other ethnic/racial, gender, and sexual-preference groups, whose leaders modeled much of their rhetoric and challenge on the consciousness-raising example of blacks and their allies, led to considerable gains. It also triggered another backlash, especially among those whom S. M. Lipset and Earl Raab once called the "once hads"—those with a greater stake in the past than in the present—and the "never hads," who argued that, if it were not for those "special-privileged minorities," we would be fine.[1]

1. Seymour Martin Lipset and Earl Raab, *The Politics of Unreason: Right-Wing Extremism in America, 1790-1970* (New York: Harper & Row, 1970), pp. 460-82.

Demands for "community control," "affirmative action," and "open enroll-ment" coupled with outbursts of civil disorder including rioting and looting in a number of cities across the country in the mid and late 1960s offered a dramatic resurgence of the old—if increasingly complex—roller-coaster phenomenon.

In the past, periods of dramatic, often violent upheaval seemed to be followed by a time of regrouping, rethinking, revision, resignation, and modest attempts at reconciliation. The classic pattern was to respond to pressure before irrevocable breakdown by stretching the tolerance limits, providing opportunities for inclusion for at least some of those who had been left behind. Viewed as co-optation by some and tokenism by others, the practice still served to cool down the simmering caldrons. Such was surely the case in the 1970s, when many solicitations of those who called for greater recognition and wider access were met with measures to do both.

In point of fact, in the days of the Nixon and Ford administrations, many of the demands—particularly those relating to affirmative action—were institutionalized. They continued to be met during the Carter administration. More and more minorities were able to find access to places from which they had formally been barred or to which it had been extremely difficult to gain admission.

While academic institutions tended to set the examples, governments, including the federal government, played a most significant role in opening doors and providing access. All of that seemed to change with the election of Ronald Reagan and the return of the Republicans to power. Almost immedi-ately, they shifted many national priorities, especially in the realm of civil rights and concern for those most marginal. The new administration not only slowed but tried to reverse the course of action that every president since FDR had followed.

Reagan had campaigned on a platform of reducing the role of government in many spheres of life, not least in the critical arena of intergroup relations. Once in control, the new president moved to keep promises made prior to his election. In addition to those on both the political and religious Right, many white working- and middle-class Americans felt that, at last, there was someone in the White House who understood their plight and was not only willing to articulate it but was acting to stop the drift of "the welfare state."

Under the first Reagan administration, hundreds of programs designed to aid the poor were disbanded, thousands of conservative judges were ap-pointed to federal courts, and millions of dollars were diverted to matters other than human services. In many ways, the representatives of the govern-ment and their sympathizers were returning to what sociologist Michael Lewis once called the "individual-as-central" sensibility,[2] the old Puritan idea that success and failure are highly personal, not collective. They contended that, in America, one must always be encouraged to strive to be the master

2. Michael Lewis, *The Culture of Inequality* (Amherst: University of Massachusetts Press, 1978).

of one's own fate, that too much reliance on others, particularly on the institutions of government, threatened the moral fiber and weakened the spirit of a true meritocracy.

While emphasizing the work ethic and praising individual initiative, the proponents of Reagan's policies reemphasized the importance of patriotism and the idea that "we are all Americans"—surely a positive message. They decried group-oriented policies as divisive threats to the *unum*.

Such concerns were expressed in many quarters. For example, many white ethnics, some of whom had become Reagan Democrats, argued that efforts designed to redress past grievances of various groups on the basis of targets and goals were unfair exercises in reverse discrimination. Others, playing a variation on the theme, argued that such favoritism was constitutionally questionable because it gave special advantages to certain designated groups.[3]

Many of the old civil rights advocates were troubled, but they were not entirely surprised by what was happening. They had seen the handwriting on the wall. Still, not a few expressed the views that the anticipated retrenchment would trigger new outbursts of protest from the quarters of those who seemed to be losing the most from new federal action—or, better put, inaction. Yet, despite their premonitions and their predictions, for almost the entire period of Reagan's presidency and, it turned out, Bush's, too, those concerned about continued discrimination against minorities watched but did little to attempt to stop the clear erosion of federal involvement and even greater abandonment of national commitment.

During the same period, the very rich got richer and the middle class as well as those in the working class began to worry about their own job security and downward mobility. Both fears were to be proven justified. At the same time, the poor, especially those in the inner cities, suffered the most as both anomie and alienation, exacerbated by family breakdown, new forms of escape through drugs, and abandonment, seemed to reach new depths. Unable to strike out at the root sources of their persisting frustration, many turned on their immediate neighbors, recapitulating a pattern familiar to students of American social history but surprising to many others. African Americans, Mexican Americans, Puerto Ricans, and some with origins in neighboring islands were among those most directly involved in these conflicts. Sometimes their antagonists were representatives of old white minorities who had stayed in the city centers when the others moved to more affluent areas; more often they were members of newer groups, recent immigrants from the Caribbean, East Asia—particularly China and Korea—and Mexico, as well as refugees from Cuba, the former USSR, and the countries of Southeast Asia. (Most of the newcomers had entered the country after the passage of the 1965 immigration amendments, which had eliminated the old quota system.)

3. See Harold Orlans and June O'Neill, eds., *Affirmative Action Revisited*, vol. 523, *The Annals* of the American Academy of Political and Social Science (Sept. 1992).

A steady stream of newspaper accounts—with datelines from Miami, Oakland, Washington, D.C., Brooklyn, and Los Angeles—recorded and described the mounting interethnic tensions, highlighting outbursts of conflict that were occurring in city after city across the country. Almost simultaneously, a spate of public debates and academic fora on identity politics became common fare on radio and television and in college lecture halls. These discussions were often responses to specific chain reactions such as that triggered by the death of an African American child hit by a car driven by an Orthodox Jew in Brooklyn, who, allegedly, jumped a red light—an accident that was almost immediately followed by the murder of a Hasidic man by a black assailant. Another such example was the Rodney King affair in Los Angeles and the trial and acquittal of the policemen involved in the beating of Mr. King, which triggered, in April 1992, the worst urban riot in U.S. history. The popular culture was caught up in such events, too.

Hard-hitting films about New York City, like Spike Lee's *Do the Right Thing*; colorful novels such as Tom Wolfe's *Bonfire of the Vanities*[4]; and journalistic commentaries such as Jim Sleeper's *Closest of Strangers*[5] brought a message of dissensus to millions. Together these media vehicles suggested that, in New York and, as Nathan Glazer and Daniel Patrick Moynihan once put it, "in those parts of America which resemble New York,"[6] we were moving way "beyond the melting pot" but in directions hardly imagined as recently as the 1960s, when their study of ethnic diversity and Milton Gordon's *Assimilation in American Life*[7] were first published.

Instead of the cautious optimism about the viability of pluralism, what was being conveyed on the air and on the screen, from the podium and in print was a depressing portrayal of the paroxysms of a city—of many cities—and of a country being torn apart by disaffected and disillusioned minorities, with each faction flying the flag of its ethnic and racial particularism.

Powerful images. And they are significant. But how consequential? Has the movement toward ever greater integration been so thoroughly reversed that we are facing what Harold Isaacs feared when he warned of reverting to "the idols of the tribe"[8] and what Arthur M. Schlesinger, Jr.,[9] now sees as an imminent "balkanization" of our own society (a phrase that has taken on renewed poignancy in the past two years)? Or are we overreacting to what is but another temporary setback, another time for reassessing and revising

    4. Tom Wolfe, *Bonfire of the Vanities* (New York: Farrar, Straus & Giroux, 1988).
    5. Jim Sleeper, *The Closest of Strangers* (New York: Norton, 1990).
    6. Nathan Glazer and Daniel Patrick Moynihan, *Beyond the Melting Pot: The Negroes, Puerto Ricans, Jews, Italians and Irish of New York City* (Cambridge: MIT Press, 1963), p. 5.
    7. Milton M. Gordon, *Assimilation in American Life: The Role of Race, Religion, and National Origins* (New York: Oxford University Press, 1964).
    8. Harold Isaacs, *The Idols of the Tribe: Group Identity and Political Change* (New York: Harper & Row, 1975).
    9. Arthur M. Schlesinger, Jr., *The Disuniting of America: Reflections on a Multicultural Society* (Knoxville, TN: Whittle Communications, 1991).

strategies to enhance inclusion on the rocky road to national unity in what is still one of the world's only truly multiethnic societies?

Taking the latter position, Deborah Sontag sees "the inter-ethnic clashes of the last year [and, presumably, of the last few years] . . . as growing pains."[10] Speaking for many, she suggests that "certainly the antagonism of the moment pales in comparison to the vehement nativism that followed World War I, or the overt hatred of the 1850's and 1890's. And few expect the situation to boil over into the bloody tensions and closing borders of some European countries."[11]

The jury is still out.

ABOUT THIS VOLUME

The present issue of *The Annals* is an attempt to carefully and critically consider the varied viewpoints and to closely examine interminority affairs in the United States today both in light of the past and in terms of the future.

What the invited contributors—historians, sociologists, economists, and political scientists—have in common is that all are specialists in the study of racial and ethnic relations in the United States. But as we differ in our approaches and research techniques and writing styles, we also differ in the assessment of what is going on today, the roles played by various actors in the streets and in the universities, in our predictions of the future, and, for those willing to make them, in recommendations for public policy relating to interminority affairs in the next century.

While not designated as such in the table of contents, the volume is divisible into three unequal parts. The first deals with a series of encounters between members of various racial and ethnic groups in the United States from its beginnings to the present day. It includes a general essay by historian Ronald H. Bayor of the Georgia Institute of Technology, editor of the *Journal of Ethnic Studies*, and another on the largely neglected story of voluntary black immigrants and their relationship to others, including other blacks, by Roy Simón Bryce-Laporte, a sociologist who is the director of Africana and Latin American studies at Colgate University. Milton D. Morris, vice president of research at the Joint Center on Political and Economic Studies in Washington, D.C., and Gary E. Rubin, director of national affairs at the American Jewish Committee, together prepared a particularly thoughtful article on what they label "the turbulent friendship" between Jewish and African Americans. Their very timely piece is complemented by another study in intergroup attitudes: American University sociologist Rita J. Simon's assessment of the aspirations, hopes, and fears of new immigrants in contrast

10. Deborah Sontag, "The Nation: Calls to Restrict Immigration Come from Many Quarters," *New York Times*, 13 Dec. 1992. Copyright © 1992 by The New York Times Company. Reprinted by permission.

11. Ibid.

to older minorities. The section ends with two comparative essays. The first is an important contribution to the literature on acculturation by two sociologists well-known for their writings on immigration and resettlement, Alejandro Portes of Johns Hopkins University and Min Zhou of Louisiana State. It introduces a new concept, segmented assimilation, and it looks at differences within the United States. The second, by Jeremy Hein, a sociologist and specialist on refugee policy currently teaching at the University of Wisconsin in Eau Claire, is entitled "Rights, Resources, and Membership." Hein compares U.S. and French models of civil rights practices and discusses their significance in the two societies.

One article bridges the other sections of this volume. It is "Multiculturalism: Battleground or Meeting Ground?" by one of the University of California's historians, Ronald Takaki, author of *Strangers from a Different Shore*.

The last five articles look, from rather different angles, at the "nation of nations" motif and the theme of civic unity in a society seen by many of its own citizens—especially the "never hads" and "once hads" referred to previously—and, increasingly, those who might be called traditional minorities, as more divided than ever. Ironically, many outside the United States still look to its practices as a possible model for resolving their own "ethnic dilemmas," the subject and title of a book by the sociologist Nathan Glazer of Harvard.

Glazer poses the broad question, "Is assimilation the answer?" and seeks to answer it. American studies specialists at the University of Hawaii in Honolulu, Glen Grant and Dennis M. Ogawa, ask a related question. Zeroing in on the situation on the islands, they ask, "Is Hawaii the answer [for the rest of America]?"

Sociologist Robert L. Bach and political scientist Lawrence H. Fuchs, both well-known scholars in the study of immigration and immigration policy, each discuss what Bach calls "recrafting the common good." Bach's article focuses on little-discussed evidence of positive interaction between new immigrants and established residents and the particular role of voluntary organizations in the reconstruction of communities riven with conflict. Fuchs's article is complementary but very different. Once a speech writer on immigration issues for John F. Kennedy and, more recently, executive director of the Select Commission on Immigration appointed by Jimmy Carter, Fuchs offers, among other things, an imaginative draft of the speech he would like President Clinton to make on immigration and intergroup policies.

The last essay is my own. While drafted before all but one of the other articles was received, it touches on many of the issues raised in each of them and, not surprisingly, provides yet another take on the key concept of pluralism and the many slogans and metaphors that occur again and again in debates over interminority affairs in the United States.

" 'Of Every Hue and Caste' " is not a summing up but, in many ways, a cautionary tale. For all the expansion of ethnic diversity and the significant achievements in lowering formal barriers to discrimination in recent years, the persistence of a specific—and specifically American—form of racism continues to be our most vexing problem. In any number of ways, tenth-generation Americans from Africa are still the odd men out. They remain, in the aggregate, more alienated than even the most recent arrivals from Asia and Latin America. Many are resentful of the influx of such newcomers poised, as they see it, to leap-frog their way into the mainstream, recapitulating an old and familiar pattern.

When it comes to considering race, immigration, and the challenges of pluralism for blacks, it seems that *plus ça change, plus c'est la même chose.*

PETER I. ROSE

ANNALS, *AAPSS*, **530**, November 1993

Historical Encounters:
Intergroup Relations
in a "Nation of Nations"

By RONALD H. BAYOR

ABSTRACT: Threats to interests and values are the basis of inter-group conflicts. This article looks historically at conflict and cooperation in America to reveal the factors and events involved in both. Various groups—Dutch, Irish, blacks, Chinese, Jews, Italians, Hispanics, and others—are discussed, and interminority relationships in New York, Philadelphia, Boston, Miami, and elsewhere are analyzed. Competition over political power, jobs, neighborhoods, and cultural values was often an essential element of conflict, as were explosive issues that quickly and forcefully pitted groups against each other. Also a factor in an emerging conflict was a group's insecurity and defensiveness within the larger society, which had often been the result of nativistic or other attacks on the minority. Interminority affairs are complex, involving both the minority groups' perceptions of each other and their treatment by the majority.

Ronald H. Bayor is a professor of history at the Georgia Institute of Technology with a joint appointment with the School of Public Policy. He is also founding and present editor of the Journal of American Ethnic History. *He has published primarily in the area of race and ethnic relations in cities and is the author of* Neighbors in Conflict: The Irish, Germans, Jews, and Italians of New York City, 1929-1941; Fiorello La Guardia: Ethnicity and Reform; *and a forthcoming study of the impact of race on the development of Atlanta.*

A S a competitive multiethnic society, the United States has seen a good deal of ethnic and racial tension and conflict. Sometimes these conflicts have been of the majority-minority type, in which the main group in the country strikes out at one of its minority elements. Other times, though, it is two or more minority groups that clash. To understand interminority friction, conflicts with the larger society must also be analyzed, since the two situations are related as to causes and have an impact on each other. They provide clues and the framework for comprehending interminority clashes and lay out the setting in which minority groups exist.

The normal tensions and frictions that develop in the process of group interaction can at times lead to conflict, which can become violent. The underlying element in these conflicts is a sense of threat—a feeling, based on realistic or unrealistic criteria, that one's own group is under attack in regard to its interests or values. The basis for a group's concern can stem from a variety of issues—jobs, political power, neighborhood control, foreign policy. Conflicts often develop in a step-by-step fashion as competitive tensions slowly increase. They can also emerge, however, with lightning speed as an explosive issue or event occurs, one that immediately puts groups into contention.[1]

1. For a more extensive discussion of competition and conflict, see Ronald H. Bayor, *Neighbors in Conflict: The Irish, Germans, Jews, and Italians of New York City, 1929-1941*, 2d ed. (Urbana: University of Illinois Press, 1988), pp. 1-2, 168-69.

There are also examples in American history of groups living together peacefully and cooperating with each other. Yet, if circumstances and perceptions change, these same groups can enter into an intense conflict. Basically, given the competitive tensions between ethnic and racial groups found in this "nation of nations," conflict occurs often and is more the norm than cooperative intergroup relations.

COLONIAL CONFLICT

Intergroup conflicts emerged early in American life and can be traced through its history to the present. One of the first examples of an ethnic clash took place in New Amsterdam/New York between the Dutch and English in the 1680s and illustrated the typical interactive tensions that were to lead so often to conflict in the subsequent three hundred years. The Dutch-English friction centered on economic and political issues as the English sought to assert their control over the city after their initial conquest of New Amsterdam in 1664 and again after the city returned to their mastery in 1674, following a brief restoration of Dutch authority. Dutch residents, reacting to the rivalry with the English, resentful of their control, and having difficulty succeeding "within the new English order," supported Leisler's Rebellion in 1689—an attempt to reassert some Dutch influence and power in the city. After initial success, the rebellion failed. Although tensions remained afterward, there was also evidence of cooperation, partly due to a slave rebellion that united the white community—an early example of European-American harmony in the face of a common racial threat.[2]

NATIVISM AND THE IRISH

Leisler's Rebellion was a relatively mild incident compared to the violence that raked America in the nineteenth century in regard to the nativism and racism of that era. The most serious outbursts involved the Irish Catholics who began arriving in large numbers in the 1820s and clashed often with white native-born Protestants in a number of cities in the subsequent decades and for various reasons. In Philadelphia, Boston, New York, and other centers where Irish immigration was strong, issues involving politics, religion, neighborhoods, jobs, and schools as well as class friction and cultural values pitted the two groups against each other.

Rivalry over employment, neighborhoods, religion, and politics was evident early, and later the question of who controlled the schools served as a particularly explosive issue in New York and Philadelphia. For native-born Protestants, the Irish came to be perceived as a very real threat to their cultural and political hegemony in a number of places, and the majority group reacted. The Irish, too, felt threatened, with their church under attack, and jobs and housing denied them. They also re-

acted. "By the late 1820s [in New York] the siege mentality of the Irish was such that they were apparently all too ready to react aggressively to any threat, real or imagined, posed by the larger Protestant society." A sense of threat, not just interaction between the groups, led to conflict.[3]

Oscar Handlin writes in his *Boston's Immigrants* that the initial interaction between religious or other groups "produced no conflict, until the old social order and the values upon which it rested were endangered."[4] In Lowell, Massachusetts, as the migration of poor Irish increased, relations between the Irish and Yankees deteriorated. "By 1850," as historian Brian Mitchell notes, "the Irish presence in Lowell had become less of a curiosity and more of a threat."[5] In New York, Philadelphia, and elsewhere, battles between Protestants and Irish Catholics grew

3. Paul A. Gilje, *The Road to Mobocracy: Popular Disorder in New York City, 1763-1834* (Chapel Hill: University of North Carolina Press, 1987), p. 137. Information on relations between Irish Catholics and native white Protestants is drawn from the following works: Oscar Handlin, *Boston's Immigrants* (1941; reprint ed., New York: Atheneum, 1968); Gilje, *Road to Mobocracy*, pp. 112, 125, 127-33, 137-42; Brian C. Mitchell, *The Paddy Camps: The Irish of Lowell, 1821-1861* (Urbana: University of Illinois Press, 1988); Ray Allen Billington, *The Protestant Crusade, 1800-1860* (1938; reprint ed., Chicago: Quadrangle Books, 1964), pp. 70-71, 73-76, 142-58, 220-37, 380-97; Amy Bridges, *A City in the Republic: Anti-Bellum New York and the Origins of Machine Politics* (New York: Cambridge University Press, 1984), pp. 31-32, 86, 92-93, 96-98; Sean Wilentz, *Chants Democratic: New York City and the Rise of the American Working Class, 1788-1850* (New York: Oxford University Press, 1984), pp. 85-86.

4. Handlin, *Boston's Immigrants*, p. 178.

5. Mitchell, *Paddy Camps*, p. 99.

2. Thomas J. Archdeacon, *New York City, 1664-1710: Conquest and Change* (Ithaca, NY: Cornell University Press, 1976), pp. 97-99, 102, 113-15, 142, 145-46.

more intense and violent in the 1830s and 1840s as migration from Ireland increased and Irish competition was more strongly felt. And so it went around the country. Of particular intensity were the 1844 riots in Philadelphia, which lasted a number of days and included the burning of Catholic churches. Fighting between the army protecting a church and native American rioters indicated the fury of this clash.

Beginning in the 1830s, local nativist political parties emerged on the basis of a fear of Catholicism; a desire to reassert Protestant power and hegemony; a concern that the Irish immigration, made up of many unskilled workers, was pushing the country to industrialize faster, thereby lowering the status and limiting the opportunities of Protestant skilled craftsmen; a perception that Catholic workers lowered wages; and a sense of political competition with Catholics. Class friction and cultural factors—religion and differing opinions about temperance—were part of the conflict as these parties developed into a national entity in the 1840s under the American Republican Party label. By the 1850s, the Know-Nothing or American party had become a formidable political organization whose growth was due to its anti-Catholic, anti-immigrant, and anti-Irish themes. Politicians who saw the nativist movement as a way to win votes often exacerbated the conflict to stay in office—a common but harmful political tool used during subsequent decades.

With Catholicism viewed as an invading, alien, authoritarian religion that would subvert America's republican institutions, and the Irish perceived as militant defenders and propagators of that faith, along with the other competitive issues involving real or imagined threats, it was inevitable that these ethnic-religious groups would clash.

One interesting element of these clashes that was to appear again among other groups 120 years later was the school-control issue. In 1840s New York, this consisted of Irish Catholic and Protestant differences in regard to the hiring of Catholic teachers, the use of schoolbooks that disparaged and belittled Catholicism, and, in general, Protestant proselytizing among Catholic schoolchildren (also an issue in Philadelphia). In turn, Catholic attempts to secure public monies to fund their own schools indicated to Protestants an attack on the public school system, a bulwark of republican values. The issue of who was to control the public schools, and the rights of minorities in them, was still a conflict flash point in the Jewish-black battles of the late 1960s in New York.

Irish battles with majority Protestants in which the minority had been abused for years and lived an insecure existence in a society dominated by its competitors produced a group strongly desirous of protecting its gains and defensive in its relations with other ethnic or racial groups. As the Irish battled with the Yankees for a place in the ethnic hierarchy, so did they clash with those minorities seen as threatening Irish advancement. Their searing early experience with the white native-born Protestant majority affected their relations with all other groups.

RACIAL CLASHES

Life in antebellum America consisted of numerous ethnic clashes over the years, but racial hostilities also occurred frequently. Once again, real or perceived threats to interests and values were the causative factors. Many whites of this period, including the Irish, saw blacks as economic competitors, as rivals for neighborhoods, and in general as a threat to white dominance. In New York, the sense of threat was enhanced during the 1830s by rumors suggesting that blacks, with abolitionist support, were imminently going to wrest control of some white areas in the city's lower-class sections. Imagined threats to white interests played a role in the ensuing clash. One indication of this conflict was the riot that occurred in 1834 in New York, which was directed at blacks and abolitionists. With large numbers of whites taking part in the assault against blacks and their institutions and property, the militia had to be called out to deal with the violence.[6]

The most significant outburst of this type in the nineteenth century was the brutal draft riots of 1863 in which mainly Irish mobs and gangs attacked blacks in New York. As Iver Bernstein, a historian who studied the riots, writes, it indicated an effort to eliminate the "presence of the black community."[7] Black-Irish class

and racial friction over jobs and neighborhoods had been evident for years and played a role in outbursts such as the 1834 assault as well as lesser incidents. This friction and occasional violence indicated a long-term conflict that reached a fever pitch and large-scale involvement when an explosive issue was added to these already strained intergroup relations. The explosive issue was twofold: the new Civil War aim of freeing the slaves and a draft policy that weighed heavily on the poor. Already feeling an assault on their interests —longshoreman and other jobs, political power, neighborhood homogeneity—and cultural values—through Republican temperance reforms and anti-Catholic abolitionists—the Irish in New York were concerned that abolition of slavery would send thousands of newly freed slaves to New York to compete for Irish-held jobs. Conscription into the army to work for this goal at a time when the draft was perceived as a Republican Party tool to weaken Irish dominance in certain occupations and exempt the rich resulted in the most serious outburst of racial violence in the nineteenth century.

While many Irish took no part in the riot and other Irish served as soldiers or policemen fighting the rioters, the riot was seen within the context of an Irish-black conflict. There were other elements in this clash—class antagonism, pro-slavery and pro-Confederate attitudes— but the essence of it was the racial friction.[8]

6. Wilentz, *Chants Democratic*, pp. 264-68, 315-17, 324, 344-46; Gilje, *Road to Mobocracy*, pp. 156-58, 160, 162-68.

7. Iver Bernstein, *The New York City Draft Riots: Their Significance for American Society and Politics in the Age of the Civil War* (New York: Oxford University Press, 1990), p. 5.

8. Ibid., pp. 5-6, 9-10, 27-28, 77-78, 113, 120, 123.

CHINESE IMMIGRATION

Racial hostility also involved Asian immigrants. The Chinese faced significant animosity in the West, especially in California. The animosity resulted from job competition, including concern about the Chinese being used as strikebreakers; fear of lowered wages; and concerns over racial homogeneity. Labor unions led the fight against Chinese immigration and workers, indicating the perceived threat to jobs. The white workers were heavily of immigrant stock. As historian Alexander Saxton writes, "Immigrants and children of immigrants (who together comprised a majority of the white labor force in California) were particularly vulnerable to the compulsions of race hostility." Politicians and union leaders used anti-Chinese fears to build their own support. The resultant violence and anti-Chinese legislation were part of the conflict as white Californians and other whites reacted to a sense of threat, of a white America under attack from nonwhite immigrants. An indication of the causes of this conflict comes from the California legislature, which in 1876 called for a study "to investigate the social, moral and political effects of Chinese immigration." The violence that occurred took place throughout the West—in Los Angeles, Denver, and Seattle and in towns in Wyoming, Alaska, and Nevada, among others. The Chinese were among a number of minority groups, white and nonwhite, who experienced initial rejection in American life from not only the majority native-born Protestants but also preceding immigrant groups who were minorities themselves.[9]

ETHNIC COOPERATION

The various points of contention between two groups are clear as is the role of an explosive issue to contribute to or exacerbate conflict. But if these are the factors that produce conflict, what are the elements that lead to cooperation between groups? While the periods of cooperation were less evident, and less reported in the press, there are illustrations of ethnic cooperation.

A good example comes from a study of Ybor City, now a section of Tampa, Florida. Here Italian, Cuban, and Spanish immigrants and later generations worked and lived peacefully together for decades from the late nineteenth into the twentieth century. The events that drew the three groups together included labor strikes in which ethnic and class solidarity against the Anglo bosses in the cigar-making industry created a united front against a common foe. Although some friction was evident between the groups, the overriding attitude was to join together in the workplace and in unions to fight for their rights. Nativism also pulled the groups together in a common defense against bigoted Anglo assailants. Ethnic cooperation was a logical and

9. Alexander Saxton, *The Indispensable Enemy: Labor and the Anti-Chinese Movement in California* (Berkeley: University of California Press, 1971), pp. 27-29, 259, 264; Shih-Shan Henry Tsai, *The Chinese Experience in America* (Bloomington: Indiana University Press, 1986), pp. 56-58, 67, 70.

beneficial way to deal with a shared adversary. It was also a logical way to deal with additional problems. Cooperative medical and other programs served to unite the ethnic groups. Yet, while cooperation was maintained, the three groups still were distinct and remained particularly so as the decades passed and earlier problems receded. "During the early years groups possessed a set of common problems and enemies, and in some cases a set of integrative institutions that by 1940 had largely fallen away." Interethnic solidarity eroded. This long-term "unity amid diversity" was relatively unique for an American community.[10]

Other indications of ethnic cooperation, such as a plan for mutual aid by B'nai B'rith and the Sons of Italy in the late 1920s in New York or joint efforts of ethnic groups during strikes or political campaigns, reveal the transitory nature of cooperation and also of conflict. The particular circumstances of the time create the response, sometimes joining diverse ethnic and racial groups in cooperative liaisons and sometimes pitting them against each other in conflict. The warm ties between Jews and Italians in the 1920s that led to mutual assistance efforts were followed in the 1930s by severe friction over both domestic and international issues.[11]

10. Gary R. Mormino and George E. Pozzetta, *The Immigrant World of Ybor City: Italians and Their Latin Neighbors in Tampa, 1885-1985* (Urbana: University of Illinois Press, 1987), pp. 11, 202, 239-47, 256, 319-21.
11. Bayor, *Neighbors in Conflict*, p. 5.

THE IRISH AND JEWS BETWEEN THE WARS— AN EXPLOSIVE PERIOD

The events of the 1930s, a time of intense interminority conflict, must be viewed in context with the era preceding it. The period of World War I and the 1920s had been difficult ones for some of America's older ethnic groups. Irish and German Americans found that they were still not accepted by majority Americans. Germans during the war years experienced abuse on a large scale, with their culture and loyalty to America under constant assault. The Irish, too, faced hostility. The insecurity of these groups, the realization that they were still outsiders in American life, was made clear for them during the war period and after. The Irish during the 1920s faced constant reminders that they were not real Americans: the anti-Catholicism of the Ku Klux Klan and the rejection of and hostility toward Al Smith in the 1928 presidential campaign. Still reeling from nineteenth-century attacks—from the anti-Catholic Know-Nothings of the 1850s to the anti-Catholic American Protective Association of the 1890s—Irish Americans were reminded again of their minority status, which made them more fearful of any other challenges to their place in American life. German Americans, who had experienced less nativism than the Irish in the nineteenth century, realized in the early decades of the twentieth century that their sense of inclusion as Americans was an illusion. Protective, insecure, and defensive, both groups were wary of any more threats.[12]

The Irish-Jewish struggles that emerged in the 1930s reveal most clearly the myriad elements of conflict, its manifestation, and its culmination. This was a situation that included a number of points of friction and few elements that served to moderate the struggle. The Irish in New York and Boston in the 1930s saw themselves as a community under siege. In both cities, the depression had reversed or frustrated their advance into the middle class, and, in New York, the political hierarchy shifted as Jews and Italians made inroads into traditional areas of Irish power in political positions and the civil service. In Boston, Jewish migration during the 1920s into Irish neighborhoods fueled resentments. Added to those factors, certain explosive issues relating to communism, the Spanish Civil War, and World War II sharply pitted the groups against each other.

The elements making up the conflict included ethnic succession, which is a normal competitive process that takes place over a number of years. But what made this competition produce more friction than usual was the nativistic abuse of the 1920s and earlier and the economic depression of the 1930s. Already insecure and threatened, the Irish faced an economic collapse and increased friction with other groups. Insecurities engendered by majority attacks merged with the threat in the 1930s of newer groups displacing them. The Irish were engulfed by this sense of displacement along with the perception that Jews, their main ethnic competitors, were more successful. The Irish felt on the defensive. This attitude was the result of some real threats to their economic wellbeing, but it also rested on some false perceptions of Jewish economic success. Jews, too, were on the defensive, insecure, and threatened during a decade when anti-Semitic attitudes and movements developed rapidly.[13]

When deeply felt economic competition and resentment merged with broader succession issues and other factors, conflict was likely. The explosive issues, such as the Spanish Civil War, made the groups more aware of who their rivals were and immediately touched off a dispute. To the Irish, the war was part of an attack on Catholicism, and they rose to defend the faith. To the Jews, the war was part of the struggle between fascism and democracy. Each supported opposite sides in the war.

The end product of the conflict in both cities was the largely Irish, anti-Semitic, and violent Christian Front and the Irish youth groups and vandals of the early 1940s that physically and verbally attacked Jews and

12. On the German American experience during World War I, see Frederick C. Luebke, *Bonds of Loyalty: German Americans and World War I* (Dekalb: Northern Illinois University Press, 1974).

13. The New York conflicts of the 1930s and 1940s are covered in Bayor, *Neighbors in Conflict*; an account of the Boston conflict is in John F. Stack, Jr., *International Conflict in an American City: Boston's Irish, Italians, and Jews, 1935-1944* (Westport, CT: Greenwood Press, 1979).

their synagogues and shops. Front meetings stressed "an extravagant picture of Jewish success in a setting of exaggerated Christian failure."[14] The Front was viewed by its supporters as a defense organization, defending against influences that were undermining Catholic interests and values. Jews were seen as the main undermining influence. Efforts were made to work against perceived Jewish dominance in unions, employment, politics, and society in general. As John Cassidy, New York and national director of the organization, said, "We are a militant group of men ... determined to use every means at our command to guarantee to the Christian people of America, that they shall never be subjected to the misfortune that befell their Christian brothers in Russia, Mexico and Spain."[15]

With this Irish-Jewish conflict, based as it was on a variety of issues and flash points, New York and Boston were faced with a prolonged and violent clash. But it eventually ended, and these two ethnic communities were able to live peacefully together, although with some bitterness about the past. By looking at ethnic and racial conflicts historically, rather than being caught up in an ongoing contemporary situation with no resolution, historians are in a unique position to analyze not only the roots and development of conflict but also its culmination—what forces muted the hostility and what impact did the clash have on the groups involved?

14. Bayor, *Neighbors in Conflict*, p. 99.
15. Ibid.

In this Irish-Jewish dispute, a number of moderating forces plus a changed neighborhood, city, and international scene ended the hostility. On the local level, groups of Irish and Jewish citizens organized tolerance committees and interfaith rallies led by the local clergy to denounce intergroup conflict. A stronger police response to anti-Semitic vandalism also helped in both cities. But essentially what ended the conflict was the elimination of the issues that had started it. The economy stabilized during World War II and jobs became more plentiful; political succession was eased as the Irish, in New York, moved back into the mayor's position when William O'Dwyer replaced Fiorello La Guardia; the explosive issues of the World War II era were no longer of such prime concern; and, with the horrendous reports and photographs of the Nazi death camps available, the anti-Jewish attitudes in the Irish community, as elsewhere, were muted. Conditions and perceptions changed, and, as they did, conflict dissipated.

GERMANS AND ITALIANS

For the German and Italian Americans of the 1930s and 1940s, some of the same factors were evident. Germans, particularly, were defensive after World War I, and they experienced some friction with Jews in New York as the Nazi regime came to power in Germany. Pressed by Jews to denounce the Nazis' anti-Semitism but loath to attack anything German, the German Americans, hesitating, found themselves faced with anti-Nazi boycotts and growing hostility from the American public as Nazi organizations made inroads into their communities. Eventually, for reasons of self-preservation, they unequivocally condemned Germany's anti-Semitism. A conflict developed with the Jews largely based on German American unwillingness to criticize Nazi policies. But moderating elements—such as the fear of going through another anti-German hysteria as in the World War I period—pushed the Germans to eliminate the causes of the conflict.

Italian Americans in New York also briefly faced conflict with the Jews over anti-Semitism, namely, Mussolini's anti-Semitic decrees; other causes included some competition and resentments in unions and workplaces. The Italian Americans, too, saw compelling reasons to end the tensions. Both German Americans and Italian Americans felt that they had more to lose than to gain in a prolonged clash with the Jews. For the Irish, it had seemed just the opposite.

The period of World War I through World War II was a troublesome one for all minority Americans, not just the ones already mentioned. The hostility toward German Americans, a relatively well-accepted group, indicated to all ethnics the tenuous nature of American inclusion. If it could happen to the Germans, who was safe? The internment of Japanese Americans during World War II revealed the extent to which majority hostility could go. The ethnic clashes of the 1930s and 1940s clearly showed that ethnic groups would have to be ever vigilant interest groups fighting for their place. The

lessons of this period were learned well.

ANTI-CATHOLICISM AND ANTI-SEMITISM

Some of the conflicts that had burned so out of control for a time became unimportant in future periods. The anti-Catholicism of the nineteenth and early twentieth centuries stirred few in the mid to late twentieth century. Beginning in the 1920s and culminating in the 1930s and 1940s, anti-Semitism largely replaced anti-Catholicism in nativist attacks. Jews were viewed by many majority and minority Americans as an alien force threatening America, much as the Irish Catholics had been perceived in the nineteenth century. In the 1890s, the American Protective Association urged Americans to beware of a papal plot and a Catholic effort to control the United States. By the 1930s William Pelley's nativist Silver Shirts were warning Americans that there was a Jewish plot to take over America and rule it from Jerusalem. In the fears of Protestant nativists, Jews had replaced Catholics, although the threatening imagery was largely the same. Anti-Catholicism was never to be the force it once was. Pelley even claimed that many Catholics were members of his organization. But the view of the alien group, whether emanating from the majority or another minority, was similar. The rhetoric of anti-Catholicism largely became the rhetoric of anti-Semitism even when uttered by Catholic mouths.[16] Seen,

16. Leo Ribuffo, *The Old Christian Right: The Protestant Far Right from Depression to Cold War* (Philadelphia: Temple University

amazingly, as both communists and plutocrats, as radicals subverting American life and as international bankers who wielded enough power to cause depressions, the Jews, like the Irish before, were blamed for all of society's ills. These images helped inspire Henry Ford's anti-Semitic ravings in the 1920s as well as those of Father Coughlin and his supporters and also Pelley's rural and native-based Silver Shirts of the 1930s.

Pelley, who viewed his movement as rescuing America from an alien Jewish menace, is also a good example of anti-Semitism appearing in areas where few Jews lived—a no-contact conflict—based on unrealistic components such as ignorance of and misinformation on the supposedly threatening group, deflected hostility (scapegoating), and historical-religious antipathy (old rivalries and hatreds that do not necessarily have relevance in the contemporary situation).

As the revelation of the horrors of the Nazi regime helped to reduce anti-Semitic activity and opinion in the United States, it did not reduce all intergroup tensions and conflicts, and these continued unabated in the

following decades with, at times, new players but the same old scenario. In cities across the country—New York, Miami, Los Angeles—conflict, sometimes violent, was still apparent between competing groups.

JEWS, BLACKS, AND SCHOOLS

In New York, racial friction, evident early in the history of the city, continued to be part of conflicts in the post-World War II period, and the causes were similar. One illustrative case was the black-Jewish battles over the school system in the late 1960s. The issue was local control over public schools, especially in black neighborhoods. As part of a general plan to decentralize the system, the schools of Brooklyn's Ocean Hill-Brownsville area were among those of three communities set up as experiments to test the new concept in 1967-68. The fight that erupted was initially between the black community and the United Federation of Teachers, but it also became a black-Jewish conflict since the union had a large Jewish constituency. The clash included a variety of issues involving such factors as teachers' rights, the educational quality at various schools, and race/religion. This was competition based on a realistic component—minority rights and control of the schools. Both the Jewish teachers and the black community felt besieged, their jobs or schools threatened by another group.[17]

Press, 1983), pp. 57-58; Geoffrey S. Smith, *To Save a Nation: American Countersubversives, the New Deal and the Coming of World War II* (New York: Basic Books, 1973), pp. 60, 202. See also Bayor, "Klans, Coughlinites and Aryan Nations: Patterns of American Anti-Semitism in the Twentieth Century," *American Jewish History*, 76:181-96 (Dec. 1986). John Higham has noted that in World War I, anti-German hostility took interest away from Catholics: "Instead of invigorating anti-Catholicism, anti-Germanism stole its thunder." See his *Strangers in the Land: Patterns of American Nativism, 1860-1925* (1955; reprint ed., New York: Atheneum, 1965), p. 201.

17. The black-Jewish school-related conflict is covered in Diane Ravitch, *The Great School Wars: New York City, 1805-1973: A History of the Public Schools as Battlefields of Social Change* (New York: Basic Books, 1974), pp. 316, 352, 354-55, 358, 365-70, 372, 385,

Based on this issue, on previous tensions between blacks and Jews (for example, over neighborhood transition), and on black and Jewish defensiveness and sensitivity due to earlier racism and anti-Semitism from the larger society and other minorities, it was not long before indications of black-Jewish conflict were evident. Similar to the Irish-Yankee school disputes of the 1840s, this particular conflict was indicative of a larger one. In the nineteenth century, the school issue was part of an extensive conflict involving Irish and Protestant efforts to assert their power and protect their interests. The school issue in the 1960s was part of a wider struggle between blacks who were trying to secure their place in New York's racial and ethnic hierarchy and the white ethnic community that was trying to maintain the status quo, with each feeling threatened. The struggle was occurring not only in the arena of the school system but in politics, neighborhoods, and employment (affirmative action programs).[18]

The Jews were not the only element making up the white group. Italian New Yorkers figured prominently in efforts to keep blacks out of white neighborhoods. In Canarsie, an Italian-Jewish neighborhood in Brooklyn studied by sociologist Jonathan Rieder, "real or imagined threats to property values and racial balance quickened the struggle over

territory." Fear of being displaced from jobs, homes, and middle-class positions fueled white ethnic animosity. Minority groups themselves, Jews and Italians fought to preserve their own uncertain place in America's competitive society as they reacted to a common racial opponent. Violent anti-black incidents in Italian neighborhoods in New York in the 1980s reveal the continuation of this conflict as do confrontations between blacks and Hasidic Jews. As in the nineteenth century, some politicians sought to use and increase the friction in order to secure power for themselves, and this had a negative effect on any conflict resolution.[19]

HISPANICS AND BLACKS: THE MIAMI STORY

Another example of a modern city convulsed by an ethnic or racial conflict that shows little sign of abating is Miami. Here blacks and Hispanics vie for control. The issues are familiar ones—political, economic, and neighborhood competition from new arrivals—Cubans, Nicaraguans, and others from Latin America—and explosive issues that have led to immediate confrontations.[20]

In the 1960s, as Cubans came to Miami after the Revolution in their

396; Maurice Berube and Marilyn Gittell, eds., *Confrontation at Ocean Hill-Brownsville* (New York: Praeger, 1969), pp. 5, 13-15, 163.

18. Ravitch makes the connection between the Irish-Protestant school conflict of the 1840s and the black-Jewish one of the 1960s. Ravitch, *Great School Wars*, pp. 31, 34-35, 40, 45, 48, 57, 61, 67-68.

19. Jonathan Rieder, *Canarsie: The Jews and Italians of Brooklyn against Liberalism* (Cambridge, MA: Harvard University Press, 1985), pp. 22-23, 26, 79, 96-97, 109, 112-13, 123-24, 127, 233; *New York Times*, 10 Apr. 1987; ibid., 1 Sept. 1989; ibid., 3 Sept. 1989; ibid., 4 Sept. 1989.

20. The tensions in the Miami area are described in Raymond Mohl, "On the Edge: Blacks and Hispanics in Metropolitan Miami since 1959," *Florida Historical Quarterly*, pp. 37-40, 42-48, 50-55 (July 1990).

country, they began to compete with blacks who were just securing some political power and new opportunities due to the civil rights movement. The large migration of Cubans immediately changed the ethnic hierarchy in Miami as the new group successfully competed for what were scarce resources and made inroads into the city's political and employment structure. Black resentment and frustration increased and found some expression in a 1968 race riot. According to the government's report on the riot, economic competition and a black perception that Cubans were favored in dealings with the federal government were clearly some of the causes of the racial outburst. As historian Raymond Mohl writes, "The economic success of the Cubans, without any comparable improvement for blacks, has been a persistent source of irritation and resentment in the Miami black community."

Housing also became an area of competition. Blacks, in need of housing due to highway displacement and urban renewal, found that they had to compete for housing with an ever growing Cuban population. Less housing was open for black use as the Cubans settled in the city and dominated certain neighborhoods.

With Cubans seemingly winning the competition and becoming the main political and economic power in metro Miami, blacks felt left out, losing whatever foothold they had had earlier in the area's economic and political hierarchy. Much like the Irish who felt under siege in the 1930s, blacks have resented and reacted to the newcomers. Explosive issues quickly pitted the groups against each other and led to violence. In the Miami case, the explosive issues consisted of various police actions—involving some Hispanic police—that led to claims of brutality against the black community.

Miami is a classic illustration of a competition-conflict situation. All the ingredients were there to turn competition into conflict. Perceptions that one group was becoming dominant, amid a sense that the second group was losing ground, plus emotionally laden explosive issues, have led to the conflict in Miami, which shows no signs of resolution.

As this article indicates, the historical encounters between ethnic and racial groups, between minority communities, or between majority and minority populations have often led to conflicts. Continued ethnic or racial friction in New York between Koreans and blacks and Jews and blacks, in Miami between Hispanics and blacks, in Los Angeles, Denver, Atlanta, Dallas, and other cities between various groups indicates the persistence of these conflicts. The interminority tensions and clashes can be understood only by also analyzing these groups' historical relations with the majority. Nativism, anti-Semitism, and racism have helped create a sense of insecurity, competitiveness, and defensiveness that is very much a part of the way in which America's minorities relate to each other.

While conflict does not have to occur and groups can cooperate, conflict has been more prevalent. "Forever lurking beneath the surface, in all ethnic relationships, are tensions, resentments, and frictions of varying degrees which are associated with living together in a competitive society." Under certain circumstances, even once friendly groups can clash. In the same way, conflicting groups can enter a period of cooperation. The examples given in this article show the complex nature of interminority relations. The main ingredient in producing conflict is a sense of threat, which can be developed on the basis of real or imagined perceptions.[21]

The outlook for the United States, based on its historical group encounters, is one of further ethnic or racial clashes and nativistic reactions. While these clashes cannot be eliminated in such a multiethnic, competitive society, efforts can be made to limit any violent outbursts and encourage cooperation.

21. Bayor, *Neighbors in Conflict*, p. 1.

ANNALS, *AAPSS*, **530**, November 1993

Voluntary Immigration and Continuing Encounters between Blacks: The Post-Quincentenary Challenge

By ROY SIMÓN BRYCE-LAPORTE

ABSTRACT: The quincentenary of Columbus's 1492 visit to America provided opportunities for scholars to engage in critical observation and observance of the event. The visit began the unended stream of voluntary crossings to the hemisphere and especially the United States. Similar crossings by blacks have been downplayed in American history; they have been located within the context of the slave trade, imposed segregation, and restricted movement. Even though, after emancipation, increasing numbers of persons immigrated to the United States from countries with predominantly black or racially mixed populations, their presence was less visible due to their relatively small numbers and their resemblance to and close association with the more numerous native-born black people. Since 1965, liberal legislation has led to increasing entry and heightened visibility of black immigrants, especially in urban and industrial centers of the country. There they bring greater ethnic diversification to the U.S. black population. These developments challenge sociology to begin to address a complex future with expanding bases of ethnic encounters and differentiation and new possibilities for inter- and intragroup relations.

Roy Simón Bryce-Laporte is the John D. and Catherine T. MacArthur Professor of Sociology and director of Africana and Latin American Studies, Colgate University. He has edited many volumes, authored several publications on black and Caribbean immigration to the United States and Central America in English and Spanish, served as guest curator at the Schomburg Center of the New York Public Library, testified before Congress, and been a consultant to governmental and international bodies on immigration and ethnic issues.

NOTE: This document is a sequel of a presentation originally delivered as the 1990 Public Humanities Lecture of the D.C. Community Humanities Council. The author wishes to acknowledge the special assistance of Cristina Delgado, Marian Holness-Gault, Mary Keys, and Norma Laird; the use of the facilities of the Gloucester County Community College Library and the North South Center of the University of Miami; and the assistance of the Special Population Statistics Programs section of the U.S. Bureau of the Census in preparing the statement. He accepts sole responsibility for any shortcomings of the document.

ALL the peoples of this hemisphere have experienced or been the products of one or more literal crossings from old worlds. While this includes even the indigenous peoples of this country, the Amerindians, who inhabited this land for thousands of years before Columbus ever set foot on their territory, in this article the term and concept of crossing-over are to be applied to one cohort of migrants: people of African descent. For reasons and circumstances historically tied to the event observed by the quincentenary, black people have usually been portrayed and treated differently in conventional American sociology and history. Pertinent to the discussion to be pursued in this article is the invisibility, nonparticipation, passiveness, immobility, and homogeneity often attributed to them in the literature. The fact is that crossing-over has been and is as much an experience for blacks as for other Americans; as a concept it is familiar, and as a term it is multiple in its meaning.[1] One meaning is the voluntariness of black immigration—the historicity and continuity of which have been downplayed for a long time in the literature, policy, scholarship, media, and art of the establishment—and the new levels of intragroup encounters and interactions that accompany such movements.

COLUMBUS'S QUINCENTENARY: A CHALLENGE TO OBSERVANCE AND OBSERVATION

In anticipation of the observance of the Columbus quincentenary, which was to take place in 1992, a short but truly stirring statement by the president of the Federation of State Councils for the Humanities was published, entitled "The Scholarly Benefits of the Columbus Quincentenary Will Reach beyond 1992."[2] Its author laid out an optimistic prediction, really a critical challenge to his colleagues in the humanities, that the then-forthcoming quincentenary would be recognized and treated as an opportunity for more than the customary relaxation and ritualistic reconstructions of the past. He posited the existence of a quiet revolution in America's celebratory culture that would result in the introduction of a new style, level, and direction in engagement and observance beyond the pageantry and filiopietism that usually mark such moments. He implored that the quincentenary be characterized by the cooperative engagement of the American public and its academy in serious thought and scholarly reflections on its nature, effects, and meanings.

His statement directs our focus toward reconsidering (1) the powerful forces that were put in motion and have resulted in crucial changes in life and relations on both sides of the Atlantic since the end of the fifteenth century and (2) the differing meanings that the October event of 500

1. For fuller discussion of the meaning of the term, see Roy Simón Bryce-Laporte, *Crossing Over: Continuing Encounters / Encuentros Continuous* (Washington, DC: D.C. Community Humanities Council, forthcoming).

2. Jamal S. Zaimalden, "The Scholarly Benefits of the Columbus Quincentenary Will Reach beyond 1992," *Chronicle of Higher Education*, 12 Apr. 1989, p. B3.

years ago has evoked from different peoples and nations of the world. Whatever may have been its motive, preconditions, or causes, it was a singular watershed that gave birth and breadth to the formation of a modern world community: one to be characterized more by international competition and conflict than by cooperation and consensus; by differences in historical trajectories, shifting alliances, political economic structures, and sociocultural formations between its member states; and by the promotion of newer levels and types of relationship within and across nations and their peoples.

Among the most persistent of the dynamics put into motion by the 1492 encounter is the continual and extensive human crossings from old to new worlds and the varied changes brought about and undergone by these immigrants in their conditions and ways of living. Generally true of the Americas, such crossings, whether over land, ocean, sea, or river, hold particular pertinence for the United States as a leading target of world immigration even through the present.

Having taken place at a moment of heightened postmodern ferment, the quincentenary of Columbus's celebrated crossing from Europe to the Americas did, indeed, elicit reactions of a wide sort, from familiar as well as strange and unexpected quarters. Many of the reactions were characterized by challenges to once axiomatically held historical claims and their subjection to intense reexamination and varied revision, to literary deconstructions and historical reconstructions, and to many public demonstrations and political protests. As for the various "discovered" peoples, their sentiments and voices reflect the deep bitterness and cynicism of people whose historical presence and critical roles in the shaping of early America have been denied, despised, and distorted, whose experience and treatment from the Age of Exploration onward have been characterized by dehumanization, discrimination, and disdain.[3] Even when professional sociology seemed to have been noticeably underrepresented in these debates, much of the discussion bordered on and reflected material of importance to critical and comparative historical sociology, to the sociology of culture, knowledge, and world systems, and to the study of race, ethnic relations, and human migration.

OVERLOOKED ASPECTS OF
BLACK AMERICAN HISTORY

Broadly defined, voluntary immigration has been a principal mode of peopling this hemisphere and has become a prominent aspect of its ideology and self-image—and projection to the world. Yet, as a term and concept, it has rarely been associated

3. For fuller discussion and examples of foreign-born black literature and artistic reaction, see Bryce-Laporte, Crossing Over, which quotes or cites the following: Winston ("Mighty Shadow") Bailey, Columbus Lie (Port-of-Spain, Trinidad and Tobago: Copyright Organization of Trinidad and Tobago, 1988); Jan Carew, Fulcrums of Change (Trenton, NJ: Africa World Press, 1988), pp. 3-4; Cubena (Carlos Guillermo Wilson), "Las Americas," Pensamientos del Negro Cubena (Los Angeles: Cubena, 1977), p. 12; Ivan Van Sertima, They Came before Columbus (New York: Random House, 1976).

with people of African descent. Perhaps this is so because it has been overshadowed by the uniqueness, magnitude, and meaning of the African slave trade and American slavery itself and by the subsequent institutionalizing of segregation and stagnation as the prevailing conditions of black life even up to the present. Neither the works of Melville Herskovits, Alex Haley, and George Fredrickson, with all their powerful consciousness-raising influences in linking America's black population to its African past, nor the instructive volumes of Marvin Lee Hensen, Oscar Handlin, John Higham, and others on the centrality of immigrants to American history have successfully penetrated the American mind in this regard. The first three of these scholars stressed slavery and most others minimized blacks—if they mentioned them at all. Thus the migratory aspects of African American life and history have escaped deserving notice and have gained recognition only as occasional phenomena and isolated events rather than consistent constituents of the historical repertoire and record of blacks' effort to survive and escape bondage and inequality.

In fact, not only American but also African American history would be rendered incomplete and unconnected without the fuller recognition of the abstract tie between the various modes of black flight, migration, crossing-over, and encounter: from the plantations to the swamps and city outskirts; from the South to the North as far as Canada via the Underground Railroad and other surreptitious means, and also to the western and Floridian territories as accomplished

by Dred Scott and the Black Seminoles, respectively; and even through spirituals or by ship to foreign lands; to Africa and the Caribbean on missions and to Europe and the Soviet Union for self-exile; and to Central and South America on work- and fortune-seeking adventures.

Once we enter this domain of black history, we discover informative revelations about what the United States of America owes not only to white European pioneers and black slaves but also to foreign-born free blacks in its midst. There in the distant past were Melendez and other black militiamen and maroons who guarded the borders of St. Augustine; the founding of the Mission of Los Angeles by a commissioned party that included blacks and mulattoes among its members; the questionable identity of the blackamoor who appeared on the muster list of Plymouth village freeholders; and the black West Indian-born patriots and French Caribbean contingents who participated in the Revolutionary War and the War of 1812.

We also begin to appreciate the early encounters and key cooperation of black immigrants with native-born African Americans in the shaping of the latter's history and culture; the fear of their presence as captains and catalysts of slave rebellion in the antebellum South; the prevalence of free Africans, West Indians, and Pacific Islanders side by side with African American slaves and freemen in the whaling fleets on both American coasts; the black workers from the Hispanic Caribbean islands who accompanied the cigar-making industry as it was transplanted to Tampa and various east coast cities; the large contingents of black emigrants from the English-speaking and French creole-speaking Caribbean who, with some African American companions, provided labor to build and maintain several North American projects in the Middle American mainland, which, in turn, resulted not only in the developing of the U.S. West but also in developing the United States' leadership of the Western world; and the later migrations of these and other West Indians and Latin American blacks to the United States itself to pursue, alongside black southerners, the great migration to northern and midwestern cities.

Together with their northern-born peers, these various groups of migrants would give new vigor, complexity, and a cosmopolitan quality to the black community and to black culture. For them, too, Harlem was in vogue; Harlem was mecca. The Harlem Renaissance, the Garvey movement, the Schomburg Center, the Hispano Theater, and the West Indian carnival all emanated from there. They were by-products of the encounters and cross-fertilization that took place in New York City between black hosts and black strangers in the earlier decades of this century. But so, too, would be discovered culture shocks and tensions between them and the derisive sentiments, stereotypes, statements, and counterstatements that arose among them as they competed for jobs and housing and jostled for status and style of living in the confines of the black ghettos.

Out of this comingling emerged a litany of leaders and a variety of tal-

ented personalities such as Marcus Garvey, Claude McKay, Asadata Dafora, Bert Williams, Hazel Scott, Machito and Graciela, Hugh Mulzac, Hubert Julian, Juano Hernández, J. A. Rogers, P. M. Savory, Maida Springer-Kemp, Kid Chocolate, Mabel Saupers, Ashley Totten, Jesús Colón, Charles Petioni, and J. Raymond Jones ("The Harlem Fox"). Like the famed social psychologist Kenneth B. Clark, who gave critical testimony in *Brown* v. *Kansas*, which led to the integration of schools and resulted in subsequent civil rights victories, these black immigrants and their progeny worked alongside their native-born peers in shaping culture, steering politics, and providing professional services to the local black communities. At the same time, they exemplified models of struggle and success for humbler black immigrants among them, who worked double time in the war industries, clothing factories, public health institutions, and private homes to raise and educate their children in emulation of their ethnic and racial heroes. They also showed unflinching concern for the political developments and welfare needs of their home countries.[4]

THE NEW BLACK IMMIGRANTS: FROM INVISIBILITY TO VISIBILITY

With the passing of the Immigration Act of 1924 and the protraction of the Great Depression, the black

4. For a fuller discussion of these migrations and encounters, see Roy Simón Bryce-Laporte, *Give Me Your Tired, Your Poor . . . ?* (New York: New York Public Library, Schomburg Center for Research in Black Culture, 1986), pp. 9-19.

immigrant stream subsided; it even reversed itself, although it never fully came to an end. The movement would not gather full momentum and magnitude again until the passing of the Immigration Act of 1965, which eliminated the quota system with its racial and geographical biases, facilitated family reunification, and identified work preferences in a manner that was compatible with labor needs of the new Western industrial power that the United States had become and also with the corpus of skills and kind of will that blacks and other immigrants of color from Third World countries could offer.

Since the historic 1965 act, there have been several other executive orders, pieces of legislation, federal policies, and court rulings that have so affected the flow and fate of foreign-born blacks in the United States. The most important of these were the Refugee Act of 1980, the Immigration Reform and Control Act of 1986, and the Immigration Act of 1990. Of these, only the act of 1986 specifically targeted a predominantly black population—undocumented Haitians and Cubans who constituted two groups of boat people who had sought asylum in Miami, escaping the duress or danger of their lives. Generally, however, while not specifying race, these immigration laws served more inadvertently to increase the number of black immigrants entering the United States and to ease their adjustment, and, despite increasing deportation and recent interdictions of black refugees, such legislation by itself has not convincingly deterred illegal entry or fraudulent extensions of residence by

them. Undoubtedly, then, such flows have their impact on the size, composition, and distribution of blacks of foreign birth as well as of recent foreign ancestry in the United States, and more particularly on its large black population that traces to the slave trade its arrival in the United States. But generalizations are risky due to statistical incomparability, undercounting, and the ill fit between the categorization of race and ethnicity. They are further complicated by the difference in definitions of race or color held by the United States versus the home societies of these black immigrants.

The latest cumulative immigration statistics show that a total of about 59 million people came to the United States as legal residents between 1920 and 1990. During the decade of 1881-90—one hundred years or so ago—the United States reportedly admitted some 5.25 million persons. Of these, Europe, as region of last residence, provided a little less than 5 million people; Asia, approximately 70,000; the Americas, some 420,000 (with Canada providing 390,000 and Mexico, only 1913; the Caribbean, 29,000; Central America, 404; and South America, 2304); Africa, 857; and Oceania, 12,500. One hundred years later, in the decade of 1981-90, the United States accepted for permanent residence slightly over 7 million legal immigrants, with Europe, as region of last residence, providing 700,000; Asia, almost 3 million; the other American states, approximately 4 million (160,000 from Canada; 2 million from Mexico; 900,000 from the Caribbean; 500,000 from Central America; and 500,000 from South America); Africa, 200,000; and Oceania, 45,000 persons. That decade also boasts the second-highest inflow of legal immigrants into the United States over the last 170 years. The numbers were surpassed only in 1901-10, the peak years of the Great Immigration, during which almost 9 million persons entered the United States, overwhelmingly from Europe.[5]

It is noteworthy that, in recent years, there have been significant increases and shifts in the sources and the people who have come to this country since 1960. There are shifts in the continents and countries of origin and in the proportion of the immigrant stream that they contribute; there are shifts also in the cultures and colors of the immigrants and consequently in the nature of their encounters, experiences, and expressions. On other occasions, I have called this post-1960 shift the New Immigration, meaning by that term the newest waves of immigrants to enter the United States.[6] But, historically speaking, the entry of Latin Americans, Caribbeans, Asians, and even free Africans into the United States is not new. Rather, as of the 1960s, it is their volume, visibility, and variety that are new.

Black, of Panamanian birth, and of Caribbean ancestry, I came to this country in 1959. I recall visiting New York City and Washington, D.C., with some frequency in those early years of residence and study and increasingly hearing strange languages and different accents from people of color who seemed to look very much like me and sometimes lived and worked in the same localities as their U.S.-born peers. Hence, in my earlier writings, I referred to the multiple levels of invisibility, characteristic of black immigrants as blacks and as foreigners.[7] Curiously enough, this invisibility was due in part to the resemblance they shared with native-born African Americans and therefore the disregard they suffered with respect to their presence, problems, or potential, as was the fate of most people of color in the society at that point in time. Not even their particularities were noticed by the larger society, its policymakers, public institutions, media, or social-scientific disciplines. Only their fellow blacks and the less naive observers among the few whites who daily engaged them perceived and sometimes reacted to those differences.

The invisibility to which black immigrants were relegated is strikingly reflected even in the literature of the social sciences. Until the present, the only book-size comprehensive treatment of this population was pub-

5. U.S., Department of Justice, *Statistical Yearbook* (Washington, DC: Department of Justice, Immigration and Naturalization Service, 1990), tab. 2, pp. 48-50. These figures refer only to the legal immigrants and not to the legal nonimmigrants or the so-called illegal immigrants who have entered and now reside in the United States.

6. Roy Simón Bryce-Laporte, "The New Immigration: A Challenge to Our Sociological Imagination," in *Sourcebook on the New Immigration*, ed. Roy Simón Bryce-Laporte et al. (New Brunswick, NJ: Transaction, 1979), pp. 459-72.

7. Roy Simón Bryce-Laporte, "Black Immigrants: The Experience of Invisibility and Inequality," *Journal of Black Studies*, 4(1):29-56 (Sept. 1972); idem, "Black Immigrants," in *Through Different Eyes*, ed. Peter Rose, Stanley Rothman, and William J. Wilson (New York: Oxford University Press, 1973), p. 44.

lished in 1939 by sociologist Ira de Augustine Reid, himself of Jamaican parentage. His classic, *The Negro Immigrant*,[8] deals primarily with the early waves of immigrants who arrived through the middle of the twentieth century. Scholarly attention to the post-1960 immigrants, whom we may want to call here the new black immigrants, was initiated with what are now regarded as two seminal pieces of mine, the article "Black Immigrants: The Experience of Inequality and Invisibility" in a special issue of the *Journal of Black Studies* dedicated to the theme of international dimensions of black inequality, and a chapter in *Through Different Eyes* entitled "Black Immigrants."[9] More recently, new scholarly treatments of these immigrants and their movements to the United States have been appearing with increasing rapidity.[10]

The photographic exhibit "Give Me Your Tired, Your Poor . . . ?" by the Schomburg Center for Research in Black Culture of the New York Public Library, on the occasion of the centennial of the Statue of Liberty, represents another level of academic visibility.[11]

With time, as these black immigrant groups became larger, their concentrations become more localized and their presence more pronounced. Their newly gained visibility is due not only to their problems and problematicalness as often may be reflected in policy-oriented studies and xenophobic anti-immigration politics—with respect to, for example, the Haitians' plight—but also to their large number and their contributions to the civic, cultural, and even economic activities of their host communities and to linkages and developments in their home countries or regions via the United States. It is also indicated by the attention they

8. Ira de Augustine Reid, *The Negro Immigrant* (New York: Columbia University Press, 1939). See also Arthur Paris, "Ira de Augustine Reid: An Alternative Approach to Immigrant Studies in Sociology" (Paper delivered at the Meeting of the Eastern Sociological Society, Boston, 25-28 Mar. 1993).

9. Bryce-Laporte, "Black Immigrants: The Experience of Invisibility"; idem, "Black Immigrants" (1973).

10. See, for example, Marcia Bayne-Smith, "Health Problems of Caribbean Immigrants in New York City: The Case for Ethnic Organizations" (Paper delivered at the annual meeting of the Eastern Sociological Society, Arlington, VA, 3-5 Apr. 1992); Christine Ho, *Salt Water Trinnies* (New York: AMS Press, 1991); Philip Kasinitz, *Caribbean New York* (Ithaca, NY: Cornell University Press, 1992); Michel Laguerre, *American Odyssey: Haitians in New York City* (Ithaca, NY: Cornell University Press, 1984); Delores Mortimer and Roy S. Bryce-Laporte, eds., *Female Immigrants to the United States: Caribbean, Latin American and African Experiences*, Research Institute on Immigration and Ethnic Studies Occasional Papers, no. 2 (Washington, DC: Smithsonian Institution, Research Institute on Immigration and Ethnic Studies, 1982); Constance R. Sutton and Elsa M. Chaney, eds., *Caribbean Life in New York City* (New York: Center for Migration Studies of New York, 1987); W. Burghardt Turner and Joyce Moore Turner, *Richard B. Moore: Caribbean Militant in Harlem* (Bloomington: Indiana University Press, 1992); John C. Walter, *The Harlem Fox* (Albany: State University of New York Press, 1989); Mary C. Waters, "From Majority to Minority Status: Expectations and Perceptions of Racism among Caribbean Immigrants and Their Children in New York City" (Paper to be delivered at the American Studies Association Conference, Boston, 4-7 Nov. 1993); Tekle Woldemikael, *Becoming Black American: Haitians and American Institutions in Evanston, Illinois* (New York: AMS Press, 1989).

11. Bryce-Laporte, *Give Me Your Tired, Your Poor . . . ?*

now obtain from the media, the market, and the academy.

Of late, the critical masses developed among these immigrants have been made particularly visible in North American cities, where their impact on urban culture can be readily felt and discerned. In the process, they have begun to participate and contribute as other earlier immigrants have and as present citizens do in the continuing Americanization of America. There are festivals, cultural and athletic clubs, radio programs, cultural programs, stores, restaurants, and churches, which constitute manifestations of successful crossing-over and continuing encounters in urban America. In our cities and suburbs everywhere, we now find ourselves confronting new black strangers with multiple experiences and different ways of expressing themselves. Among them there is an accumulating repertoire of talents and tales, which will obligate us as students in the humanities and social sciences to revisit and reevaluate the basic questions posed by our respective disciplines. As we acknowledge the differences between them, we must also realize that there are many, often considerable differences within each of their clusters. Thus the experiencing of different encounters, inequalities, and invisibilities still exists, particularly for the smaller, marginalized, and mixed minorities among them.

The 1991 immigration statistics show, for example, a total of 36,169 legal immigrants of African birth representing at least 20 countries of origin and 154,132 persons of Caribbean birth from at least 15 countries of origin, including Belize, Guyana, and various islands. While all these persons may not be black by even stringent U.S. terms, many of them would be so classified, as is true of some people from Oceania and Latin America. Of the countries with predominantly black populations, there are a few that provided 6000 or more of their nationals as legal immigrants in 1991; from largest to smallest contributor, they are the Dominican Republic, Jamaica, Haiti, Guyana, Nigeria, and Trinidad and Tobago. In addition to the countries that the immigration statistics specified, each producing more than 300 legal immigrants bound for the United States, there were also unspecified countries that provided even fewer.[12] It is particularly true among continental Africans that these populations often represent various ethnic groups that live within and across the boundaries of the sending countries, a circumstance that further complicates the level of diversity among the foreign-born black population in the United States.

Additionally, the detailed 1980 census provides information on ancestries declared by the U.S. population and thereby offers another level of appreciation of the wider diversity now characteristic of the nation's black population: 435,000 persons declared themselves to be of Jamaican ancestry; 290,000 of Haitian;

12. U.S., Department of Justice, *Statistical Yearbook* (Washington, DC: Department of Justice, Immigration and Naturalization Service, 1991), tab. 3, pp. 32-33.

82,000 of Guyanese; 76,000 of Trinidadian and Tobagonian; and 159,000 of West Indian ancestry. An additional 92,000 declared themselves Nigerian, and 244,000 as African.

Like the latter, varying proportions of the persons declaring Latin American, Hispanic, or Spanish (not Spaniard) ancestry may also have been classifiable as black or of African descent in U.S. terms. There were 11 million of them declaring Mexican, 2 million of them declaring Spanish, 2 million more declaring Puerto Rican, and 1.1 million declaring Hispanic ancestry. Of those Latin American countries with a noticeable black or mixed population, each of the following is represented by 75,000 or more persons who claimed its ancestry: Cuba, the Dominican Republic, Colombia, Guatemala, Ecuador, Nicaragua, Peru, Honduras, and Panama. Brazil fell just below the 75,000 range, and there may be a classifiable black segment among persons claiming a Pacific Island ancestry.

Even together, blacks claiming a foreign heritage are vastly outnumbered by the 24 million persons declaring themselves Afro-Americans and constituting the fourth-largest ancestry group in the United States. Nevertheless, even among the latter, there was noticeable variation in the terms used for self-classification: African American, Afro, black, Negro, colored, Creole, and so on.[13] In other words, the tendency to characterize the black population in the United States, whether native-born or foreign-born, as if it were a monolith cannot be supported in either external objective or internal subjective terms. Therefore, if a shift in parlance may be permitted here, all black people are not the same; they do not look alike, nor do they see themselves as all alike. Because of the new immigration, ancestry, ethnicity, and nationality now play an important part in the diversification of the U.S. black population, in addition to class, color, residential distribution and identity, as much of the current sociological literature has begun to suggest.[14]

13. U.S., Department of Commerce, *1990 Census of Population, Supplementary Reports:* *Detailed Ancestry Groups for States* (Washington, DC: Department of Commerce, Bureau of the Census, Oct. 1992), tab. D, pp. III 5-6; tab. 2, pp. 4-5.

14. See for example, William E. Cross, *Shades of Black* (Philadelphia: Temple University Press, 1991); F. James Davis, *Who Is Black: One Nation's Definition* (University Park: Pennsylvania State University Press, 1991); James Jackson, ed., *Life in Black America* (Newbury Park, CA: Sage, 1991); Bart Landry, *The New Black Middle Class* (Berkeley: University of California Press, 1987); National Urban League, *The State of Black America* (New Brunswick, NJ: Transaction, 1991); William O'Hare et al., *African Americans in the 1990's*, Population Bulletins, vol. 46 (Washington, DC: Population Reference Bureau, 1991); Kathy Russell, *The Color Complex: The Politics of Skin Colors among African Americans* (University Park: Pennsylvania State University Press, 1991); William Julius Wilson, *The Declining Significance of Race* (Chicago: University of Chicago Press, 1978); idem, *The Truly Disadvantaged* (Chicago: University of Chicago Press, 1987).

ETHNIC DIVERSIFICATION:
AFRO-LATINOS AND
OTHER BLACK AMERICANS

For reasons of focus, brevity, and familiarity, I call the reader's attention to blacks residing in the United States who are of Latin American birth or ancestry and some among them who have an intervening Caribbean rather than direct African heritage. Currently, some of us refer to ourselves as Afro-Latinos, a broad term which in itself connotes a motley collection of Spanish-speaking, Portuguese-speaking, and maybe French-speaking blacks of different national combinations and multiple cultural or ethnic permutations. The group stretches across the two largest segments of people of color in the United States, African Americans and Latinos. Their coming to this country with cognizance and volition qualifies them as part of its black voluntary immigrant population. While they share the stigma of their slave background and suffer no more happily the status of discrimination than do other blacks and Latinos born in the U.S. society, they often fail to gain full and unquestioned embrace from either of these two larger native-born reference groups. Thus these varied and smaller hyphenated subgroups may not only be relatively lost in the larger black population, but their specific visibilities tend to be veiled and their identities confused in the local arena, despite the serious contributions of individuals or small groups among them to popular culture, civic politics, and professional life.

The Afro-Latinos as a particular subgroup remain largely unrecognized, unheard, unattended as such, as the following literary excerpts certify:

Silently

In silence
and yet not so silently
We . . . expatriates
   from behind a veil of laughter
   we hide our pain . . .
Who are we?
Who are we?
   We sigh
Uniting two worlds
   maybe three
A bit of everything
   a lot of nothing.
We sing
We cry . . . in silence
We hide ourselves behind a mask
   but not so silently.[15]

For Ana Velford

. . . and despite it all, New York is my home.
I feel fiercely loyal to this acquired homeland.
Because of New York, I am a foreigner in
   whatever other place, . . .

But New York City is not the city of my
   infancy . . .

Because of that I will always remain on the
   margin,
a stranger between these rocks, . . .

Then, now and forever, I will always remain
   a foreigner,
even when I return to the city of my infancy.
I will always carry this marginality . . .
too *habanera* to be a New Yorker
too New Yorker to be
—ever to become again—
anything else.[16]

Whatever the level, it seems that unsettling encounters, feelings of marginality, sometimes of futility,

15. Carlos C. Russell E., "Silenciosamente," *Revista nacional de cultura*, pp. 1-5 (Oct.-Dec. 1976); English translation by R. S. Bryce-Laporte.
16. Lourdes Casals, "Para Ana Velford," *Areíto*, 3(1):52 (Summer 1976); English translation by R. S. Bryce-Laporte.

other times of dogged determination, and cries for human attention and civic recognition, are all part of the day-to-day cultural load and communicational effort of new—and old—black immigrants among us.[17] These are realities, processes, ongoing experiences that merit our attention and certainly must benefit from our greater appreciation as we reflect upon the aftermath of the Columbus visit of 1492. After all, the same holds for the entire hemisphere, including the United States, as Gordon Lewis noted with respect to the Caribbean, to which Old World immigrants began to flow at full force at least 100 years before extending to the U.S. mainland:

Migration—as the vast, restless, circulatory movement of whole peoples—has its roots, historically, in the immediate post-Discovery period. For the first century of European colonization, migration meant the influx to the colonies of European peasants and the workers of the European seaports including the riff-raff of London, Paris and Madrid. After that came the African influx, organized by the African slave trade, which did not really cease in the islands until slavery abolition in Cuba in 1886. Following that, again, was the influx of Indian indentured labor, lasting for the period 1845-1917. Every person in the Caribbean has been a newcomer; and certainly by 1700, the region's identity had been established as a series of rich, picaroon, and polyglot societies.[18]

17. See, for example, Piri Thomas, *Down These Mean Streets* (New York: Vintage Books, 1974), pp. xi-xii.
18. Gordon K. Lewis, "Foreword," in *In Search of a Better Life: Perspectives on Migration from the Caribbean*, ed. Ransford W. Palmer (New York: Praeger, 1990), p. xiii.

THE SOCIOLOGICAL FUTURE OF ETHNIC DIFFERENTIATION AND GROUP RELATIONS

But the pertinent question is, Where are we going here in the United States? Where will such reflections and projections take us—as scholars, policymakers, activists, and citizens of the larger human world community? What will it say about the character, composition, and conditions of the U.S. black population and about inter- and intragroup relations in this society?

By the year 2020, the African American population will have been numerically eclipsed by the Latino population. Much of this growth will have resulted directly and indirectly from immigration because, among other things, immigration from contemporary Africa and the Caribbean will be outnumbered significantly by the flow from Latin America—and also from Asia-Pacific regions—even though a certain percentage of the immigrants from these latter regions will also be black in U.S. terms. This motley group of black immigrants could add volume and diversity to an already diverse black population. And against the backdrop of the U.S. rule that one drop of black blood makes one black, some questions will rise concerning the location and identification of these groups of recent immigrants and their offspring, since in many of their countries of origin and ancestry the rule works quite to the inverse: there, one drop of white blood makes one white. In fact, in many of these countries, racial categorization is characterized with greater subtlety and fluidity and comprises several intermediate statuses, as opposed to the basic binary arrangements typical of U.S. society. Furthermore, often color or class, not race, becomes the salient base of social classification and mobility in many of the sending societies and in the thinking of their people, since wealth whitens and light coloring catapults one to a higher social position.

For one who struggled in obscurity and solitude for many years for the rekindling of social scientific interest in the study of immigration as an ongoing process, and more particularly for the pursuit of a fuller understanding of the intricacies and implications of black immigration to the United States, it is with an encouraging sense of fulfillment to read a recent article by Ellen Coughlin, which reviews several new and forthcoming social science publications on the growing complexities of ethnicity and race in American society. The article points out that much of the earlier research on race and ethnicity was modeled on the white European immigration experience. The shift in the racial composition of post-1960 immigration has resulted in a shift in definition so that being black does not necessarily mean being African American, narrowly defined, and therefore it no longer holds that "a black person is a black person is a black person."[19]

At present, it is more likely that new black immigrants—and native-born blacks, too—often find ethnicity to be more crucial in certain circumstances than race, although in other situations the opposite may be true. In fact, many black immigrants arrive with an acute sense of nationality while taking race for granted and placing less importance on regional or ethnic identity than is anticipated of them by others. But often they will soon find themselves branded and bonding along racial, regional, or pan-ethnic lines. Hence the pan-Caribbean dreams that have escaped the governments and political leaders of that region now find opportunities for intimate and dramatic expression in cities of the United States and other parts of the diaspora. If the same process is occurring with pan-Africanism, pan-Latinoism, pan-Asianism, and the like, what then will be the nature of politics—coalition, conflict, or competition—among the various hyphenated groups of African descent? Who is or will be considered an African American, strictly speaking, among them? When does a black person of foreign birth or ancestry become African American? What will be the character of immigration, particularly black immigration, as the world experiences further restructuring, realignment, and reduction in space and time and as its people's redefinition of "home" comes to reflect mul-

19. Ellen K. Coughlin, "Sociologists Examine the Complexities of Racial and Ethnic Identity in America," *Chronicle of Higher Education*, 24 Mar. 1993, p. A7. See also *Challenges of Measuring an Ethnic World: Science, Politics, and Reality*, preliminary version (Ottawa: Statistics Canada; Washington, DC: Department of Commerce, Bureau of the Census, 1992); Lelia De Andrade, "The Discourse of Racial-Ethnic Identity: The Social Construc-

tion of Race and Ethnicity among Cape Verdian Americans" (Paper delivered at the annual meeting of the Eastern Sociological Society, Arlington, VA, 3-5 Apr. 1992); Michael Omi and Howard Winant, *Racial Formation in the United States* (New York: Routledge & Kegan Paul, 1986).

tiple or linking places of abode, operation, and identity? Will multiethnicism become the norm or remain at the margins? Will black multiethnics become lonesome isolates or serve as critical liaisons?

We can hardly imagine what new categories and systems of human differentiation or homogenization or whether new definitions of intra- or intergroup relations will emerge in the distant future. For the foreseeable future, however, as much as we may wish to condemn racism and ethnocentrism and try to obliterate them as legitimate modes of social or political behavior, we must also realize that race and ethnicity, like class and status, are dynamic and sometimes interrelated social realities that cannot be written off or washed away by even a well-wishing but naive sociology. Events of the 1990s like those of Bosnia, Los Angeles, Crown Heights, and South Africa, call for a new sociology, new social policies, and new standards of commitment that will enable us to more fully comprehend the nature of, and to more effectively act upon the consequences and causes of, continuing human crossings-over and expanding ethnic encounters.

A true reflection on the Columbus quincentenary, then, should leave us hoping that we could and would better know our world, govern the use of our social inventions, steer the results of our discoveries, and be prepared to assume responsibility for our claims and the developments deriving from them.

The Turbulent Friendship:
Black-Jewish Relations in the 1990s

By MILTON D. MORRIS and GARY E. RUBIN

ABSTRACT: This article explores the current state of black-Jewish relations and assesses their prospects. It begins by critically examining the myths of the relationship's past. It then explores current evidence of each community's attitude toward the other, evaluating broad conclusions others have reached and offering a complex reading of mutual attitudes. It then proceeds to examine several factors critical to the relationship: socioeconomic trends, changes in political strength and representation, positions on important domestic and international issues, and developments in each group's culture and internal structure. Strengths and weaknesses in the current relationship are frankly assessed and observations offered on positive and negative developments that could take place in the future. Factors likely to determine future trends are identified. Throughout, a strong effort is made to present the views of both African Americans and Jews, including where they converge or differ and where further clarification and work is needed.

Milton D. Morris is vice president for research at the Joint Center on Political and Economic Studies. He is one of the country's leading experts on political and social trends among African Americans, on which he has published widely. He has taught at Southern Illinois and Howard universities and Smith College and served as a senior fellow at the Brookings Institution.

Gary E. Rubin is director of national affairs at the American Jewish Committee. He has extensive experience in policy development and advocacy and in coalition building with African American and other groups in the United States and has written several articles on these topics.

FOR almost three decades now, the black and Jewish communities have been debating the state of their relationship. On both sides the prevailing consensus is that a productive, long-standing relationship has been deteriorating, even though a wide variety of effective interactions continue. There is no agreement, however, about the extent of the deterioration or the forces contributing to it.

Analysts have given considerable attention to specific incidents or disagreements involving blacks and Jews as indicators of the state of their relationship. For example, disagreements over specific policy issues such as some forms of affirmative action, hostile or insensitive remarks emanating from elements in both communities, negative or anti-Semitic attitudes expressed by some or perceived in results of opinion surveys, and the tragic conflict in the Crown Heights section of New York City are, for many, definitive evidence of a relationship gone terribly bad. Invariably, commentators have viewed such incidents against a heavily retouched historical backdrop of a warm and trouble-free relationship. The result has been widespread failure to recognize and appreciate the broad currents and little complexities that have shaped black-Jewish relations historically and continue to do so now.

This article suggests that claims of serious deterioration in black-Jewish relations are exaggerated and often oversimplify a complex reality. Such claims reflect serious misperceptions of the history of black-Jewish relations; inadequate knowledge and un-derstanding of each community by the other; and failure to view the relationship in the context of profound changes in the circumstances of the two groups, in the bases for their interaction, and in the larger society. The study argues, further, that blacks and Jews continue to share a relatively strong and mutually beneficial relationship and that this relationship needs to continue. But continuing it to maximum effectiveness will not be easy. At a minimum, it will require increased efforts to broaden contacts and deepen understanding between the groups; a conscious effort to discard the myths of the past and accept the reality of changes in the circumstances of each group and in the environment within which it functions; a willingness to recognize the difference between conflicts of interest and real instances of racism or anti-Semitism; and a determination to find new bases for constructive joint action.

There is an especially great need and opportunity now to overhaul and reinvigorate black-Jewish relations. Conflicts like that in Crown Heights, and evidence of growing racial and ethnic intolerance and tensions in this increasingly diverse society, underscore the need for leadership by blacks and Jews together in reinforcing the society's pluralistic values. At the same time, the results of the November 1992 elections and the composition of the new administration dramatically underscore the maturing of black political influence and the clear entry of African Americans into the political mainstream of the society, which, together with continued strong Jewish influence, can provide new opportunities for mutually beneficial collaboration.

OUR FAULTY RECOLLECTION
OF THE PAST

A common yet appropriate observation of black-Jewish relations is that the good old days were never as good as we remember them. Claims of a rapidly deteriorating black-Jewish relationship rest in part on the false assumption that there was once a warm, conflict-free relationship. For too many, recollections of the generosity of Jews in the development of critical black institutions and in helping meet urgent needs of new black migrants to the cities, as well as of black-Jewish collaboration in the courts and on the streets in pursuit of civil rights, have blurred the memories of simultaneous conflicts and tensions between the two groups. The result is that most recent discussions aimed at improving black-Jewish relations are steeped in nostalgic recollections of these presumably good old days, and implicit advocacy of recapturing that relationship.

Reality differed substantially from these recollections, however. Black-Jewish relations throughout more than 100 years of interaction were always substantially limited in scope and depth. Both groups found common cause as their needs and circumstances permitted. Jews became very early supporters of black efforts to cope with the harsh legacy of slavery. They assisted black migrants to the northern cities from the rural south after World War I, and they became strong, resourceful allies in the long, costly struggle for civil rights in the courts and in the streets. Through-

out, the Jewish community consistently stood out to blacks as the most supportive white population group by far. Through these activities, black and Jewish leaders gradually forged strong, close ties that probably reached their peak in the major legislative triumphs of the mid-1960s.

The epic joint struggle for black civil rights had implications for the Jewish community as well. During the years of struggle, Jews had themselves been victims of discrimination throughout the United States, not to speak of the hate and discrimination to which they had been subject elsewhere in the world for centuries. They therefore felt rightfully threatened by any form of hate and intolerance, and, in fighting with blacks, they were actually fighting for their own interests. Historian Hasia Diner points out in this regard that

many of the issues raised by black civil rights groups spoke directly to the problems faced by American Jews. Job discrimination, restrictive housing markets, exclusion from universities and professional schools were concerns of Jews also. . . . Through race issues, Jews could show America how useful they had become. . . . In doing this, they not only drew links between themselves and the rhetoric of American democracy, but they illustrated the compatibility of their own heritage and culture with that of America.[1]

This sense of common interest undoubtedly constituted a special basis for the close black-Jewish relationship that emerged around civil rights. Yet, even during those years of a close, cooperative relationship be-

1. Hasia Diner, *In the Almost Promised Land* (Westport, CT: Greenwood Press, 1977), pp. xv-xvi.

tween leaders of the two communities, there were significant tensions, especially below the leadership level. Walter White, executive director of the National Association for the Advancement of Colored People (NAACP), reportedly insisted up to the mid-1940s that each of the two groups made common cause with the other when it was victimized, but it was not then appropriate to speak of a black-Jewish alliance.[2] In 1946, black sociologist Dr. Kenneth Clark's analysis of black-Jewish relations concluded that there were grounds for antagonism in virtually every area of black-Jewish relations.[3] Even at the height of the civil rights struggle, some black analysts were pointing to numerous irritants, from the daily encounters of the two groups in the urban ghetto to the chafings of black leaders at what they perceived as overly patronizing attitudes by Jews. Thus the highly successful black-Jewish collaboration on civil rights occurred alongside significant conflicts and tensions and undoubtedly some anti-Semitism.

By the late 1960s, the bases and nature of black-Jewish conflict had begun to change significantly. The change, reflected most sharply in the emergence of a young cadre of black leaders advocating Black Power, in battles for control of local schools in New York and Chicago, and in vigorous disagreements with those Jews opposed to strong forms of affirmative action, signified a major shift in direction by relative newcomers to the leadership struggle. Moving beyond the broad principles of equal rights and racial tolerance that were bases for black-Jewish cooperation, new voices sought to direct their own search for increased political influence and economic opportunity. The conflict at this juncture became more pronounced and more substantive than at any time in the past. But it hardly signified a breaking point in the relationship.

Clearly, the history of black-Jewish relations is one of both close and constructive relations as well as conflicts and tensions. Major civil rights victories were won, even as tensions were clearly evident. That this pattern continues today should not be surprising or alarming and need not indicate significant, overall deterioration in the relationship. On the contrary, amid the expressions of conflict, there are widespread indications of strong, effective relations between the two groups. In scores of communities across the nation, black and Jewish groups meet to solve common problems, improve the quality of community life, and combat expressions of hate and bigotry.[4] Indeed, the way that elements of the two communities responded to crises like Crown Heights indicates a concern about threats to the relationship and a strong interest in preserving it.

OUR POOR UNDERSTANDING OF EACH OTHER

In commenting on attitudes toward the Jews expressed by some

2. Arthur Hertzberg, *The Jews in America* (New York: Simon & Schuster, 1989), pp. 336-37.
3. Ibid.

4. See, for example, Lynne Landsberg and David Saperstein, eds., *Common Road to Justice: A Programming Manual for Blacks and Jews* (Washington, DC: Religious Action Center of Reform Judaism, 1991).

prominent African Americans, Professor Cornel West offers a perspective on Jesse Jackson's background vis-à-vis the Jews that seems easily applicable to most of the black population. Jackson, he says,

must be understood as part of a Southern Black American Protestant tradition. Blacks in the South had very infrequent contact with Jewish people. Struggles in the South were primarily between Blacks and whites, with both sides being Protestant. . . . When Jesse sees Jews he doesn't think about the expulsion of Jews from Spain in 1492, the expulsion of Jews from England in 1290, or the expulsion of Jews from France in 1306. He sees the Jews on the move in middle classes. He doesn't seem to grasp the legitimate fears or the paranoia of American Jews, nor does he seem to understand the psychological impact of the Holocaust on Jews during the past forty years.[5]

Jesse Jackson probably sees much more than Professor West suggests, but the picture does seem applicable to very large segments of the African American population whose relatively brief encounter with the Jews in urban America has been superficial and confined to the special circumstances of the northern inner cities. In fact, different images of the Jews have existed across different segments of the black population but hardly ever with the depth and coherence required as a basis for a stable, strong relationship.

Black leaders from Martin Delany to Alexander Crummell, Frederick Douglass, and Marcus Garvey all invoked the Jewish experience over the centuries for insight and inspiration

5. Cornel West, "Black-Jewish Dialogue: Beyond Rootless Universalism and Ethnic Chauvinism," *Tikkun*, p. 96 (July-Aug. 1989).

as they pondered the prospects of black people in America for dignified survival as a small and despised minority. In this century, most of the civil rights leadership encountered the Jews as generous and stalwart partners in the fight for civil rights and, in the post-civil rights era, as sometime political allies. But, in the gritty, harsh struggle to survive and make progress in the teeming urban ghettos, with their formidable barriers of racial discrimination and segregation, other blacks at times vented their frustrations on the Jews they came in contact with or even the Jews they only heard of. In their view, the Jews had functioned profitably as intermediaries between them and a hostile white establishment, and their extraordinarily rapid progress, socially and economically, merely intensified the frustrations these blacks felt. As the years of close collaboration on civil rights recede into the past, and the black civil rights leaders of that era leave the active scene, these angry urban voices seem to gain greater prominence.

A few aspirants to power in the largely black inner cities continue to find the increasingly distant image of Jews a useful target for expressing the rage of the young and poor and for gaining attention. The anti-Semitic utterances of these personalities are too often viewed benignly by much of the black public, partly because of their limited understanding of the experiences and fears of the seemingly secure and successful Jewish community and partly because of their perception that angry rhetoric has limited significance. There are notable exceptions to this reaction, however. Public officials like Mayor David Dinkins of New York City and leading black scholars like Professors Cornel West,[6] Henry Louis Gates,[7] and Randall Kennedy[8] are examples. Nonetheless, benign attitudes to anti-Semitic remarks constitute one of the prime indicators of growing black anti-Semitism for many Jews.

The Jewish community has expressed anger and anxiety with each anti-Semitic or otherwise unfriendly utterance and has demanded that more responsible black leaders denounce the statement at issue and the individuals associated with it. They worry that unrepudiated anti-Semitic utterances could help make hatred of Jews widely acceptable. However, neither black nor Jewish leaders and analysts have done enough to increase understanding of this disturbing behavior as a basis for responding to it appropriately and effectively. In the absence of such understanding, the Jewish community might well misperceive the scale of the problem in the black community and seek responses that exacerbate rather than solve it.

One of the most controversial and damaging issues in the debate about black-Jewish relations is the now routine claim by Jews that, in contrast to the rest of the population, there is a high and growing level of anti-Semitism among blacks and that this level rises as education increases. These perceptions are now a prominent part of folk wisdom in the Jewish community. These claims of a disturbing and distinctive anti-Semitic trend among blacks rest in large part on a number of survey-based studies conducted between 1967 and 1992.[9] The first major study was by Gary Marx, published in 1967 and based on 1964 data from the National Opinion Research Center.[10] Marx claims that his study was influenced in part by rumors and reports that anti-Semitism was rampant among blacks. One of the most recent studies is by Tom Smith of the National Opinion Research Center, who reviewed data from the General Social Survey for 1990. Smith underscored the specter of rising black anti-Semitism with the ominous declaration that, although on the whole anti-Semitism is declining in the United States,

there are signs of new streams feeding the old pool of anti-Semitism. Over the past two decades, Black anti-Semitism has emerged as a special problem. The traditional Black-Jewish alliance in the civil rights movement and various other liberal political activities began to break down in the late 1960s. Cooperation was replaced by Jewish-Black conflicts over various community issues in several cities. Jews became targets of Black militants like Louis Farrakhan and the objects of an ethnic slur from Jesse Jackson.[11]

6. Ibid.

7. Henry Louis Gates, "Black Demogogues and Pseudo-Scholars," *New York Times*, 20 July 1992.

8. Randall Kennedy, "Derrick Bell's Apologia for Minister Farrakhan: An Intellectual and Moral Disaster," *Reconstruction*, 2:92-96 (1992).

9. These are reviewed and analyzed in Jennifer Golub, *What Do We Know about Black Anti-Semitism?* (New York: American Jewish Committee, 1990).

10. Gary Marx, *Protest and Prejudice* (New York: Harper & Row, 1969).

11. Tom W. Smith, *What Do Americans Think about Jews?* (New York: American Jewish Committee, 1991), pp. 1-2.

Smith concludes his review of attitudes toward Jews by observing, "While Black anti-Semitism is not a major force at present, it is the only potential source of an invigorated anti-Semitism that is being pushed by leaders with non-trivial followings."[12]

This view of blacks as the only likely source of anti-Semitism is reinforced by even more recent surveys sponsored by the Anti-Defamation League (ADL) and the American Jewish Committee. The ADL survey, conducted in late 1992 by the firm of Marttila and Kiley, reported that while 20 percent of the American population "held a significant number of anti-Semitic beliefs," 37 percent of blacks did.[13] On the other hand, the ADL survey examined the claim that the level of African American anti-Semitism rises with increased education, one of the most troubling aspects of black anti-Semitism, and found no evidence to support it.[14]

Almost simultaneously, the American Jewish Committee released its own survey of New York City residents conducted by the Roper Organization. The survey showed evidence of extensive anti-Semitism among black New Yorkers. Illustrative of this is the study's finding that 47 percent of all respondents felt that Jews had too much influence, while 63 percent of blacks thought so.[15] Since Jewish analysts of anti-Semi-

tism consider this perception of too much influence the single strongest indicator of anti-Semitism, the results would seem to confirm the Smith portrayal of blacks as the source of an invigorated anti-Semitism.

The claim that anti-Semitism is most prevalent among African Americans, presumably confirmed by these surveys, raises some troubling questions for black-Jewish relations: Do the surveys reliably measure anti-Semitism among blacks or in society at large? To the extent that they do, how might we most constructively address the presence of anti-Semitism? If the findings do misrepresent reality, why? And how might we proceed to undo the damage to the relationship from this misrepresentation?

Most of the anti-Semitism surveys employ a battery of 9-11 questions that tap a variety of attitudes toward Jews. The mix of questions has varied slightly from one study to the next, but they constitute a fairly consistent anti-Semitism index. While they provide extremely valuable attitudinal information, it is not clear that they are a consistently reliable measure of anti-Semitism. For example, the survey item traditionally considered by Jewish analysts to be the strongest indicator of anti-Jewish sentiment, whether the respondent thought that Jews had too much influence, has been questioned by African American analysts as to how accurately it denotes anti-Semitic attitudes. Their assessment is that, especially among African Americans, who frequently compare influence across groups and assess their position in relation to others, the fact that Jews hold a proportion of prominent

12. Ibid., p. 27.

13. *Highlights from an Anti-Defamation League Survey on Anti-Semitism and Prejudice in America* (New York: Anti-Defamation League, 1992), pp. 30-31.

14. Ibid., pp. 32-33.

15. *1992 New York City Intergroup Relations Survey* (New York: American Jewish Committee, 1992), p. 27.

public offices much higher than their proportion of the population while the reverse is true for African Americans might make the affirmative response of the latter informed rather than hateful. In fact, in one opinion survey, 35.8 percent of Jewish respondents felt that African Americans had too little political influence.[16] A test using such measures to confirm alleged black anti-Semitism might well be unhelpful, though a response that Jews have too much power cannot be dismissed out of hand.

Even if one accepts the anti-Semitism index as reliable, it yields a mixed picture of positive and negative black attitudes toward Jews that requires further study. In the first place, the findings of the more carefully analyzed studies actually yielded much less conclusive findings about black anti-Semitism than is reflected in popular opinions among Jews. For example, in his 1967 study, Gary Marx found no consistent pattern of black-white difference in attitudes toward Jews when he controlled for education and region. When he examined those scoring very high on the anti-Semitism scale, he found that "Negroes are less likely than whites to be extreme anti-Semites in four of the five comparisons."[17] He concluded that "all in all . . . no case can be made for the prevalent notion that anti-Semitism is more widespread among Negroes than among whites."[18] A study by Selznick and

Steinberg found that, while blacks tended to score higher than whites on their index of economic anti-Semitism, they scored the same or lower on the noneconomic measures.[19]

Virtually all the surveys done by Jewish and other sponsors examining attitudes toward various ethnic groups yield two compelling findings concerning Jews. First, they are the most admired population group in the United States, and this admiration holds across every other group, including African Americans. Second, even those respondents classified as anti-Semitic because of the number of questions to which they give a qualifying answer exhibit a number of highly positive assessments of or attitudes toward Jews. Thus survey respondents, including African Americans, tend to rank Jews at or near the top of all groups in being intelligent and at or near the bottom in being lazy or prone to welfare or violence. These findings derive from the same surveys that show higher than average anti-Semitic responses among African Americans.[20] These data indicate that it is difficult to draw any simple conclusion about attitudes toward Jews from the poll findings. As for any relationship between real human beings, positive and negative attitudes combine into a complex mix. The most reliable conclusion one can draw from these findings is that the potential for both warm and tense relations coexist in attitudes toward Jews. Which will

16. Tom W. Smith, *Jewish Attitudes toward Blacks and Race Relations* (New York: American Jewish Committee, 1990), p. 22.

17. Marx, *Protest and Prejudice*, p. 147.

18. Ibid.

19. Gertrude Selznick and Stephen Steinberg, *The Tenacity of Prejudice* (New York: Harper & Row, 1969), pp. 118-19.

20. See, for example, Smith, *What Do Americans Think about Jews?* pp. 5-10; *1992 New York City Intergroup Relations Survey*.

emerge as dominant will depend on how circumstances in one's experience bring out one or the other.[21]

Paralleling the concern of Jews about anti-Semitism among African Americans are growing claims of Jewish racism. Several factors seem to contribute to this perception among African Americans. One is that the strong image of black-Jewish cooperation in pursuit of civil rights that was very pronounced up to the mid-1960s has all but disappeared even though a substantial level of such cooperation continues. A contributing factor in the declining image of cooperation in this area is the declining number of prominent civil rights issues in contention. Especially for younger African Americans, who have little or no recollection of black-Jewish collaboration on civil rights issues, Jews are distinguishable from the rest of white America only by their extraordinary successes.

A second factor is the evidence from opinion surveys that the attitudes of Jews toward African Americans is mixed, providing some evidence of racism along with friendly and supportive attitudes. Virtually all recent surveys of racial attitudes show that Jews hold consistently more favorable attitudes toward blacks than do other whites and generally favor school and housing integration. A substantial segment of the Jewish population, however, does not share these views. In his study of Jewish attitudes toward blacks, Tom

Smith used data from the National Opinion Research Center to analyze Jewish feelings toward blacks. He found that Jews had moderately favorable feelings toward blacks, but only 15.2 percent identified closely with blacks. At the same time, Jews are very cool to those blacks they identify as "militants."[22] This barely "warm" attitude combined with a handful of openly racist or socially conservative Jews contributes to the growing complaints of Jewish racism.

Third, and perhaps most important, although blacks and Jews agree on a number of important issues, there are fundamental differences between them that contribute to the perception of Jewish racism. Smith sums up these differences with the observation that among Jews, "while the principle of equal treatment and non-discrimination on the basis of race is widely endorsed, the idea of special efforts to help blacks is less popular, especially if couched in the language of preferential treatment."[23] Specifically, Smith reports, "a majority of Jews do not favor government measures to help blacks, more government spending for blacks, and the use of busing to achieve school integration, though . . . Jewish support for these positions is far from negligible."[24]

These attitudes are in sharp conflict with the expectation of most blacks that Jews would be supportive of what had become most important to blacks—civil rights. Such supportive images have not been readily evident in the post-civil rights era, how-

21. Gary E. Rubin, "A No-Nonsense Look at Anti-Semitism," *Tikkun*, 8(3):46-48, 79-81 (May-June 1993).

22. Smith, *Jewish Attitudes toward Blacks and Race Relations*, p. 6.
23. Ibid.
24. Ibid., p. 5.

ever. Instead, Jews are now seen by many African Americans as vigorous opponents of what now matters most to them—increased economic opportunities through strategies like numerically based affirmative action programs. Another factor is that for younger African Americans who have little knowledge or recollection of black-Jewish collaboration on civil rights or of Jews as strong proponents of open housing, Jews are an increasingly distant part of white America, distinguished only by their extraordinary success. This whitening of the Jews, while itself an indication of the triumph of the struggle for pluralist values, almost forces many blacks to view them as attitudinally just like the other whites. Recent survey data do not help a great deal in altering the image of an increasingly racist Jewish population, nor do the more open and heated debates on the academic front.

Survey data indicate that, as with black attitudes toward Jews, the attitudes of Jews toward blacks are mixed. Virtually all the recent polls show that compared to other whites, Jews consistently hold more favorable attitudes toward blacks. On measures of social distance, Jews rate themselves as having moderately warm feelings toward blacks, feeling neither particularly distant nor intimate. While most Jewish respondents favor school integration and would have little hesitancy sending their children to racially integrated schools, most would not send their children to schools with a black-majority enrollment. While most Jews had a favorable opinion of "black civil rights leaders," they were decidedly less favorable toward those they characterized as "black militants."[25] Furthermore, virtually all the opinion surveys indicate that in sharp contrast to Jews, African Americans consistently fall at or very near the bottom of every ranking of distinct racial or ethnic groups. Along with Hispanics, they consistently are given the highest negatives and lowest positives by others, including Jews.[26] When these findings are linked to the whitening phenomenon, they lead to perceptions of Jewish racism, especially in the absence of significant offsetting experiences. Still, higher than average positive attitudes of Jews toward blacks consistently emerge from the surveys. Among Jews, then, as among blacks, positive attitudes coexist with negative ones.

CHANGING TIMES
AND PRIORITIES

Relationships like those involving blacks and Jews are subject to changing times and circumstances. Unfortunately, discussions about the relationship by both communities occur with little attention to how profound changes in the circumstances of both communities and in the rest of society affect the relationship. At a minimum, efforts to understand and improve black-Jewish relations require that we take into account the changing context of the relationship. At least four broad, interrelated areas of change seem especially noteworthy: the socioeconomic circumstances of

25. Ibid., passim.
26. Smith, *What Do Americans Think about Jews?* pp. 5-12; *1992 New York City Intergroup Relations Survey.*

the two groups, the level and character of their political participation, their issue orientations, and the treatment of ethnicity and diversity in the society. Together, these will determine both the form and the substantive bases of future relations.

Different socioeconomic experiences

The ink had hardly been dry on the Voting Rights Act of 1965, one of the major legislative products of the civil rights revolution, when blacks began to stress the need to secure economic gains paralleling those in civil and political rights. Concern about economic opportunity became central to black social and political activism, and a major force behind changes in the composition and style of black leadership. For, although the black population had been experiencing substantial gains in education and income since the end of World War II, and the pace of those gains was picking up in the 1960s, blacks still lagged very far behind the rest of the population. The urban disorders of the mid-1960s dramatically underscored the demand for economic opportunity, spawned a cadre of angry and impatient urban leaders, and prompted a combination of urban development initiatives and race-specific policies to expand opportunities. Although analysts and politicians disagree about the effectiveness of these policies, they clearly provided important new economic opportunities. By the late-1970s, however, black economic progress had stalled and a painful stagnation had begun to set in. Black families, already handicapped by the strains of rapid urbanization, began to disintegrate under the strain of economic stagnation and the social dislocations resulting from increased migration from the central cities by those blacks able to benefit from open housing opportunities. By the early 1980s, analysts were describing what they characterized as a "new urban underclass," consisting mostly of black urban residents hopelessly mired in poverty, lacking many of the social structures essential to effective community life, and enmeshed in crime and other dysfunctional life-styles.

Even though many blacks continue to experience significant progress, overall, their economic gains have all but stalled, and about a third of the population remains in poverty. In 1991, the average black family income was only 57 percent of that for white families, down a full percentage point from the previous year. Moreover, the large poverty population hangs like a dark cloud over the black community, defining the status of the group and its policy priorities. The crises of long-term poverty and social disintegration, coupled with the twin scourges of illegal drugs and violent crime, have contributed to a profound sense of disillusionment and hopelessness, even among those blacks not directly affected. This grim economic outlook continues to define the world of black America.

On the other hand, by virtually any measure, the Jewish population has experienced dramatic social and economic gains in the postwar years and especially in the past three decades. These gains were not primarily the result of the civil rights movement, but the movement undoubtedly helped to remove some remaining barriers to opportunity for Jews. Rapid socioeconomic advancement enabled most of those Jews who were inner-city residents to move to the suburbs or to wealthier urban neighborhoods. Success also enabled them to give up the roles of inner-city merchants, landlords, and other service providers of the black inner-city poor. Thus the sharply contrasting experiences of the two communities have helped increase the physical distance and, to an extent, decrease their common concerns.

The changed political relationship

Easily the most dramatic change in the experience of African Americans is their greatly increased political participation as voters and officeholders. In the nearly three decades since enactment of the Voting Rights Act of 1965, African Americans have moved from the position of a largely excluded group on the margins of the political system to the political mainstream. Their level of voting in national elections is now only slightly lower than that of the rest of the electorate. That change, combined with major expansion of the concept of equal representation by the courts and the gradually increasing willingness of whites to vote for black candidates, has resulted in dramatic increases in the number and types of elective offices they hold. After the November 1992 elections, there were over 8000 African Americans in elective offices of all types in the country, including 39 members of the House of Representatives and one Senator. After playing prominent roles in the presidential primaries, general elections, and leadership of the Democratic Party, blacks now hold four cabinet and at least three top subcabinet positions. These accomplishments constitute considerable potential political influence. Especially noteworthy is the fact that recent black gains have been substantial in the national security and foreign policy areas—a black Chairman of the House Armed Services Committee and two senior State Department positions, along with the recent Chairman of the Joint Chiefs of Staff.

What has not changed significantly over the past three decades is the similarity in black-Jewish voting patterns, a fact that continues to contribute to the image of a black-Jewish political alliance. For example, in the 1992 presidential elections, voting patterns of the two groups were virtually identical. According to Voter Research Surveys, blacks cast 82 percent of their votes for Bill Clinton, 11 percent for George Bush, and 7 percent for Ross Perot.[27] Jews voted 78 percent for Clinton, 12 percent for Bush, and 10 percent for Perot. No other two communities in the electorate were as close in their voting patterns.

The 1992 vote continues a pattern in which blacks and Jews have consistently backed the Democratic Party and Democratic presidential candidates, though rarely by near identical margins. In 1988, for example, 86 percent of blacks and 64 per-

27. Milton D. Morris, "African Americans and the Clinton Victory," *The World & I* (Feb. 1993).

cent of Jews voted for the Democratic candidate, Michael Dukakis, in contrast to 45 percent of the nation at large and 40 percent of whites. In 1984, 90 percent of blacks and 67 percent of Jews voted for Democrat Walter Mondale, while 40 percent of all Americans and 35 percent of whites did. Similarities in partisan voting show up in the partisanship of blacks and Jews in Congress. The Congress, beginning in 1993, has 39 black representatives—38 Democrats and 1 Republican. It also has 33 Jewish representatives—27 Democrats and 6 Republicans. In the Senate, there is 1 black Democrat, along with 9 Jewish Democrats and 1 Jewish Republican.

The perception of black-Jewish political collaboration has been particularly strong at the municipal level. In a number of highly visible mayoral races involving black candidates, Jewish voters provided the critical margin of victory, emerging, as a result, as a critical ally. This was true starting with the first of the major mayoral races of the 1960s, those involving Carl Stokes in Cleveland, Ohio, and Richard Hatcher in Gary, Indiana. It was true again later for Harold Washington in Chicago and Wilson Goode in Philadelphia and, most recently, David Dinkins in New York City. In all these elections, victory represented an important political milestone for blacks and was achieved partly because of the support of Jewish voters in racially polarized elections.

In spite of their similar voting patterns, strong identification with the Democratic Party, and support for black candidates in key mayoral races, the black-Jewish political relationship has never been as deliberate or deep as the term "alliance" might suggest. Although Jewish votes did provide the margin of victory in key mayoral races when the electorate was otherwise divided along racial lines, the level of Jewish support never reached a majority of their votes. What was distinctive was that a much higher proportion of Jews supported these candidates than was the case for other whites. The 1989 New York mayoral race illustrates this situation. Mr. Dinkins, the black candidate and a long-time highly visible friend of the Jewish community, won about a third of the Jewish vote in his successful mayoral race, well above the percentage for other whites.

But even the modest level of Jewish electoral support for black candidates may be shrinking as relations between the two groups become increasingly complex. Some of this shrinkage may well be coincidental as prominent black mayoral figures were followed by less prominent ones or as the political climate changed in some cities. For example, black candidates for mayor in Chicago and Philadelphia failed to muster significant Jewish support in what were relatively lackluster primary bids. The same is likely to be true in Los Angeles and other cities in the near future. Even in New York, as Mayor Dinkins approaches reelection, he does so against a backdrop of highly visible, often intense, ethnic conflict and persistent criticism from elements of the Jewish community. Heightened ethnic and racial tensions in major cities, the growing preoccupation by the Jewish community with anti-Semitic expressions by some blacks, and the declining novelty of black electoral success are likely to weaken black-Jewish electoral alliances at the municipal level. Simultaneously, growing differences in overall policy agendas as well as on specific issues may be diminishing prospects for meaningful alliances at this level in the future.

Black-Jewish political collaboration may be declining for major substantive reasons as well. Their collaboration has been most effective on basic civil rights issues, but the number of such issues has been declining. Although blacks and Jews both support liberal policies and activist government, the two communities seem to mean very different things by "liberal policies." On racial matters, most Jews see the goal of activist government as that of achieving equal opportunity; however, they oppose policies they view as favoring one group over another. Thus, while they support programs in job training, education, and health care, most Jews oppose racially targeted programs, as well as school busing. For blacks, on the other hand, the goal of equal opportunity requires some race-specific policies to help achieve a level playing field. The sharp disagreements between the two groups over numerically based affirmative action programs illustrate the deep substantive division between the two communities. Most Jews view strong forms of affirmative action programs as a form of racial quotas that threaten their continued access to opportunities and violate their strong commitment to performance or merit-based achievement. Of course,

many Jews do support some affirmative action programs, but they distinguish between those programs that rely on general equal opportunity goals and timetables from those that appear to impose firm numerical quotas. For example, the American Jewish Committee has been on record in support of several affirmative action programs while opposing others.

Although black-Jewish political collaboration at the municipal level appears to be eroding, recent broad gains by blacks in state legislatures, in Congress, and in the federal executive branch are likely to provide important new bases for cooperation. The more than 500 black state legislators are close to composing an average of 10 percent of the approximately 40 state legislatures in which they serve. Because most are Democrats in Democratic Party-controlled legislatures, they have been moving rapidly into key leadership positions. As state governments have gained prominence in policymaking over the past decade, this black presence has become an increasingly important source of influence.

The growing black presence in Congress is an even more promising basis for a future political relationship between blacks and Jews. As of the November 1992 elections, blacks outnumber Jews in the House of Representatives, 39 to 33. Furthermore, these black members now serve on some of the key congressional committees, and they chair three: Armed Services, Government Operations, and Post Office and Civil Service. They also hold 13 subcommittee chairmanships. Together, these provide unprecedented opportunities to lead and otherwise influence major areas of national policy. Although the two communities disagree on some domestic policy issues, they also share a broad range of domestic policy concerns. The emerging Clinton policy agenda with its emphasis on education, job training, rebuilding cities, and universal access to health care is one on which black and Jewish legislators are likely to cooperate closely. The same is true for a number of important civil and individual rights issues still facing the nation.

The interests of the Jewish community have come to focus increasingly on defense and foreign policy issues relevant to Israel's well-being. African Americans, too, after having been only occasionally involved with foreign affairs, are becoming more interested in U.S. foreign policy, especially in relation to Africa and other developing areas. It is likely that future black-Jewish collaboration might focus more on common interests in Congress and particularly in international affairs. The prospects here are for important new successes for their joint efforts on such issues as humanitarian and development aid to developing countries. On the other hand, there may be new conflicts over policies in the Middle East on what constitutes fair treatment of Palestinians or security for Israel and over allocations of foreign assistance dollars. What seems clear is that, in any future political collaboration, blacks and Jews will be operating from positions closer to equality than at any time in the past. The primary currency of the relationship will be each group's power to achieve shared objectives.

Changing attitudes toward diversity and identity

Black-Jewish relations have been complicated by powerful new currents in group attitudes toward race and ethnicity and in the way these attitudes are expressed. Historically, the great divide in American society has been racial. The civil rights struggle was fundamentally about whether blacks would be fully incorporated into society with the same rights and opportunities as whites. Although blacks had long debated issues of their identity and status in the society, the overwhelming sentiment and drive were for inclusion in a multiracial, multiethnic community. Gradually, this simple black-white dichotomy has been changing to a more complex multiethnic picture, aided in large part by the heavy immigration of the past two decades. Along with this change has come a broader range of group conflicts, new concerns and insecurities by African Americans about their position and opportunities, and greater emphasis on group identity than at any time in the recent past.

In this changing environment, African Americans have been seeking to affirm their identity and assert their cultural autonomy with renewed vigor and controversy. They are demanding greater attention to their African heritage and their distinctive contributions to a common American culture. In part, this continues a centuries-long struggle with these issues, and in part, it is a response to disillusionment with the deteriorating socioeconomic circumstances and growing despair of large segments of the black population.

Use of the term "African American," demands for an Afrocentric curriculum in the public schools, increased conflicts with some newly arrived groups like Koreans, and increasingly angry expressions in speech, music, and literature are all reflections of this development.

In this environment, the black community has tended to accommodate or tolerate a very wide range of expression, some of it angry, distinctly antiwhite, and anti-Semitic, and some thoughtfully challenging their place in the common culture but most deeply committed to their heritage as part of an American society made richer by its diversity. Such accommodation of widely diverse views on matters of race, culture, and status have been a long-standing tradition in black America. The Black Panthers, the Republic of New Africa, the Nation of Islam, the National Urban League, the NAACP—all vastly different entities with different beliefs and behaviors—have nevertheless coexisted in the black community at various times, some gradually disappearing as others remain and grow. This tradition of accommodating diverse viewpoints has made many blacks less perturbed about, and less condemnatory of, extremist rhetoric and hateful expressions than might be expected or desirable.

Of course, such acceptance of within-group diversity is not peculiar to blacks. The Jewish community, too, has long been characterized by a very wide array of beliefs and attitudes about most major issues, including race relations. Indeed, the conflict that plagued the Crown Heights neighborhood is a clear ex-ample of the diversity within each of the two communities, involving as it did a small sect of Jews and a mostly Caribbean-born black population. So is the current, highly charged debate about race and ethnicity in the two communities. There are visible, vocal Jewish proponents of racist views, opponents of relationship building, and opportunistic proponents of the view that blacks are enemies of the Jews. More broadly, a concern with Jewish continuity and fears of population erosion through intermarriage have caused many in the Jewish community to turn inward and place less emphasis on building relations with others. In many respects, these trends parallel similar attitudes and expressions in the black community. What is noteworthy and encouraging is the fact that the hostile fringes in both communities have been and remain small. For all the many years of Jewish fears of rising black anti-Semitism, militant and overt anti-Semitic expression has remained confined to a relatively small segment of the black community, though its appeal to a larger audience is unknown and worrisome. Anti-Semitic behavior has also been prevalent among groups of whites who are both anti-Semitic and racist, notably skinheads and other neo-Nazis.

One factor that now magnifies black anti-Semitic expression and tends to exacerbate black-Jewish tensions is the communications revolution, which allows easy access to mass media, and the greater availability of major public forums for nontraditional, angry, even hateful expression. Thus the Nation of Islam preached its antiwhite and anti-Semitic views in the 1950s much as it does now, but today those views are expressed via talk radio and from the podium of major universities. We live in an age when outrageous expression has market appeal and when little is taboo. Yet, public and widely broadcast expressions of hatred have unprecedented potential to affect public attitudes. A major challenge both black and Jewish communities face is trying to maintain the taboo against hateful and bigoted expressions while being mindful of the rights of free speech and the dangers of overreacting in the current climate.

REVITALIZING THE RELATIONSHIP

This article has suggested that the black and Jewish communities have had a long and mutually beneficial relationship through most of this century. That relationship, based in part on mutual self-interest and always more limited and contentious than most commentators now recall, has been changing. To some observers this change amounts to a serious deterioration that threatens a once-potent alliance.

While claims of serious deterioration seem exaggerated, there clearly has been change, and it is important that both communities use those changes as starting points in revitalizing the relationship. A strong cooperative black-Jewish relationship is important because over time it has been clearly beneficial to both groups and it has demonstrated the efficacy of coalitions or alliances across social groups in the political system; because the two groups of necessity

share a strong interest in combatting hate and intolerance and fostering support for a diverse yet cohesive society; and because they have a broad array of shared policy interests. The challenge, therefore, is to determine how they can most effectively proceed to forge a relationship that appears likely to meet their respective interests. Three steps seem essential in that effort: to accept the principle of limited partnership, one that acknowledges the inevitability of disagreements and builds on areas of agreement; to choose issue areas of importance to both sides for long-term collaboration—a social policy agenda for expanding opportunities is one such area; and to resolve to serve as special guardians of the society's pluralist values.

Limited partnerships

Black-Jewish relations have been set back by a tendency on both sides to stress the issues on which there is disagreement and to overlook the broad areas of agreement and common interests. For many blacks, the Jewish community's failure to fully support affirmative action programs defines the state of the relationship, in much the same way that some black leaders' failure to swiftly denounce Louis Farrakhan and his anti-Semitic statements does for many Jews. But it is unrealistic to expect full, across-the-board agreement on issues or approaches to problems from two large, diverse communities. The success of black-Jewish relations depends in large part on the willingness of both sides to accept the inevitability of differences, to respect reasoned disagreements, and to keep litmus-test issues to a minimum.

The Jewish and African American communities already share a commitment to the core issues for each group. Both sides, for practical reasons as well as on principle, share an especially strong opposition to hate and bigotry whether expressed as anti-Semitism or racism. Both sides, too, share a strong commitment to basic civil and human rights and equal opportunity. In addition, the black community has a long unassailable commitment to the security of Israel, a fundamental concern of the Jewish community, and Jews have been prominent in the struggles against apartheid in South Africa and oppression in Haiti. On this foundation, it should be possible to build a trusting relationship able to cope with occasional differences in policy and strategy.

Fundamental to this view of relationship is mutual respect as equals in society. In the rhetoric of the 1960s' Black Power movement, there was often the assertion that equality was a prerequisite for coalition politics. Although African Americans are nowhere close to the economic status of the Jewish community, in the political arena there has been dramatic movement toward the kind of equality that makes for a trusting coalition of equals.

Focused collaboration

Relationships invariably are forged through cooperative action rather than through debates. It is not surprising that the two groups seemed closer and may have felt closer as they worked toward a clear set of shared goals. Currently, those goals —the civil rights agenda—have been partly replaced by a quality-of-life or economic opportunity agenda for African Americans. The relationship might be considerably enhanced by a joint effort on this front.

Already, there is evidence of general agreement about several major social policy issues, many being promoted by the Clinton administration. African Americans and Jews in Congress and in the public interest community are likely to form the core of support for new social policy initiatives. Such a development could have a strong reinforcing effect on the working relationship between the two communities. But there is hard work beyond the ready, almost automatic areas of agreement. Leaders of the two communities need to work to narrow their differences on strategies to expand black economic opportunities beyond general and essential steps like expanded educational opportunities.

The data show clearly that while education helps, it does not do nearly enough to narrow the black-white opportunity gap. Some form of affirmative action that pushes both public and private sectors to expand opportunities is critical. Yet indications are that the strategies that evolved out of the 1960s and 1970s affirmative action efforts might need rethinking, not only because of Jewish opposition but because the expanding categories of beneficiaries are rapidly undermining their effectiveness. Those sectors of the Jewish community like the American Jewish Committee that already provide qualified support for affirmative action by distinguishing between those that have the effects of firm quotas and those that do not might be in a good position to help fashion more effective and widely supportive measures. Such an effort would respond to the concern among many blacks that, while Jews support the broad principle of equal opportunity, they oppose any practical means of getting there.

Guardians of pluralism

Finally, this collaboration would not only serve to advance the interests of both communities and improve economic fairness in society broadly; it would also demonstrate that two communities can overcome differences to work toward common goals. In the current fractured atmosphere of American life, this demonstration of working pluralism would reaffirm the value of diversity and the potential for cooperation to overcome ethnic and racial division. The future of relations between the Jewish and African American communities will tell much about the potential of U.S. society to live fruitfully within its pluralistic structure, repudiate hatred, and secure a better future for all.

ANNALS, *AAPSS*, **530**, November 1993

Old Minorities, New Immigrants: Aspirations, Hopes, and Fears

By RITA J. SIMON

ABSTRACT: Contrary to the image attributed to American society—that it loves and welcomes immigrants—public opinion polls over the past 50-plus years show that the current cohort of immigrants, whoever they may be, is viewed with suspicion and distrust. Most Americans, even those of relatively recent immigrant origins, do not favor allowing more immigrants to enter, and a large plurality favor admitting fewer than the law permits. Historical analysis of the print media, political party platforms, and the Quota Acts beginning in the 1920s also reveals the United States' ambivalence about immigrants seeking admission at any time since the 1880s. In retrospect, those who came earlier are viewed as making important and positive contributions to our society and culture, but those who seek entry now, whenever "now" happens to be, are viewed, at best, with ambivalence and, more likely, with distrust and hostility.

Rita J. Simon, a sociologist, is a University Professor at the American University in Washington, DC. Previously, she was a member of the faculty at the University of Illinois. Her work on immigration includes The Ambivalent Welcome: Print Media, Public Opinion and Immigration *(with Susan Alexander; 1993);* New Lives: The Adjustment of Soviet Jewish Immigrants in the United States and Israel *(1985);* International Migration: The Female Experience *(with Caroline Brettell; 1986); and a special issue of* The Annals *of the American Academy of Political and Social Science entitled* Immigration and American Public Policy *(1986). From 1978 to 1981, Professor Simon served as editor of the* American Sociological Review.

IN a 1992 national poll of 2817 Americans of Mexican, Puerto Rican, and Cuban descent, 65 percent agreed with the statement "There are too many immigrants in this country." The poll was conducted by the Latino National Political Survey.[1] The respondents are citizens or residents of the United States. The views expressed by these Hispanic respondents are consistent with the long-term views of most Americans that there are too many immigrants in this country. For example, as represented in Table 1, responses to national polls show that between 1946 and 1990 most respondents favored a decrease in the number of immigrants permitted to enter this country, and at no point in this 45-year time span did more than 13 percent believe the United States should admit more immigrants than the law permitted.

But when the American people, most of whom are the descendants of immigrants, are asked to look back on what immigrants have contributed to this country, many find that the contributions have been a good thing for the country. They are proud to proclaim, "We are a country of immigrants." How does one explain the seeming inconsistency between the responses in Table 1 along with the responses by the Hispanic community to the 1992 poll, on the one hand, and the general pride that most Americans express about their immigrant roots, on the other? We can shed some light on these seemingly inconsistent and contradictory views by looking at the responses to the question posed in Table 2.

1. *Washington Post*, 16 Dec. 1992.

The responses to the question suggest that immigrants who arrived long ago are the ones who are valued and who are perceived as having made positive contributions to our cultural, social, and economic life. But the contemporary immigrants, those about whom decisions—such as whom to admit and under what circumstances—have to be made, receive negative evaluations by a majority of Americans. Of course, we recognize that many of the former immigrant communities who currently enjoy the positive status—the Irish, Jews, Italians, Poles—were themselves the subjects of vicious attacks a hundred or so years earlier, when they began to arrive in great numbers. It is also important to remember that the majority of the current respondents are themselves descendants of the more than 20 million Southern and Eastern European Catholic, Orthodox, and Jewish immigrants who arrived in this country between the 1880s and the 1920s. The majority also consists of the more than 10 million immigrants from Mexico, the Caribbean, Central and Latin America, and Asia in the post-World War II era. Overall, then, the responses show that most descendants of immigrants hold the view that once their relatives are safely on the other side of the door, it is right and proper to shut and lock the door behind them.

The various ethnic organizations that dot the American social and political landscape today generally do not advocate more liberal immigration policies across the board. In the 1980s, for example, when several immigration bills were being debated in

TABLE 1

PUBLIC OPINION ON THE NUMBER OF IMMIGRANTS THAT SHOULD BE PERMITTED TO ENTER THE UNITED STATES: DISTRIBUTION OF RESPONSES (Percentage)

Response	Years								
	1946*	1953	1965	1977	1981	1982	1986	1988	1990‡
More/increase	5	13	8	7	5	4	7	6	9
Same/present level	32	37	39	37	22	23	35	34	29
Fewer/decrease	37 [14]†	39	33	42	65	66	49	53	48
No opinion/don't know	12	11	20	14	8	7	9	7	14

SOURCE: Roper Center, University of Connecticut, Storrs, 1991.

*In 1946, the question was phrased, "Should we permit more persons from Europe to come to this country each year than we did before the war, should we keep the number about the same, or should we reduce the number?" In the subsequent polls, the question was usually phrased as follows: "Should immigration be kept at its present level, increased, or decreased?"

†1946 was the one time "none" was offered as a choice of response, and 14 percent selected that choice.

‡In 1990, the question was phrased, "Is it your impression that the current immigration laws allow too many immigrants, too few immigrants, or about the right number of immigrants into this country each year?"

TABLE 2

PERCEPTION OF IMMIGRANTS IN LIGHT OF THEIR CONTRIBUTIONS TO THE UNITED STATES: DISTRIBUTION OF RESPONSES (Percentage)

Since the beginning of our country, people of many different religions, races, and nationalities have come here and settled. Here is a list of some different groups. Would you read down the list and, thinking both of what they have contributed to this country and have gotten from this country, for each one tell me whether you think, on balance, they have been a good thing or a bad thing for this country?

	Good	Bad	Difference
English	66	6	60
Irish	62	7	55
Jews	59	9	50
Germans	57	11	46
Italians	56	10	46
Poles	53	12	41
Japanese	47	18	29
Blacks	46	16	30
Chinese	44	19	25
Mexicans	25	34	−9
Koreans	24	30	−6
Vietnamese	20	38	−18
Puerto Ricans	17	43	−26
Haitians	10	39	−29
Cubans	9	59	−50

SOURCE: Gallup Poll, Gallup Organization, 1982.
NOTE: The two categories not shown are "mixed feelings" and "don't know."

congressional committees and on the floor of the Congress, the various ethnic groups did most of their lobbying in favor of maintaining the priority for family unification as the primary criterion for admission; they did not lobby for admitting more immigrants generally or for giving technical skills and qualifications higher priority.

In "Mexican Americans, Mexican Immigrants and Immigration Reform," Rudolfo De La Garza argued that "Mexican Americans are less supportive of Mexican immigration than Anglo observers have suggested."[2] He claimed, "Their attitudes are best understood within the context of that population's historical effort to establish itself as a legitimate and permanent part of American society."[3]

De La Garza reported the results of a 1984 survey of Texan Chicanos that showed that 40 percent of the respondents believed that undocumented workers were harmful to this country, in contrast to 32 percent who thought they were beneficial. In addition, 48 percent agreed that the undocumented abuse welfare privileges in contrast to 40 percent who disagreed. Fifty-two percent approved of employer sanctions, and over 40 percent were either neutral about or supportive of national identity cards.[4] These results are consistent with the findings of the 1992 Latino Political Survey commented on at the outset of this article. The

larger point, however, is that the opinions of Mexican Americans are not atypical. Other hyphenated Americans, be they of European or Asian backgrounds, share those beliefs. Immigration is either not a salient issue for them or they favor restrictionist policies.

In a survey conducted in 1985 of 82 eminent social scientists—anthropologists, economists, historians, political scientists, psychologists, and sociologists—about the consequences of immigration to the United States, one of the questions asked was, "Do you believe that recent immigrants are: less likely to assimilate, as likely to assimilate, more likely to assimilate, do not know?" While most respondents—52 percent—thought recent immigrants were as likely to assimilate as those who came earlier, 36 percent thought the recent immigrants would not be as likely to assimilate as ones who had come earlier. These eminent social scientists believe, as have most Americans for the past 140 years, that the current cohort of immigrants is special —especially different, especially incapable of assimilating, and especially dangerous to our values and institutions.[5]

The current controversy over the Haitians is a case in point and not atypical. The large majority of Americans of European, Asian, or Latin American descent either do not support or actively oppose admitting the Haitians. There are some black jour-

2. Rudolfo O. De La Garza, "Mexican Americans, Mexican Immigrants and Immigration Reform," in *Clamor at the Gates*, ed. Nathan Glazer (San Francisco: ICS Press, 1985), pp. 93-109.

3. Ibid., p. 105

4. Ibid., p. 102.

5. Stephen Moore, "Social Scientists' Views on Immigrants and U.S. Immigration Policy: A Postscript," *The Annals* of the American Academy of Political and Social Science, 487:213-17 (Sept. 1986).

nalists and free-market black economists such as Walter Williams and Thomas Sowell who have strongly and publicly advocated admitting the Haitians and granting them refugee status. But most of the white ethnic community and the hyphenated Asian and Hispanic groups have maintained a noisy silence on the issue. The reasons Americans oppose admitting the Haitians are basically the same reasons that all other previous cohorts beginning in the mid-nineteenth century have not been welcomed by those already here. The newcomers, it was believed then and most current citizens believe now, would compete for jobs, housing, education, and social services with those who are already here. The newcomers would never "adjust," "assimilate," or "integrate" into the larger culture. The newcomers would "marginalize" American society. They would threaten our basic political institutions. For example, they would not understand separation of church and state and would not be capable of self-governance.

EARLY ANTI-IMMIGRATION SENTIMENTS

These have been the arguments used against all of the "current cohorts" from the time the new immigrants began arriving, first from Ireland, then a decade or two later from Southern and Eastern Europe. The term "new immigrants" was applied to these groups, who were non-English speaking, largely Catholic, urban dwellers; they were not landowners; and they lacked technical skills. Before the mid-1850s, most newcomers to the United States

looked like and enjoyed the same religious and cultural heritage as the white Americans already here. They were largely of English-speaking, Protestant backgrounds and they came to settle the land. Many were fair-skinned, with blond hair and blue eyes. They shared the heritage of "free men" who understood and were part of a great democratic tradition. In contrast, new immigrants were described by Francis Walker, then Commissioner General of the Immigration Service, in the following terms:

The entrance into our political, social and industrial life of such vast masses of peasantry, degraded below our utmost conceptions, is a matter which no intelligent patriot can look upon without the gravest apprehension and alarm. These people have no history behind them which is of a nature to encouragement. They have none of the inherited instincts and tendencies which made it comparatively easy to deal with the immigration of the older time. They are beaten men from beaten races; representing the worst failures in the struggle for existence. Centuries are against them, as centuries were on the side of those who formerly came to us. They have none of the ideas and aptitudes which fit men to take up readily and easily the problem of self care and self government, such as belong to those who are descended from the tribes that met under the oak-trees of old Germany to make laws and choose chieftains.[6]

Even earlier in American history, there were always manifestations of fear and hostility against people who were different. For example, all of the New England colonies except Rhode Island excluded non-Puritans. In

6. Francis Walker's article in *Atlantic Monthly* (June 1896).

1666, Maryland passed the first naturalization act in the colonies and, in doing so, limited the privilege of citizenship to foreign-born Protestants. In 1671, Virginia adopted similar legislation, followed by South Carolina in 1696. During the French and Indian wars in 1689, Huguenot communities in New York, Pennsylvania, Virginia, and Rhode Island were attacked because the Huguenots were suspected of loyalty to the French. German settlers were attacked in Pennsylvania in the 1750s. All of the colonies passed laws against voting and officeholding by Catholics and Jews.

In the decades before the Civil War, anti-Catholic and anti-immigrant sentiments coalesced into political parties bearing such names as the "Native American Party" (1840s) and, the most famous of all, the "Know-Nothing Party" (1850s). Supporters of these parties rioted in the port cities, they burned Catholic churches, and they sought to extend the naturalization requirement to 21 years and to exclude Catholics and all foreign-born from holding public office. The leaders of the Know-Nothing Party developed the slogan, "Whose country is this anyway?" They claimed that the foreigners were degrading American character and morals.

At no time were these views expressed more blatantly than in the U.S. treatment of Chinese and Japanese immigrants in the late nineteenth century and first decade of the twentieth century. In 1882, Congress passed the Chinese Exclusion Act, which suspended entry of Chinese workers for 10 years and barred all foreign-born Chinese from acquiring U.S. citizenship. In 1907, the U.S. accomplished much the same objectives with respect to the Japanese with its Gentlemen's Agreement. Never before had U.S. immigration policy exhibited such overt racist behavior, nor has it since. The Chinese Exclusion Act remained in effect until 1943. Congress repealed it in the midst of World War II, when the United States and China were allies.

Both the Democratic and the Republican Party platforms from 1884 to the onset of World War I emphasized their support of Chinese exclusion and, indeed, the exclusion of all Asians from the United States. The 1884 platform of the Democratic Party stated, "American civilization demands that against the immigration of Mongolians to these shores our gate be closed."[7] The Republican platform included this plank: "We pledge ourselves to sustain the present law restricting Chinese immigration and to provide such further legislation as is necessary to carry out its purposes."[8]

In 1900, the Democrats favored "the continuance and strict enforcement of the Chinese Exclusion Law and application to the same class of all Asiatic races."[9] In 1908, that party stated, "We are opposed to the admission of Asiatic immigrants who cannot be amalgamated with our population or whose presence among us would raise a race issue and involve

7. E. P. Hutchinson, *Legislative History of American Immigration Policy 1798-1965* (Philadelphia: University of Pennsylvania Press, 1981), p. 626.

8. Ibid., p. 627.

9. Ibid., p. 629.

us in diplomatic controversies with Oriental powers."[10]

In all of the national political campaigns of the 1920s, the two major parties carried planks in their platforms that supported restriction of immigrants and the newly enacted Quota Laws.

In 1932, the Republican Party reminded the voters that it was the party that passed the Quota Acts of 1921 and 1924:

The restriction of immigration is a Republican policy. Our party formulated and enacted into law the quota system, which for the first time has made possible an adequate control of foreign immigration. Rigid examination of applicants in foreign countries prevented the coming of criminals and other undesirable classes, while other provisions of the law have enabled the President to suspend immigration of foreign wage earners who otherwise, directly or indirectly, would have increased unemployment among native-born and legally resident foreign-born wage-earners in this country. As a result, immigration is now less than at any time during the past one hundred years. We favor the continuance and strict enforcement of our present laws upon this subject.[11]

The Quota Act of 1921 limited the annual number of entrants to the United States of each admissible nationality to 3 percent of the foreign-born of that nationality as recorded in the U.S. census of 1910. It also set the limit on European immigration at 350,000. Quotas were established for countries in Europe, the Near East, Africa, Australia, and New Zealand. No quotas were imposed on im-

10. Ibid., p. 631.
11. Ibid., pp. 635-36.

migrants from countries in the Western hemisphere.

In 1924, the year that the 1921 Quota Act expired, Congress passed the National Quota Act, which was even more restrictive than the previous Quota Act. This new act set national quotas at 2 percent of the number of the respective nationalities in the 1890 population. The Quota Act of 1924 also provided that beginning on 1 July 1927, the quota limit would be 150,000, allocated on the basis of the estimated national origins distribution of the population of the continental United States in 1920. That portion of the 1924 act was postponed twice, but it finally became effective on 1 July 1929. The act barred from entry all aliens who were ineligible for citizenship.

In the first two decades of the twentieth century, Congress passed other pieces of restrictionist legislation that limited groups on the basis of political activities and ideologies and medical histories. Anarchists and epileptics, for example, were excluded by these measures.

NATIONAL POLLS

Much of the anti-immigrant sentiment expressed in the decade before the United States entered what became World War II grew out of strong isolationist beliefs and the specific belief that the United States had made a mistake when it joined the allied forces during World War I. For example, when the American public was asked, "If the question of the United States going to war against Germany and Italy came up for a national vote within the next two weeks, would you vote to go into the war or stay out?" 86 percent preferred, in May 1940, to "stay out"; in January 1941, 88 percent preferred to "stay out." Even in October 1941, two months before the attack on Pearl Harbor, 79 percent of the respondents said they would "vote to . . . stay out."[12]

During the 1930s, in response to questions about helping refugees from Nazi Germany come to the United States, large majorities of the American public consistently indicated their unwillingness to help. In May 1938, the public was asked, "What is your attitude toward allowing German, Austrian, and other political refugees to come to the United States?" Five percent responded that they would "encourage [the refugees to come to the United States], even if we have to raise immigration quotas"; 18 percent felt that the country should "allow them to come, but [should] not raise quotas"; 68 percent responded that, "with conditions as they are, we should keep them out"; and 9 percent "didn't know." When asked in January 1939, after Germany had annexed Austria and invaded Czechoslovakia, "Should we allow a large number of Jewish exiles from Germany to come to the United States to live?" 71 percent answered "no." When asked, again in January of 1939, "If you were a member of the incoming Congress, would you vote yes or no on a bill to open the doors of the United States to a larger number of European refugees than are now admitted under our immigration

quota?" 83 percent said they would vote "no."[13]

As shown in Table 3, support for refugees increased after the end of World War II and remained strong until the 1970s, when the origins of the refugees shifted from Europe to Southeast Asia and Cuba; then support dropped sharply.

CURRENT ANTI-IMMIGRATION SENTIMENTS

A description of the contemporary anti-immigration alliance would show that it is made up of groups who have strong organized labor, environmental, and zero-population-growth support, along with support from traditional conservatives and right-wingers in the form of Senator Alan Simpson (R-Wyoming), Pat Buchanan, and David Duke. The pro-immigrant alliance have their share of support from traditional conservatives, such as the American Enterprise Institute and the Hudson Institute; from libertarians, such as Cato; and from Democrats such as Congresspersons Pat Schroeder, William Lipinski, and Howard Berman.

The Federation for American Immigration Reform (FAIR) is the major anti-immigration organization. It operates with an annual budget of $1.7 million and a membership of some 50,000 supporters. Immigration is FAIR's only business, and its platform covers a wide range of immigration issues. Basically, FAIR advocates setting a ceiling on immigration at roughly 300,000 newcomers per year. (As of the 1990 Immigration

12. Rita J. Simon, *Public Opinion in America: 1936-1970* (Chicago: Rand McNally, 1974), p. 125.

13. *Fortune*, Roper Center, University of Connecticut, Storrs, May 1938.

Act, that figure is less than 40 percent of current levels.) FAIR contends that immigration contributes to higher social welfare costs, overpopulation, and resource depletion.

The Immigration Reform Law Institute, which is the legal offspring of FAIR, files amicus briefs in suits dealing with illegal immigration and suits against the Immigration and Naturalization Service. The institute was formed in 1986, after FAIR had successfully lobbied Congress to pass the Immigration Reform and Control Act, which imposes penalties on employers who hire illegal immigrants.

Larger in membership than FAIR and operating with a $2.2 million budget, the American Immigration Control Foundation (AICF) assumes more extreme anti-immigrant positions than FAIR. It believes that immigrants take U.S. jobs, go on welfare, and waste law enforcement resources. It faults immigration for weakening the incentives of Third World nations to adopt population control policies, and it accuses Third World nations of allowing excessive population growth with the intent of exporting their excessive numbers to the United States. AICF has argued that people from authoritarian countries appreciate freedom but that they lack the heritage and the habits to maintain it. AICF has lobbied consistently against the passage of any bills that would increase immigration or provide amnesty to illegal aliens.

The Rockford Institute, under the presidency of Allan Carlson, advocates much the same position as AICF. In its magazine *Chronicles: A Magazine of American Culture*, it has stated that immigrants are a threat to U.S. cultural norms. Immigrants cannot comprehend certain intangible notions of U.S. politics, art, literature, religious morality, and work ethic. The *Chronicles* has accused liberal elites of bringing in new immigrants and aliens to bolster their power base in the underclass.

Although smaller in its number of active supporters and budget than either FAIR or AICF, the Center for Immigration Studies (CIS) is another broad-based anti-immigration organization. It holds current immigration policies responsible for the existence of Asian organized crime rings. The center has published studies on the negative effects of immigration on public education, housing, and job opportunities for U.S. workers. In the past, it has criticized U.S. immigration policy as "complicating the pursuit of more traditional political, security and trade concerns" with such countries as Cuba, Vietnam, and the Soviet Union.[14]

The most extreme anti-immigrant message is spread by the National Association for the Advancement of White People (NAAWP), whose chairperson is David Duke and which reports a membership of some 40,000. The NAAWP warns that Hispanic immigrants are engaged in a secretive irredentist movement to seize the U.S. Southwest and give it back to Mexico. The NAAWP also claims that most immigrants from non-European origins are not assimilable

14. Quoted from testimony by Rose M. Hanes, executive director, Population Environment Balance, Inc., before U.S., Congress, House, Committee on the Judiciary, 27 Sept. 1989, p. 3.

TABLE 3

PUBLIC OPINION ON THE NUMBER OF REFUGEES THE
UNITED STATES SHOULD ADMIT: DISTRIBUTION OF RESPONSES (Percentage)

Response	Years												
	1938 (1)	1939 (2)	1946 (3)	1947 (4)	1953 (5)	1956 (6)	1957 (7)	1965 (8)	1975 (9)	1975 (10)	1978 (11)	1979 (12)	1980 (13)
Allow to enter	5[a] 18[b]		10[a] 43[b]		47	11	60	64	36	37	32	34	26
Keep out	68[c]	83	23[c] 17[d]	72	48	48	31	23	52	49	57	57	66
Don't know	9[d]		7		5	7	9	13	12	14	11	9	8

1. What is your attitude toward allowing German, Austrian, and other political refugees to come to the United States?
   a. Encourage.
   b. Allow them to come, but do not raise quotas.
   c. With conditions as they are, we should keep them out.
   d. Don't know.
2. If you were a member of the incoming Congress, would you vote yes or no on a bill to open the doors of the United States to a larger number of European refugees than are now admitted under our immigration quota?
3. There are still a lot of refugees or displaced persons in European camps who cannot go back to the homes they had before the war. Which of these four statements comes closest to what you think this country should do about these refugees?
   a. We should admit all of these refugees who are well and strong to the United States, no matter what other countries do.
   b. We should take only our share of these refugees and insist that other countries do the same.
   c. There are still too many here now and we should not admit any more at all. But we should help to get them settled elsewhere.
   d. They are a problem for the European countries to worry about and we should let those countries handle the problem.

4. Would you vote yes or no on a bill in Congress to let 100,000 selected European refugees come to this country in each of the next four years in addition to the 150,000 immigrants now permitted to enter every year under our present quota?

5. Do you favor a law that President Eisenhower asked the Congress to pass that would admit 240,000 refugees to enter the United States over a two-year period?

6. Do you feel the United States is letting in too many refugees from Hungary, about the right number, or not enough?

7. There are an estimated 15 million refugees in different parts of the world. These people have been forced to leave their home countries or have fled for various reasons. Are you in favor of or against allowing any of those refugees to come to the United States to make their new home?

8. Do you think the United States' immigration policy should or should not have provisions for admitting people who escape from communism?

9. If [the] South Vietnamese are evacuated, should they be permitted to live in the United States or not?

10. Do you favor or oppose 130,000 Vietnamese refugees coming to live in the United States?

11. Thinking now about the Indochinese refugees, the so-called "boat people," would you favor or oppose the United States' relaxing its immigration policies so that many of these people could come to live in the United States?

12. Should the U.S. government permit . . . Cubans to come and live in the United States?

13. Some people say that the U.S. government should permit persons who leave other countries because of political oppression to come and live in the United States. Others say that the federal government should halt all immigration until the national unemployment rate falls below five percent. Which point of view comes closer to the way you feel—that political refugees should be permitted to immigrate to the United States or that immigration should be halted until the unemployment rate in the United States drops?

SOURCE: Roper Center, University of Connecticut, Storrs, 1981.

into white American culture. It favors a return to the pre-1965 national origins system, whereby immigrants are permitted to enter as a national origins percentage base equal to the proportion of people from a given country already living in the United States as of a certain time period. The NAAWP advocates bringing home all the military forces stationed overseas and employing them on the Mexican border to catch illegals.

U.S. Citizens, Inc., worries about immigrants' imposition upon citizen rights in the areas of political representation, public services, and natural resources. It charges immigrants with seeking affirmative action units and utilizing civil rights laws in order to secure unfair advantages.

These organizations provide a flavor of the platforms assumed by the major generally anti-immigrant groups in the country. They view immigrants as threats to American culture and ideals and as competitors for jobs, housing, and educational opportunities. They believe that immigrants take undue advantage of our welfare system and that they do not understand how to live in a free society. They believe immigrants threaten population stabilization and depletion of our natural resources.

Another category of anti-immigrant organization comprises those for whom immigration is a by-product of their central concerns: population stabilization and preserving the environment. These groups include Zero Population Growth, Californians for Population Stabilization, Population Crisis Committed, the Sierra Club, Population Environment Balance, and Negative Population Growth (NPG).

NPG's primary objective is to achieve negative population growth for the United States, and immigrant control is an important part of that strategy. NPG states that zero net migration should be the cornerstone of U.S. immigration policy. Annual net migration—immigration minus emigration—should no longer be allowed to contribute to U.S. population growth. Zero net migration means that total immigration should never exceed emigration in any given year. To achieve zero net migration, NPG advocates tallying illegal immigration and reducing legal immigration so that it does not exceed an overall ceiling of 100,000 a year. According to NPG, immigration is an environmental and resource issue. "Each additional immigrant, regardless of his or her personal qualifications and merit, swells our numbers and further increases the already dangerous level of environmental pollution. In addition, most immigrants have low skills and are illiterate. They add nothing positive to the labor market."[15] About illegal immigration NPG holds this view: "Illegal immigration constitutes a massive and criminal invasion of our country. It is inconceivable that any other country would allow its laws to be violated, with almost complete impunity, by millions of illegal aliens each year."[16]

Population Environment Balance has assumed much the same stance on immigration as has NPG, but for

15. Negative Population Growth, "Zero Net Immigration," *NPG Forum*, p. 2 (1990).
16. Ibid., p. 1.

Population Environment Balance, the major focus is the environment. Population Environment Balance estimates that approximately 200,000 Americans leave the United States in a given year; therefore, it recommends that an equal number, 200,000, should be allowed to enter, and refugees should be included in that ceiling.

The Sierra Club, with its membership of half a million and an annual budget of $29.9 million, shares the sentiments of NPG and Population Environment Balance. Population Crisis Committee perceives immigration as a serious economic drain on the United States. Immigrants take jobs from poor people and force them onto welfare. Many immigrant children, according to Population Crisis Committee, are illiterate or cannot speak English and will not be able to find jobs and will end up on welfare.

CONCLUDING REMARKS

To return to the opening theme of this article, contemporary immigrants are no less popular than the immigrants who began coming to this country after the Civil War and for all the years in between. The only popular or valued immigrants are those who came long ago, whenever "long ago" happened to be. Thus, today, we look back and feel what a good thing it has been for this country that people from Italy, Russia, Greece, Poland, Hungary, and so on came to settle in the United States. Even the Chinese and Japanese immigrants of the last century are remembered warmly, and their contributions valued. But for those coming now, the story has not changed. The refrain is, "They are unassimilable. They are a threat to our institutions and values. They deplete and draw upon scarce natural and human resources. We should keep them out." Unfortunately, the descendants of immigrants over the past 100-plus years have never made common cause with the immigrants arriving during any contemporary period and said to them, "We made it; so will you. We overcame obstacles; so will you. We became a part of the civic culture, indeed we contributed to that culture; we know you will, too. We welcome you and we will help you."

The New Second Generation:
Segmented Assimilation and Its Variants

By ALEJANDRO PORTES and MIN ZHOU

ABSTRACT: Post-1965 immigration to the United States has given rise to a vigorous literature focused on adult newcomers. There is, however, a growing new second generation whose prospects of adaptation cannot be gleaned from the experience of their parents or from that of children of European immigrants arriving at the turn of the century. We present data on the contemporary second generation and review the challenges that it confronts in seeking adaptation to American society. The concept of segmented assimilation is introduced to describe the diverse possible outcomes of this process of adaptation. The concept of modes of incorporation is used for developing a typology of vulnerability and resources affecting such outcomes. Empirical case studies illustrate the theory and highlight consequences of the different contextual situations facing today's second generation.

Alejandro Portes is John Dewey Professor of Sociology and International Relations at the Johns Hopkins University. He is coauthor, with Rubén G. Rumbaut, of Immigrant America: A Portrait *(1990) and, with Alex Stepick, of* City on the Edge: The Transformation of Miami *(1993).*

Min Zhou is assistant professor of sociology at Louisiana State University. She is the author of Chinatown: The Socioeconomic Potential of an Urban Enclave *(1992).*

NOTE: The data on which this article is partially based were collected by the project Children of Immigrants: The Adaptation Process of the Second Generation, supported by the Andrew W. Mellon Foundation, the National Science Foundation (grant no. SES-9022555), and the Spencer Foundation. The article was written while the senior author was in residence at the Russell Sage Foundation, whose support is also gratefully acknowledged. The authors are exclusively responsible for the contents of this article.

My name is Herb
and I'm not poor;
I'm the Herbie that you're looking for,
like Pepsi,
a new generation
of Haitian determination—
I'm the Herbie that you're looking for.

A beat tapped with bare hands, a few dance steps, and the Haitian kid was rapping. His song, titled "Straight Out of Haiti," was being performed at Edison High, a school that sits astride Little Haiti and Liberty City, the largest black area of Miami. The lyrics captured well the distinct outlook of his immigrant community. The panorama of Little Haiti contrasts sharply with the bleak inner city. In Miami's Little Haiti, the storefronts leap out at the passersby. Bright blues, reds, and oranges vibrate to Haitian merengue blaring from sidewalk speakers.[1] Yet, behind the gay Caribbean exteriors, a struggle goes on that will define the future of this community. As we will see later on, it involves the second generation—children like Herbie— subject to conflicting pressure from parents and peers and to pervasive outside discrimination.

Growing up in an immigrant family has always been difficult, as individuals are torn by conflicting social and cultural demands while they face the challenge of entry into an unfamiliar and frequently hostile world. And yet the difficulties are not always the same. The process of growing up American oscillates between smooth acceptance and traumatic confrontation depending on the characteristics that immigrants and their children bring along and the social context that receives them. In this article, we explore some of these factors and their bearing on the process of social adaptation of the immigrant second generation. We propose a conceptual framework for understanding this process and illustrate it with selected ethnographic material and survey data from a recent survey of children of immigrants.

Research on the new immigration —that which arose after the passage of the 1965 Immigration Act—has been focused almost exclusively on the first generation, that is, on adult men and women coming to the United States in search of work or to escape political persecution. Little noticed until recently is the fact that the foreign-born inflow has been rapidly evolving from single adult individuals to entire family groups, including infant children and those born to immigrants in the United States. By 1980, 10 percent of dependent children in households counted by the census were second-generation immigrants.[2] In the late 1980s, another study put the number of students in kindergarten through twelfth grade in American schools who spoke a lan-

1. Alejandro Portes and Alex Stepick, *City on the Edge: The Transformation of Miami* (Berkeley: University of California Press, 1993), chap. 8.

2. Defined as native-born children with at least one foreign-born parent or children born abroad who came to the United States before age 12. See Leif Jensen, *Children of the New Immigration: A Comparative Analysis of Today's Second Generation,* paper commissioned by the Children of Immigrants Research Project, Department of Sociology, Johns Hopkins University, reprinted as Institute for Policy Research and Evaluation Working Paper no. 1990-32 (University Park: Pennsylvania State University, Aug. 1990).

guage other than English at home at 3 to 5 million.[3]

The great deal of research and theorizing on post-1965 immigration offers only tentative guidance on the prospects and paths of adaptation of the second generation because the outlook of this group can be very different from that of their immigrant parents. For example, it is generally accepted among immigration theorists that entry-level menial jobs are performed without hesitation by newly arrived immigrants but are commonly shunned by their U.S.-reared offspring. This disjuncture gives rise to a race between the social and economic progress of first-generation immigrants and the material conditions and career prospects that their American children grow to expect.[4]

Nor does the existing literature on second-generation adaptation, based as it is on the experience of descendants of pre-World War I immigrants, offer much guidance for the understanding of contemporary events. The last sociological study of children of immigrants was Irving Child's *Italian or American? The Second Generation in Conflict*, published fifty years ago.[5] Conditions at the time were quite different from those confronting settled immigrant groups today.

Two such differences deserve special mention. First, descendants of European immigrants who confronted the dilemmas of conflicting cultures were uniformly white. Even if of a somewhat darker hue than the natives, their skin color reduced a major barrier to entry into the American mainstream. For this reason, the process of assimilation depended largely on individual decisions to leave the immigrant culture behind and embrace American ways. Such an advantage obviously does not exist for the black, Asian, and mestizo children of today's immigrants.

Second, the structure of economic opportunities has also changed. Fifty years ago, the United States was the premier industrial power in the world, and its diversified industrial labor requirements offered to the second generation the opportunity to move up gradually through better-paid occupations while remaining part of the working class. Such opportunities have increasingly disappeared in recent years following a rapid process of national deindustrialization and global industrial restructuring. This process has left entrants to the American labor force confronting a widening gap between the minimally paid menial jobs that immigrants commonly accept and the high-tech and professional occupations requiring college degrees that native elites occupy.[6] The gradual disappearance of intermediate

3. Joan N. First and John W. Carrera, *New Voices: Immigrant Students in U.S. Public Schools* (Boston: National Coalition of Advocates for Students, 1988).

4. Michael Piore, *Birds of Passage* (New York: Cambridge University Press, 1979); Herbert Gans, "Second-Generation Decline: Scenarios for the Economic and Ethnic Futures of the Post-1965 American Immigrants," *Ethnic and Racial Studies* 15:173-92 (Apr. 1992).

5. Irving L. Child, *Italian or American? The Second Generation in Conflict* (New Haven, CT: Yale University Press, 1943).

6. See, for example, Saskia Sassen, "Changing Composition and Labor Market Location of Hispanic Immigrants in New York City, 1960-1980," in *Hispanics in the U.S. Economy*, ed. George J. Borjas and Marta Tienda (New York: Academic Press, 1985), pp. 299-322.

opportunities also bears directly on the race between first-generation economic progress and second-generation expectations, noted previously.

THE NEW AMERICANS AT A GLANCE

Before examining this process in detail, it is important to learn a little more about today's second generation. In 1990, the foreign-born population of the United States reached an estimated 21.2 million. In absolute terms, this is the highest number in the history of the nation, although relative to the native-born population, the figure is lower than that at the turn of the century. A century ago, in 1890, immigrants represented 14.8 percent of the total population, almost double today's figure of 8.6 percent. The foreign-stock population, composed of immigrants and their descendants, is, however, much higher. In 1990, roughly 46 million, or 18.5 percent of the total U.S. population, were estimated to be of foreign stock. This yields a net second-generation total of 24.8 million, or 10.9 percent of the American population.[7]

As an estimate of the new second generation, this figure is inflated by the presence of offspring of older immigrants. A team of demographers at the Urban Institute have estimated the contribution of post-1960 immigration, including immigrants and their children, to the total 1990 U.S. population. According to their esti-

mate, if immigration had been cut off in 1960, the total population in 1990 would have been 223.4 million and not the 248.7 actually counted. Hence post-1960 immigration contributed approximately 25.3 million. Subtracting estimates of net immigration for 1960-90 provided by the same researchers, the new second generation, formed by children of post-1960 immigrants, represents 7.7 million, or 3.4 percent of the native-born population. This is a lower-bound estimate based on a demographic model and not on an actual count. It excludes children born to mixed foreign-native couples who are also normally counted as part of the second generation.[8]

More important, however, is the prospect for growth in future years. Given the record increase of immigration since 1960, the second generation as a whole is expected to grow rapidly, surpassing its former peak of roughly 28 million in 1940 sometime during this decade. As noted previously, however, the racial and ethnic composition of the component of the second generation attributable to post-1960 immigration is quite different from that which peaked just before World War II. Over 85 percent of children of immigrants in 1940 were born to Europeans, or, in current terminology, non-Hispanic whites. By contrast, approximately 77 percent of post-1960 immigrants are non-Europeans. Of the post-1960 immigrants, 22.4 percent are classi-

7. Jeffrey S. Passel and Barry Edmonston, "Immigration and Race: Recent Trends in Immigration to the United States" (Paper no. PRIP-UI-22, Urban Institute, May 1992), tab. 2.

8. The new immigration is defined as that which started after the 1965 Immigration Act. Inclusion of 1960-65 immigrants in the totals just mentioned leads to only a slight overcount due to the relatively low numbers arriving before passage of the act. See ibid., tab. 9.

fied as Asians, 7.6 as blacks, and 47 percent as Hispanics. The latter group, which originates in Mexico and other Latin American countries, poses a problem in terms of phenotypical classification since Hispanics can be of any race.[9]

According to the 1990 census, 51.7 percent of the 22.3 million Hispanics counted were white, 3.4 percent black, and 42.7 percent of another race. The latter figure, possibly corresponding to the category of mixed race, or mestizos, was slightly larger among Mexicans, who constitute 60.4 percent of the total Hispanic population. Applying these figures with some adjustments to the post-1960 immigrant flow, it is reasonable to assume that approximately half of Hispanic immigrants would be classified as nonwhite. This phenotypical category would hence comprise a majority, roughly 54 percent, of the total inflow.[10]

Individual data from the 1990 census have not been released as of this writing. In an effort to learn more about the new second generation, Leif Jensen conducted an analysis of the one-in-a-thousand version of the Public Use Microdata Sample A (PUMS) from the 1980 census. He identified 3425 children living in households with at least one foreign-born parent and who themselves were either native-born or had immigrated to the United States at a

9. Ibid.

10. U.S., Department of Commerce, Bureau of the Census, *Race by Hispanic Origin, 1990 Census of Population and Housing*, special tabulation prepared by the Ethnic and Hispanic Branch (Washington, DC: U.S. Department of Commerce, 1992).

young age.[11] The number represented 5.1 percent of native-born native-parentage children identified in the sample, a figure that is close to the estimated contribution of post-1960 immigration to the 1980 U.S. population, 5.8 percent.

The ethnic classification of Jensen's sample of new second-generation children in 1980 also corresponds closely with that of post-1965 immigrants reported previously. In Jensen's sample, 17.9 percent were classified as Asians, 6.8 percent as blacks, and 45.5 percent as Hispanics. The data do not provide a racial breakdown of Hispanics, but they do contain information on their national origin. Sixty-five percent of the 1564 post-1965 Hispanic children were of Mexican origin; 7.5 percent of Cuban origin; and the remaining 27.5 percent were from all other Latin American nationalities. Table 1 presents selected sociodemographic characteristics of this sample and compares them with those of native-born children of native parentage.

Not surprisingly, second-generation youths are far more likely to be bilingual than their native-parentage counterparts. Less than half of the children of immigrants speak English only, and two-thirds speak a language other than English at home in contrast with the overwhelming English exclusivity among native-parentage youth. However, linguistic assimilation is evident in the fact that only 12 percent of the second generation reports speaking English poorly. Households with immigrant parents are far more likely to be

11. In most cases, before age 12. See Jensen, *Children of the New Immigration.*

TABLE 1

**SELECTED CHARACTERISTICS OF POST-1965
SECOND-GENERATION YOUTHS AND NATIVE YOUTHS
OF NATIVE PARENTAGE, 1980 (Percentage unless noted)**

Children's Characteristics	Post-1965 Immigrant Parent ($N = 3,425$)	Native-born Parents ($N = 67,193$)
Female	46.8	47.4
Mean age	7.5 years	11.9 years
Race or ethnicity		
White	27.4	78.9
Black	6.8	14.4
Hispanic	45.7	5.4
Mexican	29.7	3.3
Cuban	3.5	0.0
Other	12.5	2.1
Asian	19.5	0.5
Chinese	4.3	0.1
Filipino	5.1	0.1
Korean	2.6	0.0
Vietnamese	1.4	0.0
Other	6.1	0.3
English ability		
Speaks English only	47.7	95.5
Very well	26.5	2.7
Well	13.8	1.3
Not well or not at all	12.0	0.5
Language spoken at home		
English	33.6	94.9
Other	66.4	5.1
Household type		
Couple	89.7	79.0
Single male head	1.5	2.7
Single female head	8.8	18.3
Area of residence		
Central city	39.6	17.4
Non-central-city metropolitan area	48.4	49.8
Mixed	6.5	11.7
Nonmetropolitan	5.5	21.1
State of residence*		
California	32.4	8.1
New York	12.8	7.2
Texas	9.9	6.1
Illinois	5.7	5.2
Florida	5.0	3.5
New Jersey	4.9	3.1

(continued)

TABLE 1 Continued

Children's Characteristics	Post-1965 Immigrant Parent (N = 3,425)	Native-born Parents (N = 67,193)
Mean family income	$19,502	$23,414
Poverty rate	20.8	13.8
Mean education of family head	10.9 years	12.2 years
Mean education, self[†]	11.5 years	12.0 years
High school dropout[†]	22.8	22.9
School type		
Public	83.4	86.6
Private	16.6	13.4

NOTE: The youths in this sample reside in households with at least one parent present. This table is based on U.S. Census Public Use Microdata Sample A as reported in Leif Jensen, *Children of the New Immigration: A Comparative Analysis of Today's Second Generation*, paper commissioned by the Children of Immigrants Research Project, Department of Sociology, Johns Hopkins University, reprinted as Institute for Policy Research and Evaluation Working Paper no. 1990-32 (University Park: Pennsylvania State University, Aug. 1990), tabs. 1-8.

*The six states with the largest concentrations of post-1965 immigrant parents.

†Restricted to those aged 20 or more and not enrolled in school.

urban and to be found in central cities. Their geographic distribution by state also differs significantly from native-headed households. Just six states account for 71 percent of immigrant households while the same states contain only 33 percent of the natives. Not surprisingly, immigrant parents tend to have more modest socioeconomic characteristics, as indicated by their lower family income, higher poverty rates, and lower education of the family head. However, they are about twice less likely to head single-parent households than are natives. Greater family cohesiveness may have something to do with second-generation educational outcomes. Figures in Table 1 indicate that children of immigrants are as likely to attend private schools, as unlikely to be dropouts, and as likely to graduate from high school as native-parentage youth.[12]

These comparisons are, of course, based on averages that conceal great diversity within each universe. Among second-generation youths in particular, preliminary field research indicates wide differences in educational, linguistic, and social psychological outcomes. None is more important than the forms that an inexorable process of cultural assimilation takes among different immigrant nationalities and its effects on their youths. We explore these differences and pro-

12. Because of data limitations, comparisons of years of education completed and high school dropouts are limited to persons aged 20 or older still living with their parents. These results may not be representative of the respective universes of adult individuals. See ibid.

vide a theoretical explanation of their causes in the next sections.

ASSIMILATION
AS A PROBLEM

The Haitian immigrant community of Miami is composed of some 75,000 legal and clandestine immigrants, many of whom sold everything they owned in order to buy passage to America. First-generation Haitians are strongly oriented toward preserving a strong national identity, which they associate both with community solidarity and with social networks promoting individual success.[13] In trying to instill national pride and an achievement orientation in their children, they clash, however, with the youngsters' everyday experiences in school. Little Haiti is adjacent to Liberty City, the main black inner-city area of Miami, and Haitian adolescents attend predominantly inner-city schools. Native-born youths stereotype Haitians as too docile and too subservient to whites and they make fun of French and Creole and of the Haitians' accent. As a result, second-generation Haitian children find themselves torn between conflicting ideas and values: to remain Haitian they would have to face social ostracism and continuing attacks in school; to become American—black American in this case—they would have to forgo their parents' dreams of making it in America on the basis of ethnic solidarity and preservation of traditional values.[14]

An adversarial stance toward the white mainstream is common among inner-city minority youths who, while attacking the newcomers' ways, instill in them a consciousness of American-style discrimination. A common message is the devaluation of education as a vehicle for advancement of all black youths, a message that directly contradicts the immigrant parents' expectations. Academically outstanding Haitian American students, "Herbie" among them, have consciously attempted to retain their ethnic identity by cloaking it in black American cultural forms, such as rap music. Many others, however, have followed the path of least effort and become thoroughly assimilated. Assimilation in this instance is not into mainstream culture but into the values and norms of the inner city. In the process, the resources of solidarity and mutual support within the immigrant community are dissipated.

An emerging paradox in the study of today's second generation is the peculiar forms that assimilation has adopted for its members. As the Haitian example illustrates, adopting the outlooks and cultural ways of the native-born does not represent, as in the past, the first step toward social and economic mobility but may lead to the exact opposite. At the other end, immigrant youths who remain firmly ensconced in their respective

---

13. See Alex Stepick, "Haitian Refugees in the U.S." (Report no. 52, Minority Rights Group, London, 1982); Alex Stepick and Alejandro Portes, "Flight into Despair: A Profile of Recent Haitian Refugees in South Florida," *International Migration Review*, 20:329-50 (Summer 1986).

14. This account is based on fieldwork in Miami conducted in preparation for a survey of immigrant youths in public schools. The survey and preliminary results are described in the final section of this article.

ethnic communities may, by virtue of this fact, have a better chance for educational and economic mobility through use of the material and social capital that their communities make available.[15]

This situation stands the cultural blueprint for advancement of immigrant groups in American society on its head. As presented in innumerable academic and journalistic writings, the expectation is that the foreign-born and their offspring will first acculturate and then seek entry and acceptance among the native-born as a prerequisite for their social and economic advancement. Otherwise, they remain confined to the ranks of the ethnic lower and lower-middle classes.[16] This portrayal of the requirements for mobility, so deeply embedded in the national consciousness, stands contradicted today by a growing number of empirical experiences.

A closer look at these experiences indicates, however, that the expected consequences of assimilation have

15. On the issue of social capital, see James S. Coleman, "Social Capital in the Creation of Human Capital," *American Journal of Sociology*, supplement, 94:S95-121 (1988); Alejandro Portes and Min Zhou, "Gaining the Upper Hand: Economic Mobility among Immigrant and Domestic Minorities," *Ethnic and Racial Studies*, 15:491-522 (Oct. 1992). On ethnic entrepreneurship, see Ivan H. Light, *Ethnic Enterprise in America: Business and Welfare among Chinese, Japanese, and Blacks* (Berkeley: University of California Press, 1972); Kenneth Wilson and W. Allen Martin, "Ethnic Enclaves: A Comparison of the Cuban and Black Economies in Miami," *American Journal of Sociology*, 88:135-60 (1982).

16. See W. Lloyd Warner and Leo Srole, *The Social Systems of American Ethnic Groups* (New Haven, CT: Yale University Press, 1945); Thomas Sowell, *Ethnic America: A History* (New York: Basic Books, 1981).

not entirely reversed signs, but that the process has become segmented. In other words, the question is into what sector of American society a particular immigrant group assimilates. Instead of a relatively uniform mainstream whose mores and prejudices dictate a common path of integration, we observe today several distinct forms of adaptation. One of them replicates the time-honored portrayal of growing acculturation and parallel integration into the white middle-class; a second leads straight in the opposite direction to permanent poverty and assimilation into the underclass; still a third associates rapid economic advancement with deliberate preservation of the immigrant community's values and tight solidarity. This pattern of segmented assimilation immediately raises the question of what makes some immigrant groups become susceptible to the downward route and what resources allow others to avoid this course. In the ultimate analysis, the same general process helps explain both outcomes. We advance next our hypotheses as to how this process takes place and how the contrasting outcomes of assimilation can be explained. This explanation is then illustrated with recent empirical material in the final section.

VULNERABILITY AND RESOURCES

Along with individual and family variables, the context that immigrants find upon arrival in their new country plays a decisive role in the course that their offspring's lives will follow. This context includes such broad variables as political relations between sending and receiving countries and the state of the economy in the latter and such specific ones as the size and structure of preexisting coethnic communities. The concept of modes of incorporation provides a useful theoretical tool to understand this diversity. As developed in prior publications, modes of incorporation consist of the complex formed by the policies of the host government; the values and prejudices of the receiving society; and the characteristics of the coethnic community. These factors can be arranged in a tree of contextual situations, illustrated by Figure 1. This figure provides a first approximation to our problem.[17]

To explain second-generation outcomes and their segmented character, however, we need to go into greater detail into the meaning of these various modes of incorporation from the standpoint of immigrant youths. There are three features of the social contexts encountered by today's newcomers that create vulnerability to downward assimilation. The first is color, the second is location, and the third is the absence of mobility ladders. As noted previously, the majority of contemporary immigrants are nonwhite. Although this feature may appear at first glance as an individual characteristic, in reality it is a trait belonging to the host society. Prejudice is not intrinsic to a particular skin color or racial type, and, indeed, many immigrants never experienced it in their native lands. It is by virtue of moving into a new social environment, marked by different values and prejudices, that physical features become redefined as a handicap.

The concentration of immigrant households in cities and particularly in central cities, as documented previously, gives rise to a second source of vulnerability because it puts new arrivals in close contact with concentrations of native-born minorities. This leads to the identification of the condition of both groups—immigrants and the native poor—as the same in the eyes of the majority. More important, it exposes second-generation children to the adversarial subculture developed by marginalized native youths to cope with their own difficult situation.[18] This process of socialization may take place even when first-generation parents are moving ahead economically and, hence, their children have no objective reasons for embracing a countercultural message. If successful, the process can effectively block parental plans for intergenerational mobility.

The third contextual source of vulnerability has to do with changes in the host economy that have led to the evaporation of occupational ladders for intergenerational mobility. As noted previously, new immigrants may form the backbone of what remains of labor-intensive manufacturing in the cities as well as in their growing personal services sector, but these are niches that seldom offer channels for upward mobility. The new hourglass economy, created by

17. See Alejandro Portes and Rubén G. Rumbaut, *Immigrant America: A Portrait* (Berkeley: University of California Press, 1990), chap. 3.

18. See Mercer L. Sullivan, *"Getting Paid"*: *Youth, Crime, and Work in the Inner City* (Ithaca, NY: Cornell University Press, 1989), chaps. 1, 5.

FIGURE 1

MODES OF INCORPORATION: A TYPOLOGY

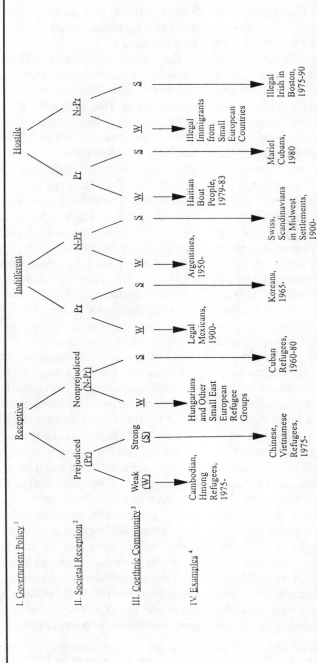

SOURCE: Adapted from Alejandro Portes and Rubén G. Rumbaut, *Immigrant America: A Portrait* (Berkeley: University of California Press, 1990), p. 91. Copyright © 1990 by The Regents of the University of California.

1. Receptive policy is defined as legal entry with resettlement assistance, indifferent as legal entry without resettlement assistance, hostile as active opposition to a group's entry or permanence in the country.

2. Prejudiced reception is defined as that accorded to nonphenotypically white groups; nonprejudiced is that accorded to European and European-origin whites.

3. Weak coethnic communities are either small in numbers or composed primarily of manual workers; strong communities feature sizable numerical concentrations and a diversified occupational structure including entrepreneurs and professionals.

4. Examples include immigrant groups arriving from the start of the century to the present. Dates of migration are approximate. Groups reflect broadly but not perfectly the characteristics of each ideal type.

economic restructuring, means that children of immigrants must cross a narrow bottleneck to occupations requiring advanced training if their careers are to keep pace with their U.S.-acquired aspirations. This race against a narrowing middle demands that immigrant parents accumulate sufficient resources to allow their children to effect the passage and to simultaneously prove to them the viability of aspirations for upward mobility. Otherwise, assimilation may not be into mainstream values and expectations but into the adversarial stance of impoverished groups confined to the bottom of the new economic hourglass.

The picture is painted in such stark terms here for the sake of clarity, although in reality things have not yet become so polarized. Middle-level occupations requiring relatively modest educational achievements have not completely vanished. By 1980, skilled blue-collar jobs—classified by the U.S. census as "precision production, craft, and repair occupations"—had declined by 1.1 percent relative to a decade earlier but still represented 13 percent of the experienced civilian labor force, or 13.6 million workers. Mostly clerical administrative support occupations added another 16.9 percent, or 17.5 million jobs. In 1980, occupations requiring a college degree had increased by 6 percent in comparison with 1970, but they still employed less than a fifth—18.2 percent—of the American labor force.[19] Even in the largest cities, oc-cupations requiring only a high school diploma were common by the late 1980s. In New York City, for example, persons with 12 years or less of schooling held just over one half of the jobs in 1987. Clerical, service, and skilled blue-collar jobs not requiring a college degree represented 46 percent.[20] Despite these figures, there is little doubt that the trend toward occupational segmentation has increasingly reduced opportunities for incremental upward mobility through well-paid blue-collar positions. The trend forces immigrants today to bridge in only one generation the gap between entry-level jobs and professional positions that earlier groups took two or three generations to travel.

Different modes of incorporation also make available, however, three types of resources to confront the challenges of contemporary assimilation. First, certain groups, notably political refugees, are eligible for a variety of government programs including educational loans for their children. The Cuban Loan Program, implemented by the Kennedy administration in connection with its plan to resettle Cuban refugees away from South Florida, gave many impoverished first- and second-generation Cuban youths a chance to attend college. The high proportion of professionals and executives among Cuban American workers today, a figure on a par with that for native white work-

A (MRDF) (Washington, DC: Department of Commerce, 1983).

20. Thomas Bailey and Roger Waldinger, "Primary, Secondary, and Enclave Labor Markets: A Training System Approach," *American Sociological Review*, 56:432-45 (1991).

19. U.S., Department of Commerce, Bureau of the Census, *Census of Population and Housing, 1980: Public Use Microdata Samples*

ers, can be traced, at least in part, to the success of that program.[21] Passage of the 1980 Refugee Act gave to subsequent groups of refugees, in particular Southeast Asians and Eastern Europeans, access to a similarly generous benefits package.[22]

Second, certain foreign groups have been exempted from the traditional prejudice endured by most immigrants, thereby facilitating a smoother process of adaptation. Some political refugees, such as the early waves of exiles from Castro's Cuba, Hungarians and Czechs escaping the invasions of their respective countries, and Soviet Jews escaping religious persecution, provide examples. In other cases, it is the cultural and phenotypical affinity of newcomers to ample segments of the host population that ensures a welcome reception. The Irish coming to Boston during the 1980s are a case in point. Although many were illegal aliens, they came into an environment where generations of Irish Americans had established a secure foothold. Public sympathy effectively neutralized governmental hostility in this case, culminating in a change of the immi-

gration law directly benefiting the newcomers.[23]

Third, and most important, are the resources made available through networks in the coethnic community. Immigrants who join well-established and diversified ethnic groups have access from the start to a range of moral and material resources well beyond those available through official assistance programs. Educational help for second-generation youths may include not only access to college grants and loans but also the existence of a private school system geared to the immigrant community's values. Attendance at these private ethnic schools insulates children from contact with native minority youths, while reinforcing the authority of parental views and plans.

In addition, the economic diversification of several immigrant communities creates niches of opportunity that members of the second generation can occupy, often without a need for an advanced education. Small-business apprenticeships, access to skilled building trades, and well-paid jobs in local government bureaucracies are some of the ethnic niches documented in the recent lit-

---

21. Professionals and executives represented 25.9 percent of Cuban-origin males aged 16 years and over in 1989; the figure for the total adult male population was 26 percent. See Jesus M. García and Patricia A. Montgomery, *The Hispanic Population of the United States: March 1990*, Current Population Reports, ser. P-20, no. 449 (Washington, DC: Department of Commerce, 1991).

22. Portes and Rumbaut, *Immigrant America*, pp. 23-25; Robert L. Bach et al., "The Economic Adjustment of Southeast Asian Refugees in the United States," in *World Refugee Survey, 1983* (Geneva: United Nations High Commission for Refugees, 1984), pp. 51-55.

23. The 1990 Immigration Act contains tailor-made provisions to facilitate the legalization of Irish immigrants. Those taking advantage of the provisions are popularly dubbed "Kennedy Irish" in honor of the Massachusetts Senator who coauthored the act. On the 1990 act, see Michael Fix and Jeffrey S. Passel, "The Door Remains Open: Recent Immigration to the United States and a Preliminary Analysis of the Immigration Act of 1990" (Working paper, Urban Institute and RAND Corporation, 1991). On the Irish in Boston, see Karen Tumulty, "When Irish Eyes Are Hiding . . . ," *Los Angeles Times*, 29 Jan. 1989.

erature.[24] In 1987, average sales per firm of the smaller Chinese, East Indian, Korean, and Cuban enterprises exceeded $100,000 per year and they jointly employed over 200,000 workers. These figures omit medium-sized and large ethnic firms, whose sales and work forces are much larger.[25] Fieldwork in these communities indicates that up to half of recently arrived immigrants are employed by coethnic firms and that self-employment offers a prime avenue for mobility to second-generation youths.[26] Such community-mediated opportunities provide a solution to the race between material resources and second-generation aspirations not available through competition in the open labor market. Through creation of a capitalism of their own, some immigrant groups have thus been able to circumvent outside discrimination and the threat of vanishing mobility ladders.

24. Bailey and Waldinger, "Primary, Secondary, and Enclave Labor Markets"; Min Zhou, *New York's Chinatown: The Socioeconomic Potential of an Urban Enclave* (Philadelphia: Temple University Press, 1992); Wilson and Martin, "Ethnic Enclaves"; Suzanne Model, "The Ethnic Economy: Cubans and Chinese Reconsidered" (Manuscript, University of Massachusetts at Amherst, 1990).

25. U.S., Department of Commerce, Bureau of the Census, *Survey of Minority-Owned Business Enterprises, 1987*, MB-2 and MB-3 (Washington, DC: Department of Commerce, 1991).

26. Alejandro Portes and Alex Stepick, "Unwelcome Immigrants: The Labor Market Experiences of 1980 (Mariel) Cuban and Haitian Refugees in South Florida," *American Sociological Review*, 50:493-514 (Aug. 1985); Zhou, *New York's Chinatown*; Luis E. Guarnizo, "One Country in Two: Dominican-Owned Firms in New York and the Dominican Republic" (Ph.D. diss. Johns Hopkins University, 1992); Bailey and Waldinger, "Primary, Secondary, and Enclave Labor Markets."

In contrast to these favorable conditions are those foreign minorities who either lack a community already in place or whose coethnics are too poor to render assistance. The condition of Haitians in South Florida, cited earlier, provides an illustration of one of the most handicapped modes of incorporation encountered by contemporary immigrants, combining official hostility and widespread social prejudice with the absence of a strong receiving community.[27] From the standpoint of second-generation outcomes, the existence of a large but downtrodden coethnic community may be even less desirable than no community at all. This is because newly arrived youths enter into ready contact with the reactive subculture developed by earlier generations. Its influence is all the more powerful because it comes from individuals of the same national origin, "people like us" who can more effectively define the proper stance and attitudes of the newcomers. To the extent that they do so, the first-generation model of upward mobility through school achievement and attainment of professional occupations will be blocked.

THREE EXAMPLES

Mexicans and Mexican Americans

Field High School (the name is fictitious) is located in a small coastal community of central California whose economy has long been tied to

27. Stepick, "Haitian Refugees in the U.S."; Jake C. Miller, *The Plight of Haitian Refugees* (New York: Praeger, 1984).

agricultural production and immigrant farm labor. About 57 percent of the student population is of Mexican descent. An intensive ethnographic study of the class of 1985 at Field High began with school records that showed that the majority of U.S.-born Spanish-surname students who had entered the school in 1981 had dropped out by their senior year. However, only 35 percent of the Spanish-surname students who had been originally classified by the school as limited English proficient (LEP) had dropped out. The figure was even lower than the corresponding one for native white students, 40 percent. LEP status is commonly assigned to recently arrived Mexican immigrants.[28]

Intensive ethnographic fieldwork at the school identified several distinct categories in which the Mexican-origin population could be classified. Recent Mexican immigrants were at one extreme. They dressed differently and unstylishly. They claimed an identity as Mexican and considered Mexico their permanent home. The most academically successful of this group were those most proficient in Spanish, reflecting their prior levels of education in Mexico. Almost all were described by teachers and staff as courteous, serious about their schoolwork, respectful, and eager to please as well as naive and unsophisticated. They were commonly classified as LEP.

The next category comprised Mexican-oriented students. They spoke Spanish at home and were generally classified as fluent English proficient (FEP). They had strong bicultural ties with both Mexico and the United States, reflecting the fact that most were born in Mexico but had lived in the United States for more than five years. They were proud of their Mexican heritage but saw themselves as different from the first group, the *recién llegados* (recently arrived), as well as from the native-born Chicanos and Cholos, who were derided as people who had lost their Mexican roots. Students from this group were active in soccer and the Sociedad Bilingue and in celebrations of May 5th, the anniversary of the Mexican defeat of French occupying forces. Virtually all of the Mexican-descent students who graduated in the top 10 percent of their class in 1981 were identified as members of this group.

Chicanos were by far the largest Mexican-descent group at Field High. They were mostly U.S.-born second- and third-generation students whose primary loyalty was to their in-group, seen as locked in conflict with white society. Chicanos referred derisively to successful Mexican students as "schoolboys" and "schoolgirls" or as "wannabes." According to M. G. Matute-Bianchi,

To be a Chicano meant in practice to hang out by the science wing . . . *not* eating lunch in the quad where all the "gringos" and "schoolboys" hang out . . . cutting classes

28. M. G. Matute-Bianchi, "Ethnic Identities and Patterns of School Success and Failure among Mexican-Descent and Japanese-American Students in a California High School," *American Journal of Education*, 95:233-55 (Nov. 1986). This study is summarized in Rubén G. Rumbaut, "Immigrant Students in California Public Schools: A Summary of Current Knowledge" (Report no. 11, Center for Research on Effective Schooling for Disadvantaged Children, Johns Hopkins University, Aug. 1990).

by faking a call slip so you can be with your friends at the 7-11 . . . sitting in the back of classes and not participating . . . *not* carrying your books to class . . . *not* taking the difficult classes . . . doing the minimum to get by.[29]

Chicanos merge imperceptibly into the last category, the Cholos, who were commonly seen as "low riders" and gang members. They were also native-born Mexican Americans, easily identifiable by their deliberate manner of dress, walk, speech, and other cultural symbols. Chicanos and Cholos were generally regarded by teachers as "irresponsible," "disrespectful," "mistrusting," "sullen," "apathetic," and "less motivated," and their poor school performance was attributed to these traits.[30] According to Matute-Bianchi, Chicanos and Cholos were faced with what they saw as a forced-choice dilemma between doing well in school or being a Chicano. To act white was regarded as disloyalty to one's group.

The situation of these last two groups exemplifies losing the race between first-generation achievements and later generations' expectations. Seeing their parents and grandparents confined to humble menial jobs and increasingly aware of discrimination against them by the white mainstream, U.S.-born children of earlier Mexican immigrants readily join a reactive subculture as a means of protecting their sense of self-worth. Participation in this subculture then leads to serious barriers to their chances of upward mobility because school achievement is defined as antithetical to ethnic solidarity. Like Haitian students at Edison High, newly arrived Mexican students are at risk of being socialized into the same reactive stance, with the aggravating factor that it is other Mexicans, not native-born strangers, who convey the message. The principal protection of *mexicanos* against this type of assimilation lies in their strong identification with home-country language and values, which brings them closer to their parents' cultural stance.

Punjabi Sikhs in California

Valleyside (a fictitious name) is a northern California community where the primary economic activity is orchard farming. Farm laborers in this area come often from India; they are mainly rural Sikhs from the Punjab. By the early 1980s, second-generation Punjabi students already accounted for 11 percent of the student body at Valleyside High. Their parents were no longer only farm laborers, since about a third had become orchard owners themselves and another third worked in factories in the nearby San Francisco area. An ethnographic study of Valleyside High School in 1980-82 revealed a very difficult process of assimilation for Punjabi Sikh students. According to its author, M. A. Gibson, Valleyside is "redneck country," and white residents are extremely hostile to immigrants who look different and speak a different language: "Punjabi teenagers are told they stink . . . told to go back to India . . . physically abused by majority students who spit at them, refuse to sit by them in class

29. Matute-Bianchi, "Ethnic Identities and Patterns," p. 253.

30. Rumbaut, "Immigrant Students," p. 25.

or in buses, throw food at them or worse."[31]

Despite these attacks and some evidence of discrimination by school staff, Punjabi students performed better academically than majority Anglo students. About 90 percent of the immigrant youths completed high school, compared to 70-75 percent of native whites. Punjabi boys surpassed the average grade point average, were more likely to take advanced science and math classes, and expressed aspirations for careers in science and engineering. Girls, on the other hand, tended to enroll in business classes, but they paid less attention to immediate career plans, reflecting parental wishes that they should marry first. This gender difference is indicative of the continuing strong influence exercised by the immigrant community over its second generation. According to Gibson, Punjabi parents pressured their children against too much contact with white peers who may "dishonor" the immigrants' families, and defined "becoming Americanized" as forgetting one's roots and adopting the most disparaged traits of the majority, such as leaving home at age 18, making decisions without parental consent, dating, and dancing. At the same time, parents urged children to abide by school rules, ignore racist remarks and avoid fights, and learn useful skills, including full proficiency in English.[32]

31. M. A. Gibson, *Accommodation without Assimilation: Sikh Immigrants in an American High School* (Ithaca, NY: Cornell University Press, 1989), p. 268.

32. Gibson, *Accommodation without Assimilation*. The study is summarized in Rumbaut, "Immigrant Students," pp. 22-23.

The overall success of this strategy of selective assimilation to American society is remarkable because Punjabi immigrants were generally poor on their arrival in the United States and confronted widespread discrimination from whites without the benefit of either governmental assistance or a well-established coethnic community. In terms of our typology of vulnerability and resources, the Punjabi Sikh second generation was very much at risk except for two crucial factors. First, immigrant parents did not settle in the inner city or in close proximity to any native-born minority whose offspring could provide an alternative model of adaptation to white-majority discrimination. In particular, the absence of a downtrodden Indian American community composed of children of previous immigrants allowed first-generation parents to influence decisively the outlook of their offspring, including their ways of fighting white prejudice. There was no equivalent of a Cholo-like reactive subculture to offer an alternative blueprint of the stance that "people like us" should take.

Second, Punjabi immigrants managed to make considerable economic progress, as attested by the number who had become farm owners, while maintaining a tightly knit ethnic community. The material and social capital created by this first-generation community compensated for the absence of an older coethnic group and had decisive effects on second-generation outlooks. Punjabi teenagers were shown that their parents' ways paid off economically, and this fact, plus their community's cohesiveness, endowed them with a source of pride to counteract outside discrimination. Through this strategy of selective assimilation, Punjabi Sikhs appeared to be winning the race against the inevitable acculturation of their children to American-style aspirations.

Caribbean youths in South Florida

Miami is arguably the American city that has been most thoroughly transformed by post-1960 immigration. The Cuban Revolution had much to do with this transformation, as it sent the entire Cuban upper class out of the country, followed by thousands of refugees of more modest backgrounds. Over time, Cubans created a highly diversified and prosperous ethnic community that provided resources for the adaptation process of its second generation. Reflecting this situation are average Cuban family incomes that, by 1989, approximated those of the native-born population; the existence in 1987 of more than 30,000 Cuban-owned small businesses that formed the core of the Miami ethnic enclave; and the parallel rise of a private school system oriented toward the values and political outlook of this community.[33] In terms of the typology of vulnerability and resources, well-sheltered Cuban American teenagers lack any extensive exposure to outside discrimination, they have little contact with youths from disadvantaged minorities, and the development of an en-

clave creates economic opportunities beyond the narrowing industrial and tourist sectors on which most other immigrant groups in the area depend. Across town, Haitian American teenagers face exactly the opposite set of conditions, as has been shown.

Among the other immigrant groups that form Miami's ethnic mosaic, two deserve mention because they represent intermediate situations between those of the Cubans and Haitians. One comprises Nicaraguans escaping the Sandinista regime during the 1980s. They were not as welcomed in the United States as were the Cuban exiles, nor were they able to develop a large and diversified community. Yet they shared with Cubans their language and culture, as well as a militant anti-Communist discourse. This common political outlook led the Cuban American community to extend its resources in support of their Nicaraguan brethren, smoothing their process of adaptation.[34] For second-generation Nicaraguans, this means that the preexisting ethnic community that provides a model for their own assimilation is not a downtrodden group but rather one that has managed to establish a firm and positive presence in the city's economy and politics.

The second group comprises West Indians coming from Jamaica, Trinidad, and other English-speaking Caribbean republics. They generally arrive in Miami as legal immigrants, and many bring along professional and business credentials as well as the advantage of fluency in English. These individual advantages are dis-

33. García and Montgomery, *Hispanic Population*; U.S., Department of Commerce, Bureau of the Census, *Survey of Minority-Owned Business Enterprises*, MB-2.

34. Portes and Stepick, *City on the Edge*, chap. 7.

counted, however, by a context of reception in which these mostly black immigrants are put in the same category as native-born blacks and discriminated against accordingly. The recency of West Indian migration and its small size have prevented the development of a diversified ethnic community in South Florida. Hence new arrivals experience the full force of white discrimination without the protection of a large coethnic group and with constant exposure to the situation and attitudes of the inner-city population. Despite considerable individual resources, these disadvantages put the West Indian second generation at risk of bypassing white or even native black middle-class models to assimilate into the culture of the underclass.

A recently completed survey of eighth- and ninth-graders in the Dade County (Miami) and Broward County (Ft. Lauderdale) schools includes sizable samples of Cuban, Haitian, Nicaraguan, and West Indian second-generation children. The study defined "second generation" as youths born in the United States who have at least one foreign-born parent or those born abroad who have lived in the United States for at least five years. All eligible students in the selected schools were included. The survey included both inner-city and suburban public schools, as well as private schools and those where particular foreign-origin groups were known to concentrate. The sample was evenly divided between boys and girls, and the students ranged in age between 12 and 17.[35]

35. Alejandro Portes and Lisandro Perez, Children of Immigrants: The Adaptation Pro-

Table 2 presents the responses of second-generation students from these nationalities to a battery of attitudinal and self-identification questions. The large Cuban-origin sample is divided between those attending public and private school. Large socioeconomic differences between the four groups are highlighted in the first panel of Table 2. Cuban children in private schools have the best-educated parents and those with the highest-status occupations. Haitians in public schools have parents who rank lowest on both dimensions. Nicaraguans and West Indians occupy intermediate positions, with parents whose average education is often higher than that of the parents of public school Cubans but whose occupational levels are roughly the same. Reflecting these differences, over half of private school Cuban respondents define their families as upper middle class or higher, while only a third of Haitians and Nicaraguans do so.[36]

The next panel of the table presents differences in ethnic self-identification. Less than one-fifth of these second-generation students identify themselves as nonhyphenated Americans. The proportion is highest among higher-status Cubans, but

cess of the Second Generation (Project conducted at the Department of Sociology, Johns Hopkins University, in progress).

36. Because of the large sample size, .001 is used as the criterion of statistical significance in these tabulations. Cramér's V^2 is used as the principal measure of strength of association. In comparison with other coefficients, it has the advantage of a constant range between 0 and 1. Higher values indicate stronger association. Eta is similarly defined but is used only for the continuous parental occupational status variables.

TABLE 2
SECOND-GENERATION EIGHTH- AND NINTH-GRADE STUDENTS
BY NATIONAL ORIGIN, SOUTH FLORIDA SCHOOLS, 1992 (Percentage unless noted)

	Cubans in Private School (N = 172)	Cubans in Public School (N = 968)	Haitians (N = 136)	Nicaraguans (N = 319)	West Indians (N = 191)	Total (N = 1,786)	p <	V^2 or Eta
Socioeconomic characteristics								
Father college graduate	50.0	21.4	11.0	38.6	18.8	26.1	.001	.27
Mother college graduate	39.0	17.5	11.0	28.2	26.2	21.9	.001	.15
Father occupation, mean prestige scores*	52.6	44.2	37.6	43.7	43.6	44.5	.001	.22
Mother occupation, mean prestige scores*	51.1	45.1	39.7	40.1	44.8	44.3	.001	.23
Family wealthy or upper-middle class†	57.0	42.7	37.5	35.4	49.2	43.1	.001	.10
Self-identification								
American	33.1	19.9	16.2	10.0	16.2	18.8	.001	.64
Black American	—	—	12.5	—	9.9	2.2	.001	.64
Hispanic American	3.5	7.6	1.5	39.5	0.5	11.7	.001	.64
Cuban‡	61.6	67.5	—	0.3	—	42.6	.001	.64
Haitian‡	—	—	53.7	—	3.1	4.4	.001	.64
Nicaraguan‡	—	0.6	—	44.8	—	8.3	.001	.64
Other nationality§	1.8	4.4	16.2	5.3	70.2	12.2	.001	.64
Aspirations								
College education or higher‖	97.1	82.6	86.7	79.0	84.8	83.9	.001	.11
Professional or business occupation	72.1	70.0	75.0	69.9	71.2	70.6	n.s.	.06

(continued)

93

TABLE 2 Continued

	Cubans in Private School (N = 172)	Cubans in Public School (N = 968)	Haitians (N = 136)	Nicaraguans (N = 319)	West Indians (N = 191)	Total (N = 1,786)	p <	V^2 or Eta
Perceptions of discrimination								
Has ever been discriminated against	29.1	38.2	67.6	50.8	64.4	44.6	.001	.23
Discriminated against by teachers	5.2	12.5	16.2	13.5	23.6	13.4	.001	.13
Attitudes toward U.S. society								
There is racial discrimination in economic opportunities	91.3	79.2	84.6	81.5	89.5	82.3	.001	.11
Nonwhites have equal opportunities	30.8	53.6	44.9	52.4	41.9	49.3	.001	.14
The United States is the best country in the world	79.7	68.9	36.0	49.8	35.1	60.4	.001	.30
Friends								
Many or most friends have foreign-born parents	93.6	73.1	46.3	75.2	43.5	70.2	.001	.22
Friends' parents are								
Cuban	89.5	58.7	2.9	11.3	4.2	43.1	.001	.44
Haitian	—	1.2	30.1	1.3	12.6	4.5	.001	.44
Nicaraguan	7.6	24.8	2.9	69.0	2.1	26.9	.001	.44
West Indian	—	6.2	46.3	7.2	62.8	14.9	.001	.44
Other	2.9	9.1	17.7	11.2	18.3	10.6	.001	.44

SOURCE: Alejandro Portes and Lisandro Perez, Children of Immigrants: The Adaptation Process of the Second Generation (Project conducted at the Department of Sociology, Johns Hopkins University, in progress).

*Employed parents only; Treiman international prestige scale scores.
†Respondent's class self-classification.
‡Includes hyphenated self-identifications of the same nationality, for example, Nicaraguan American.
§West Indian self-identifications not classified individually by country.
‖ Respondents' statements of the level of education that they realistically expect to attain.

94

even among this group almost two-thirds see themselves as Cuban or Cuban American, a proportion close to their peers in public schools. Very few Cubans opt for the self-designation "Hispanic." Nicaraguan students, on the other hand, use this label almost as commonly as that of "Nicaraguan" itself. None of the Latin groups identify themselves as "black." Among Haitians and West Indians, however, roughly one-tenth already assume an identity as black American. Haitian self-identifications are similar to Nicaraguan in being less attached to the country of origin and in using pan-national labels more often than either Cubans or West Indians do. In total, about half of the Haitian children identified themselves as something other than "Haitian."[37]

Aspirations are very high in the entire sample, as indicated in the next panel of Table 2. Although significant differences in expectations of completing college do exist, at least four-fifths of every group expects to achieve this level of education. Similarly, roughly 70 percent of students from every nationality aspire to professional or business careers. These consistently high aspirations contrast with the reported wide differences in parental socioeconomic backgrounds and the differential effects of discrimination. The next panel of the table addresses the latter point, documenting the awareness that these teenagers have about the realities of American society. The two mostly black groups report discrimination against themselves twice to three times more frequently than do Cubans. Majorities of both Haitian and West Indian youths reported having been discriminated against, and about 20 percent said that discrimination was by their teachers. In contrast, only 5 percent of Cubans in private school report such incidents. Nicaraguans occupy an intermediate position, with half reporting discrimination against themselves and 13 percent pointing to their teachers as the source.

Congruent with these personal experiences, Haitian and West Indian teenagers are more likely to agree that there is racial discrimination in economic opportunities in the United States and to disagree that non-whites have equal opportunities. Interestingly, they are joined in these negative evaluations by private school Cubans. This result may reflect the greater information and class awareness of the latter group relative to their less privileged Latin counterparts. However, all Cuban students part company with the rest of the sample in their positive evaluation of the United States. Roughly three-fourths of second-generation Cubans endorse the view that "the United States is the best country in the world"; only half of Nicaraguans do so and the two mostly black groups take a distinctly less enthusiastic stance. These significant differences illustrate the contrasting levels of identification with their country and their local community by children of nationalities affected more or less by outside discrimination.

Introducing controls for native versus foreign birth of respondents attenuates these differences some-

37. West Indian self-identification was not coded separately and hence is classified under "Other nationality" in Table 2.

what, but the overall pattern remains. Results of this survey illustrate the race between generalized career aspirations and the widely different vulnerabilities and resources created by first-generation modes of incorporation. Aspirations are very high for all groups, regardless of origin; however, parental socioeconomic backgrounds, resources of the coethnic community—as exemplified by the existence of a private school system —and experiences of discrimination are very different. They influence decisively the outlook of second-generation youths, even at a young age, and are likely to have strong effects on the course of their future assimilation. Illustrating these differences is the enthusiasm with which children of advantaged immigrants embrace their parents' adopted country and the much less sanguine views of those whose situation is more difficult.

CONCLUSION

The last panel of Table 2 highlights another intriguing fact about today's second generation. The best-positioned group—private-school Cubans—is the one least likely to step out of the ethnic circle in their interpersonal relationships, while the group in the most disadvantaged position—Haitians—is most likely to do so. Overall, the three Latin groups overwhelmingly select friends who are also children of immigrants, mostly from the same nationality. Less than half of the Haitians and West Indians do so, indicating much

greater contact with native-parent-age youths. Other Haitian American teenagers are not even the majority of foreign-parentage friends among our Haitian respondents.

Fifty years ago, the dilemma of Italian American youngsters studied by Irving Child consisted of assimilating into the American mainstream, sacrificing in the process their parents' cultural heritage in contrast to taking refuge in the ethnic community from the challenges of the outside world. In the contemporary context of segmented assimilation, the options have become less clear. Children of nonwhite immigrants may not even have the opportunity of gaining access to middle-class white society, no matter how acculturated they become. Joining those native circles to which they do have access may prove a ticket to permanent subordination and disadvantage. Remaining securely ensconced in their coethnic community, under these circumstances, may be not a symptom of escapism but the best strategy for capitalizing on otherwise unavailable material and moral resources. As the experiences of Punjabi Sikh and Cuban American students suggest, a strategy of paced, selective assimilation may prove the best course for immigrant minorities. But the extent to which this strategy is possible also depends on the history of each group and its specific profile of vulnerabilities and resources. The present analysis represents a preliminary step toward understanding these realities.

ANNALS, *AAPSS*, **530**, November 1993

Rights, Resources, and Membership: Civil Rights Models in France and the United States

By JEREMY HEIN

ABSTRACT: Civil rights are usually conceptualized as a minority-majority issue. Comparison of public policy to promote racial and ethnic equality in the United States and France indicates that civil rights also influence interminority relations. American policy is based on rights to resources. It emphasizes racial and ethnic differences, interest groups, and distribution of jobs and other social goods. French policy is based on rights to membership. It emphasizes commonalities between ethnic minorities, majority group responsibility, and a social contract of interdependence. Limiting the expression of racism is the centerpiece of French civil rights law. The American approach to civil rights contributes to interminority conflict because it is primarily a method for influencing institutions rather than, as in France, a model of ideal race and ethnic relations.

Jeremy Hein is assistant professor of sociology at the University of Wisconsin—Eau Claire. Specializing in comparative social policy and race and ethnic relations, he has received support for his research from the National Science Foundation and the Centre National de la Recherche Scientifique. His publications include States and International Migrants: The Incorporation of Indochinese Refugees in the United States and France *(1992).*

NOTE: I wish to thank Martine Segalen and Jean-Pierre Hassoun of the Centre d'Ethnologie Française for sponsoring my fellowship from the Centre National de la Recherche Scientifique in the fall of 1991, which supported the research upon which this article is based.

CIVIL rights policies are methods for ameliorating racial and ethnic inequality. But they also are models of race and ethnic relations. Social activism, court decisions, and legislation accumulate into a simplified, collective representation of complex racial and ethnic realities. In this transformation from method to model, policies designed to change social inequality come to embody social relations.

A leading example is provided by U.S. civil rights policies in that they are conceptualized as the political dimension of minority-majority relations, although they also influence interminority relations. The history of African American and Jewish American convergence and divergence over rights for ethnic minorities provides ample evidence.[1] Contemporary tensions between blacks, Asians, and Hispanics also concern perceived inequalities in government assistance.[2] The increasing proportion of the U.S. population that comprises ethnic minorities—16.5 percent in 1970, 24.4 percent in 1990—and the foreign-born status of many minorities—66 percent of Asians, 41 percent of Hispanics—means that the American civil rights model is one mechanism for incorporating international migrants into American pluralism.[3]

How civil rights affect race and ethnic relations is most apparent through cross-national comparison, and the United States and France provide ideal contrasts. Both countries ban discrimination on the basis of race, religion, and national origin. But they differ in what constitutes a fundamental right. France does not hire to promote diversity nor redistrict voting along racial or ethnic lines. But at about the time that the U.S. Supreme Court ruled unconstitutional a municipal law punishing cross burning as a hate crime, France forbade contesting the veracity of the Holocaust and imposed more severe penalties on racial and ethnic insults.

American policy focuses on rights to resources, such as minorities' access to jobs and political power. Conversely, French policy seeks to ensure minorities' rights to membership, such as protection against hate speech and a general limitation on the expression of racism. The American emphasis on resources rather than membership heightens conflict between minorities because such policies, while operating with great precision as a method for influencing institutions, serve poorly as a model depicting how race and ethnic relations ought to be. The first study of interminority relations in France suggests less conflict than in the United States, although the rights-to-membership approach

1. Jonathan Kaufman, *Broken Alliance: The Turbulent Times Between Blacks and Jews in America* (New York: Scribner, 1988).

2. Michael C. Thornton and Robert J. Taylor, "Intergroup Attitudes: Black American Perceptions of Asian Americans," *Ethnic and Racial Studies*, 11(4):474-88 (1988); Federation for American Immigration Reform, *Hispanic and Black Attitudes toward Immigration Policy* (Washington, DC: Federation for American Immigration Reform, 1983).

3. Jeremy Hein, "Do 'New Immigrants' Become 'New Minorities'?: The Meaning of Ethnic Minority for Indochinese Refugees in the United States," *Sociological Perspectives*, 34(1):61-78 (1991).

to civil rights is only one cause of this outcome.[4]

RIGHTS TO RESOURCES IN THE UNITED STATES

Mobilization and collective action by blacks during the 1950s and 1960s produced executive, judicial, and legislative action that dramatically altered the facts and perception of racial inequality. White violence in reaction to nonviolent black protest, along with state and local government's resistance to federal policy, forced the American state to sequentially expanded citizenship for blacks, particularly by dismantling the southern caste system.[5]

The Birmingham campaign in 1965 marked a change in movement goals from desegregation to employment, housing, and political power, although black organizations had long considered these issues important.[6] A number of factors converging during the mid-1960s and early 1970s augmented this shift from gaining rights to obtaining resources.[7] Neoliberal criticism errs in dismissing this new approach to civil rights as rights without reciprocity, as social engineering, or as abandoning integration for pluralism. The shift from pro-testing for rights to politicking for resources is entirely consistent with American political traditions.[8]

In his prophetic 1965 essay, "From Protest to Politics," Bayard Rustin wrote of macrolevel changes in American society that required a new civil rights strategy:

Hearts are not relevant to the issue; neither racial affinities nor racial hostilities are rooted there. It is institutions—social, political, and economic—which are the ultimate molders of collective sentiments. Let these institutions be reconstructed today, and let the ineluctable gradualism of history govern the formation of a new psychology.[9]

Rustin's vision of a rights-to- resources civil rights strategy came to pass, and some of its material successes are beyond doubt, particularly at the municipal level.[10] But subordinating the search for meaningful group relations to the manipulation of institutional resources made civil rights a method without a model. This imbalance left American civil rights unprepared for increased immigration in the 1970s and 1980s, with some unforeseen consequences

4. Véronique de Rudder, *Autochones et immigrés en quartier populaire: D'Aligre à l'îlot Châlon* (Paris: CIEMI and L'Harmattan, 1987).

5. Doug McAdam, *Political Process and the Development of Black Insurgency, 1930-1970* (Chicago: University of Chicago Press, 1982).

6. Aldon Morris, *The Origins of the Civil Rights Movement: Black Communities Organizing for Change* (New York: Free Press, 1984).

7. Hugh D. Graham, *The Civil Rights Era: Origins and Development of National Policy* (New York: Oxford University Press, 1990).

8. Charles V. Hamilton, "Social Policy and the Welfare of Black Americans: From Rights to Resources," *Political Science Quarterly*, 101(2):239-55 (1986).

9. Bayard Rustin, "From Protest to Politics: The Future of the Civil Rights Movement," in *The Civil Rights Reader*, ed. L. Friedman (New York: Walker, 1968), p. 339.

10. Rufus P. Browning, Dale R. Marshall, and David H. Tabb, *Protest Is Not Enough: The Struggle of Blacks and Hispanics for Equality in Urban Politics* (Berkeley: University of California Press, 1986); James W. Button, *Blacks and Social Change: Impact of the Civil Rights Movement in Southern Communities* (Princeton, NJ: Princeton University Press, 1989).

for blacks' relations with Asians and Hispanics.

By the mid-1970s, more than one in four blacks worked in the public sector—very often, servicing the black poor—compared to one in six whites.[11] Since then, Asian and Hispanic immigrants have become more numerous among the urban populations needing public programs, which are disproportionately staffed by blacks. A second economic consequence concerns the transition from an industrial to a service economy. In New York City during the 1970s, blacks' concentration in government jobs limited their self-employment, thus indirectly contributing to conflict with Asian small businesses. More important, blacks' concentration in public sector occupations enabled immigrants, particularly Asians, to enter private sector occupations vacated by whites through retirement and out-migration.[12]

Politically, the community-control component of the rights-to-resources approach is ill suited to the new complexities of multiethnic urban areas. Black boycotts of Korean businesses provide one example. This conflict has complex causes, including white corporations' use of Asian businesses as middlemen in poor neighborhoods.[13] But black leaders organizing a long boycott of Korean stores in

Brooklyn drew upon a repertoire of tactics from the 1960s.[14] Demanding that white chain stores hire blacks is quite different from demanding that blacks be hired by Korean stores, which rely on unpaid family labor. Similarly, formative political experiences with community action programs have been a liability to black leaders seeking political alliances with Caribbean immigrants, whose interests are less parochial.[15]

Finally, the rights-to-resources civil rights approach inevitably leads to conflict over who is included under the rubric "minority." In *City of Richmond* v. *Corson* (1989), the Supreme Court ruled that racial discrimination against one group—blacks—did not justify municipal set-aside contracts for all minority firms, since populations like the Vietnamese lacked a historical experience of discrimination in the free-market system.[16] Social identity also is a civil rights issue in voting protection for linguistic minorities, the U.S. census's tabulation of people who are "Other Spanish," and the inclusion of recent Asian and Hispanic immigrants—regardless of legal status—in public policies designed to compensate for past inequality.[17]

11. Michael K. Brown and Steven P. Erie, "Blacks and the Legacy of the Great Society: The Economic and Political Impact of Federal Social Policy," *Public Policy*, 29(3):299-330 (1981).

12. Roger Waldinger, "Changing Ladders and Musical Chairs: Ethnicity and Opportunity in Post-Industrial New York," *Politics and Society*, 16(4):369-402 (1987).

13. U.S., Commission on Civil Rights, *Recent Activities against Citizens and Residents*

of Asian Descent (Washington, DC: Commission on Civil Rights, 1987).

14. Jim Sleeper, *The Closest of Strangers: Liberalism and the Politics of Race in New York* (New York: Norton, 1990).

15. Philip Krasnitz, *Caribbean New York: Black Immigrants and the Politics of Race* (Ithaca, NY: Cornell University Press, 1992).

16. George R. LaNoue, "Split Visions: Minority Business Set-Asides," *The Annals* of the American Academy of Political and Social Science, 523:104-16 (Sept. 1992).

17. Abigail M. Thernstrom, *Whose Votes Count? Affirmative Action and Minority Voting*

These interminority conflicts indicate that policy based on rights to resources functions well as a method for influencing institutions but poorly as a model providing guidance on race and ethnic relations. French civil rights policy is particularly instructive in this respect because it is based on rights to membership. In France, civil rights defend a social contract between the individual and society, which in practice means limiting the expression of racism. As a result, civil rights are at once a method for changing inequality and a model of what intergroup relations should look like.

DEFINITIVE MOMENTS
IN CONTEMPORARY
FRENCH CIVIL RIGHTS

Four events between 1986 and 1990 typify the rights-to-membership approach. The cases involve different ethnic groups—Jews and North Africans—and interacted with the civil rights movement in different ways, from transitory to definitive. But they share a common attribute: a conception of civil rights that both protects individuals through a social contract and provides an affirmative collective representation of race and ethnic relations.[18]

A challenge to citizenship

In November 1986, Socialist election losses forced President François Mitterrand to appoint a right-wing prime minister, Jacques Chirac. One proposal from the new administration concerned modification of the naturalization process.

In contrast to the United States, children born in France to immigrant parents who have not become naturalized retain their parents' nationality until the age of 18. Acquisition of French citizenship is then automatic. The children of Algerian immigrants are citizens at birth if one parent was born prior to 1962, when Algeria ceased being part of France. The proposal would have required second-generation immigrants to make an affirmative request in writing to become citizens, rather than having the certification arrive unsolicited. Extensive protest by North African youths and civil rights organizations forced Chirac to withdraw the proposal.[19]

Citizenship became a political issue in the mid-1980s because membership is central to the French conception of civil rights. Public opinion surveys support this conclusion. In 1985, 62 percent of the French public favored the existing naturalization

---

Rights (Cambridge, MA: Harvard University Press, 1987); William Petersen, "Politics and the Measurement of Ethnicity," in *The Politics of Numbers,* ed. W. Alonso and P. Starr (New York: Russell Sage Foundation, 1987), pp. 187-233; Peter Skerry, "Borders and Quotas: Immigration and the Affirmative-Action State," *Public Interest,* 96:86-102 (Summer 1989).

18. In 1983, 40 North African youths marched 750 miles from Marseilles to Paris to protest a surge in racist killings. Although the trek of one and one-half months is the forma-

tive event in contemporary North African mobilization against racism in France, its primary relevance was for social movements rather than civil rights policy. See Adil Jazouli, *L'action collective des jeunes Maghrébins de France* (Paris: CIEMI and L'Harmattan, 1986).

19. Rogers Brubaker, *Citizenship and Nationhood in France and Germany* (Cambridge, MA: Harvard University Press, 1992). The massive electoral victory of right-wing parties in the March 1993 parliamentary election once again threatens immigrants' right to French citizenship.

law, while 29 percent felt it was too liberal.[20] Despite subsequent publicity and debate—the extreme Right propagated the slogan "One must deserve being French"—attitudes on French citizenship remained largely unchanged. A 1989 survey found that 57 percent of the public felt it was appropriate for the children of immigrants to automatically become French citizens upon reaching adulthood; 37 percent disagreed.[21] One year later, 63 percent still agreed that children born in France to immigrant parents should be entitled to French citizenship; 30 percent disagreed.[22]

Le point du détail

In September 1987, Jean-Marie Le Pen, the anti-Arab and anti-Semitic leader of the extreme-Right National Front, was interviewed on a radio talk show.[23] The host asked his opinion of revisionist French historians who deny that gas chambers were used to exterminate Jews during the 1940s. Le Pen responded, " 'I am not saying that gas chambers did not exist. . . . But I believe that it is a minor point in the history of World War II.' "[24]

The remark immediately became a civil rights issue by breaking a so-

cietal consensus on France's complicity in the Holocaust. It rallied resistance against the new Right and entered French political lexicon as the "point du détail." Eighty-eight percent of the public disapproved of defaming the gas chambers—2 percent approved—and Le Pen's national approval rating dropped from 14 to 8 percent.[25] Mainstream right-wing parties—the Rally for the Republic and the Union for French Democracy—canceled agreements with the National Front that would have withdrawn candidates in closely contested municipal elections to prevent a split vote aiding a Socialist or Communist candidate. Leading civil rights organizations brought suit against Le Pen. In January 1988, the Supreme Court of Appeal let stand a lower court ruling finding Le Pen guilty of "exceeding the limits of free expression" and fining him a nominal sum.

L'affaire des foulards

In October 1989, a school principal, citing a ban on religious displays in public institutions, expelled three North African girls for refusing to lower their head-enveloping scarves (*foulards*). The incident ignited a political debate on whether or not secularization was a disguised version of racism against Muslims. The Left, which had traditionally supported "immigrant rights," now found its cherished ideal of church and state separation unexpectedly questioned in the case of a non-European population.

20. "Les Français et l'immigration," *Convergence et institutions*, 1:30-35 (1985).

21. Robert Schneider, "Immigrés: L'enquête qui dérange," *Actualités migrations*, 20-26 Nov. 1989, pp. 18-20.

22. Gérard Le Gall, "L'éffet immigration," in *L'état de l'opinion* (Paris: Editions du Seuil, 1991), pp. 119-36.

23. In national elections since 1986, Le Pen has regularly received about 15 percent of the vote, but approximately 25 percent in southern cities like Nice and Marseilles. His position on immigrants has a national approval rating of about 30 percent.

24. Steven Greenhouse, "French Rightist Belittles Gas Chambers," *New York Times*, 16 Sept. 1989. Copyright © 1989 by The New York Times Company. Reprinted by permission.

25. Schneider, "Immigrés."

Intervention by the Minister of Education secured the teenagers' reinstatement. But the Council of State ruled that local school authorities should decide on a case-by-case basis if wearing Islamic scarves was acceptable in public schools. Yet religious freedom never became a rallying point for protest by North Africans or civil rights organizations, suggesting a consensus on the meaning of membership in French society. Public opinion provides part of the explanation.

By 66 to 26 percent, the French public disapproved of the Education Minister's action, but sympathizers of the Right exceeded those on the Left by only 14 percentage points. The Left and Right diverged by only 5 percentage points—they scored 68 and 73 percent, respectively—on the need to maintain French schools' secular tradition.[26] Moreover, 71 percent of the public agreed with the statement, "It is up to the immigrants living in France to make efforts to adapt themselves to French society even if they aren't able to practice their religion under the same conditions as in their original country."[27] Opinions remained unchanged a year later: 78 percent of the French public deemed it unacceptable for young Muslims to wear Islamic scarves in school.[28] Among Muslims, who were surveyed seven months before the incident, 73 percent felt they could satisfactorily practice their re-

ligion, and 71 percent preferred public to private, Muslim schools for Muslim children.[29]

The Carpentras desecration

In May 1990, vandals desecrated a Jewish cemetery in Carpentras, a small city fifty miles north of Marseilles. Massive demonstrations erupted throughout the country.

About 200,000 people protested in Paris, the third-largest demonstration about civil rights and racism since these issues had become central to French politics in the early 1980s.[30] Television stations broadcast *Night and Fog*, a film about the Nazi concentration camps. At the time, the Senate and National Assembly were deadlocked over a new antiracism law. It subsequently passed by a slim margin but required some members of Right parties to vote with the Left, a very rare occurrence in French politics.

When asked if Carpentras was "an indication of an unhealthy atmosphere in which anti-Semitism is trivialized," 55 percent of the French public agreed. Concerning proposals to combat anti-Semitism, publicizing the Holocaust received the most support, from 51 percent of the public, followed by banning anti-Semitic

26. "Le Pen," in *L'état de l'opinion* (Paris: Editions du Seuil, 1988), pp. 131-42.

27. Elizabeth H. Hastings and Philip K. Hastings, eds., *Index to International Public Opinion, 1989-1990* (Westport, CT: Greenwood Press, 1991), p. 511.

28. Le Gall, "L'effet immigration."

29. Hastings and Hastings, *Index to International Public Opinion*, p. 511.

30. The largest protest occurred in 1986 following the killing by police of a French university student of Algerian ancestry during student demonstrations; the crowd was estimated at 300,000. The second-largest was a 1985 antiracism rally by the new youth organization SOS-Racism, which drew a crowd of about 275,000.

publications, remarks, and organizations, from 28 percent. Thirty-five percent of the public attributed the desecration to the influence of the extreme Right and 30 percent to overlooking events during World War II. The Carpentras event had such significance that, by 40 to 21 percent, the public felt it would revive rather than curtail anti-Semitism.[31]

PROTECTION AGAINST HATE
SPEECH: THE SINE QUA NON
OF MEMBERSHIP

Naturalization, irreverence for the Holocaust, Islamic scarves, and a cemetery desecration became civil rights issues in France because the most important right of an ethnic minority is membership in the society. The essence of membership is protection against being identified on the basis of racial or ethnic affiliation, an element of what the French call *solidarité* (translated as interdependence or mutual responsibility).[32] In practice, this social contract requires limiting hate speech, since expressing racism is inherently unjust— ethnic minorities receive, but do not produce, racism—and entails an unacceptable level of social conflict.

In France, racist slander or publicly provoking racist hate can result in a $50,000 fine and a prison term up to one year. Even insults based on race, ethnicity, nationality, or religion are punishable, with maximum penalties of $25,000 and six months

in prison. A 1990 law made contesting the existence of crimes against humanity—a reference to the Holocaust—an offense.[33]

One of the first and most celebrated hate-speech cases occurred in Grenoble. In December 1973, a tribunal ruled that a newspaper had committed racial defamation and provocation by publishing a cartoon suggesting that North Africans migrated to France to receive social welfare payments. The tribunal fined each defendant about $200.[34]

The leading litigation-oriented civil rights organizations are the Movement against Racism and for Friendship between Peoples (the French acronym is "MRAP") and the International League against Racism and Anti-Semitism (LICRA). Preliminary analysis of their 331 legal actions between 1973 and 1989 documents the centrality of prosecuting verbal, written, and depicted racism in French civil rights cases.[35]

With respect to charges, only one-fifth of cases involve standard U.S. civil rights issues: 14 percent concern discrimination in employment, education, housing, and government ser-

31. Hastings and Hastings, *Index to International Public Opinion*, pp. 513-14.
32. Paul Spicker, "Equality versus Solidarity," *Government and Opposition*, 27:66-77 (Winter 1992).

33. Dominique Bouder, "Racisme, étrangers et lois pénales," *Regard sur l'actualité*, 116: 3-25 (Dec. 1985); Jacqueline Costa-Lascoux, "Le droit contre le racisme," *Migrations société*, 11(11):21-36 (1990).
34. Jacqueline Costa-Lascoux, "La loi du 1er juillet 1972 et la protection pénale des immigrés contre la discrimination raciale," *Droit social*, 5:181-87 (May 1976).
35. Movement against Racism and for Friendship between Peoples and International League against Racism and Anti-Semitism, *Le racisme en justice, 1972-1989* (Paris: Movement against Racism and for Friendship between Peoples and International League against Racism and Anti-Semitism, 1989).

vices, and 5 percent involve threats and violence. Provoking racial hatred, the leading offense, accounts for 34 percent of all cases. Racist insults are the reason for 21 percent; defamation, 11 percent; and negation of the Holocaust, 7 percent. Miscellaneous cases account for the remainder.

With respect to defendants, Jean-Marie Le Pen, the National Front, and other extreme Right organizations and personalities account for 20 percent of all cases. Publishers, newspapers, and other media compose 13 percent. Government agencies, such as employment bureaus and municipalities, constitute 8 percent of all defendants. Individuals, some of whom are no doubt associated with the extreme Right, account for 59 percent.

The modal case involves a man charged with expressing racism through provocative activity, defamation, or insults. A Strasbourg tribunal found a man guilty of provocation for publishing a tract that stated, "There are too many immigrants in the public housing project." The defendant and charge accounting for the single largest number of cases—19 percent—are a racist insult by an individual. A tribunal gave a Toulouse man a $350 fine and a 15-day suspended sentence for saying "dirty Arab."

MRAP and LICRA achieved complete wins—as opposed to partial wins or complete losses—in 58 percent of cases. They were least successful in suits against government institutions (48 percent) and the media (50 percent). But they won 66 percent of the time against Le Pen and the National Front, although only 55 percent against extreme Right defen-

dants. Wins were least likely on charges of threats and violence (43 percent) and most likely on racist insults (64 percent).

Defamation suits against the media were the least likely to end in a conviction; only 1 of 6 such cases resulted in a conviction. Negation-of-genocide suits against the extreme Right also were difficult to win; only 6 of 12 such cases were won. Conversely, discrimination suits against individuals had a higher probability of conviction; conviction occurred in 14 of 21 such cases. But freedom-of-speech cases achieved similar conviction rates. MRAP and LICRA won 14 of 20 cases against media for provoking racial hatred. A Parisian tribunal found a newspaper guilty of provocation for comparing the fertility of Algerian women to termite queens. Similarly, individuals charged with making racist insults, the modal case, ended in conviction in 38 of 59 cases. A tribunal in Mulhouse fined a man about $450 for calling someone a "dirty Jew."

ASSIMILATION: A PREREQUISITE FOR MEMBERSHIP?

The social context of civil rights in France is quite distinct from that in the United States. An ideology of cultural conformity rather than cultural pluralism is the most salient difference, although immigrants from former colonies and a law of codes rather than cases are significant as well. Determining if rights to membership are an extension of the French nation-state tests the generalizability of the French approach to civil rights.

Assimilation, in the form of, for example, a host-society code of conduct, is central to French race and ethnic relations. Forty-five percent of the French public agrees that political support for Le Pen is understandable given the behavior of some foreigners. Eighty-four percent agree that a racist reaction is sometimes justified given the behavior of particular foreigners.[36]

An acute sensitivity to the spatial distribution of foreigners is another consequence of an assimilationist nation-state. Of nine policies to promote immigrant adjustment, the most popular among the French public is more evenly distributing immigrants; 76 percent were in favor. The second most popular also involves collective space; 72 percent favor rehabilitating undesirable neighborhoods where many immigrants live.[37]

A final dimension of assimilation concerns the number of immigrants. A 1989 survey found that 82 percent of the French public agreed that integrating foreigners already in France is a good solution to the "immigrant problem." But 74 percent of these respondents also agreed that France risked losing its national identity if the number of foreigners was not limited; foreigners constitute about 7 percent of the population in France.[38]

There is a degree of sociological symmetry between race and ethnic relations founded on assimilation

and civil rights based on membership. But the two positions are distinct, as evidenced by an apparent decline in public expectation of cultural conformity but stronger support for antiracist activities. In 1985, 50 percent of the public agreed—but 42 percent disagreed—that it was only a question of time before immigrants were integrated into France. By 1990, the proportions were reversed to 43 and 49 percent, respectively.[39]

Midway through this waning of the assimilationist ideology, a 1988 survey of opinion in 11 Western European countries found strong support for civil rights among the French. Forty-one percent of the French public consider "the struggle against racism" a great cause worth sacrificing for, a proportion exceeded only in Italy, with 44 percent, and Portugal, with 42 percent. Only 31 percent of Germans prioritize the struggle against racism. Moreover, 8 percent of Germans consider immigrants "one of the most important problems nowadays," compared to 3 percent of the French—Muslims comprise similar proportions of the population in Germany and France. Indeed, 19 percent of Germans, but 6 percent of the French, associate the term "another social class" with immigrants and foreigners.[40]

Antiracist values in France stem from a social contract between the individual and society—*solidarité*—not from assimilationist norms. A 1989 survey found that 51 percent of

36. Marie-Laurie Colson, "Plus d'un Français sur trois s'avoue un peu ou plutôt raciste," *Libération*, 22 Mar. 1991.

37. Hastings and Hastings, *Index to International Public Opinion*, p. 513.

38. "Un Français sur deux est contre la construction d'une mosquee dans sa commune," *Paris Match*, 14 Dec. 1989.

39. Le Gall, "L'effet immigration."

40. Hastings and Hastings, *Index to International Public Opinion*, pp. 589-93. The Luxembourg sample of 300 is excluded from analysis.

the French public felt immigrants made little or no effort to integrate themselves, but a greater proportion, 64 percent, also felt the French did little or nothing to bring about their integration.[41] The French public's mea culpa indicates that the interdependence that frames civil rights as membership presumes the reciprocal obligations of majorities and minorities.

This social contract ultimately is the responsibility of the state rather than of civil society. In 1985, 65 percent of the French public felt that the children of foreigners were more integrated into French society than their parents were. Only 21 percent disagreed. Yet among affirmative respondents, a greater proportion attributed the second generation's integration to the French educational system (56 percent) rather than to their birth in France (42 percent).[42]

French perceptions of antiracist organizations further document that the rights-to-membership model requires state intervention. SOS-Racism, a moderate, youth-based movement that formed in 1984, is the best-known antiracist organization. It draws members from all racial and ethnic groups and espouses a philosophy epitomized by the slogan, "Against racism and xenophobia and for integration, equal rights, and the defense of democratic values." Although 63 percent of the French agree that France has become more racist in the past few years, they are divided over the role of SOS-Racism. Forty-eight percent believe the organization prevents racism, but 37 percent believe it actually incites racism.[43]

A survey of youths aged 11 to 20, the most liberal segment of the French population, offers additional evidence that the state is expected to play a central role in the rights-to-membership approach to civil rights. Eighty-seven percent of the youths agree that it is necessary to combat racism. However, 70 percent rank "the state (the government, president of the Republic)" as the most efficient means to combat racism, compared to 65 percent for "associations like SOS-Racism," and 56 percent for teachers. Only 13 percent express readiness to work with an antiracist organization to combat racism, while 78 percent prefer simply to respect differences in everyday life.[44]

CONCLUSION

The American approach to civil rights should be added to international migration, urban dislocation, and economic transformation to explain patterns of interminority relations in the United States, particularly those characterized by conflict. Policies based on rights to resources are consistent with American political traditions, such as interest group formation on the basis of ethnicity. But one irony of race and ethnic relations is that what works for majority groups has hidden consequences for ethnic minorities. This is the case with U.S. civil rights policies, which distribute institutional resources on

41. Ibid., p. 513.
42. "Les Français et l'immigration."

43. "Racisme: Les réponses des Français," *Le journal du dimanche*, 14 Feb. 1988.
44. Marie-Odile Fargier, "Sondage: Je ne suis pas raciste mais," *Science et vie junior*, 18:26-31 (Sept. 1990).

the basis of group membership. The fact that relations between American minorities are more frequently patterned on conflict and competition than on coalitions and cooperation is congruent with the rights-to-resources approach.

The French policy of rights to membership does not increase racial and ethnic conflict because of a symmetry between civil rights as methods for changing social conditions and as models of what better conditions ought to be like. First, French policy focuses on majority-group behavior and responsibility, while the American approach, such as affirmative action, makes minorities the agents of change. Second, rights to membership do not require the individual to claim a group affiliation in order to merit state protection. The American policy of rights to resources requires individuals to identify with a racial or ethnic group in order to share collective benefits. Finally, the French approach is future oriented in that it clearly depicts idealized race and ethnic relations. The American approach is meant to compensate for past injustice, and the mechanisms for adjudicating these wrongs are themselves conceived as necessary evils until full equality is achieved.

The persistent economic inequalities experienced by nonwhites in the United States, including lower returns on human capital investments like education, is one reason why rights to resources cannot be simply abandoned. French public policy has yet to demonstrate that it can address racial and ethnic inequalities in housing, education, and employment. But the principal French critique of the American approach is its overemphasis on materialism and its neglect of the social contract between the individual and society. The reluctance of the United States to limit the expression of racism and to designate certain illegal behavior as a hate crime signals that the American approach to civil rights fares poorly in protecting ethnic minorities' membership in society.

Methods cannot substitute for models, and distributing resources along racial and ethnic lines presumes a level of social conflict that American society will be increasingly unable to bear as ethnic minorities become a larger proportion of the population. The French approach to civil rights suggests that rights to resources cannot be achieved without rights to membership.

ANNALS, *AAPSS*, **530**, November 1993

Multiculturalism:
Battleground or Meeting Ground?

By RONALD TAKAKI

ABSTRACT: Is multiculturalism a battleground or a meeting ground? To answer this question, Ronald Takaki identifies two emerging perspectives—particularism and pluralism. The culture war over the content of the curriculum is presented as a debate, a clash of ideas: Allan Bloom, Diane Ravitch, and Arthur Schlesinger versus Gerald Graff, Henry Louis Gates, and Takaki himself. The university should be a stimulating contested terrain where scholars of different viewpoints engage each other over the meaning and content of culture, but whether it can become such a place of intellectual encounters may be in doubt.

Ronald Takaki is professor of ethnic studies at the University of California, Berkeley, where he was instrumental in the establishment of an American cultural-diversity requirement. He is the author of A Different Mirror: A History of Multicultural America *(1993).*

"It is very natural that the history written by the victim does not altogether chime with the story of the victor."

Jose Fernandez of California, 1874[1]

In 1979, I experienced the truth of this statement when I found myself attacked by C. Van Woodward in the *New York Review of Books*. I had recently published a broad and comparative study of blacks, Chinese, Indians, Irish, and Mexicans, from the American Revolution to the U.S. war against Spain. But, for Woodward, my *Iron Cages: Race and Culture in Nineteenth-Century America* was too narrow in focus. My analysis, he stridently complained, should have compared ethnic conflicts in the United States to those in Brazil, South Africa, Germany, and Russia. Such an encompassing view would have shown that America was not so "bad" after all.

The author of scholarship that focused exclusively on the American South, Woodward was arguing that mine should have been cross-national in order to be "balanced." But how, I wondered, was balance to be measured? Surely, any examination of the "worse instances" of racial oppression in other countries should not diminish the importance of what happened here. Balance should also insist that we steer away from denial or a tendency to be dismissive. Woodward's contrast of the "millions of corpses" and the "horrors of genocide" in Nazi Germany to racial violence in the United States seemed both heartless and beside the point. Enslaved

1. David J. Weber, ed., *Foreigners in Their Native Land: Historical Roots of the Mexican Americans* (Albuquerque: University of New Mexico Press, 1973), p. vi.

Africans in the American South would have felt little comfort to have been told that conditions for their counterparts in Latin America were "worse." They would have responded that it mattered little that the black population in Brazil was "17.5 million" rather than "127.6 million" by 1850, or whether slavery beyond what Woodward called the "three-mile limit" was more terrible and deadly.

What had provoked such a scolding from this dean of American history? One might have expected a more supportive reading from the author of *The Strange Career of Jim Crow*, a book that had helped stir our society's moral conscience during the civil rights era. My colleague Michael Rogin tried to explain Woodward's curious reaction by saying that the elderly historian perceived me as a bad son. History had traditionally been written by members of the majority population; now some younger scholars of color like me had received our Ph.D.'s and were trying to "re-vision" America's past. But our critical scholarship did not chime with the traditional version of history. Noting my nonwhiteness, Woodward charged that I was guilty of reverse discrimination: my characterization of whites in terms of rapacity, greed, and brutality constituted a "practice" that could be described as "racism." Like a father, Woodward chastised me for catering to the "current mood of self-denigration and self-flagellation." "If and when the mood passes," he lamented, "one would hope a more balanced perspective on American history will prevail."[2]

2. C. Van Woodward, "America the Bad?" *New York Review of Books*, 22 Nov. 1979; Ron-

Looking back at Woodward's review today, we can see that it constituted one of the opening skirmishes of what has come to be called the culture war. Some of the battles of this conflict have erupted in the political arena. Speaking before the 1992 Republican National Convention, Patrick Buchanan urged his fellow conservatives to take back their cities, their culture, and their country, block by block. This last phrase was a reference to the National Guard's show of force during the 1992 Los Angeles riot. On the other hand, in his first speech as President-elect, Bill Clinton recognized our ethnic and cultural diversity as a source of America's strength.

But many of the fiercest battles over how we define America are being waged within the academy. There minority students and scholars are struggling to diversify the curriculum, while conservative pundits like Charles J. Sykes and Dinesh D'Souza are fighting to recapture the campus.[3]

The stakes in this conflict are high, for we are being asked to define education and determine what an educated person should know about the world in general and America in particular. This is the issue Allan Bloom raises in his polemic, *The Closing of the American Mind*. A leader of the intellectual backlash against cultural diversity, he articulates a con-

servative view of the university curriculum. According to Bloom, entering students are "uncivilized," and faculty have the responsibility to "civilize" them. As a teacher, he claims to know what their "hungers" are and "what they can digest." Eating is one of his favorite metaphors. Noting the "large black presence" at major universities, he regrets the "one failure" in race relations—black students have proven to be "indigestible." They do not "melt as have *all* other groups." The problem, he contends, is that "blacks have become blacks": they have become "ethnic." This separatism has been reinforced by an academic permissiveness that has befouled the curriculum with "Black Studies" along with "Learn Another Culture." The only solution, Bloom insists, is "the good old Great Books approach."[4]

Behind Bloom's approach is a political agenda. What does it mean to be an American? he asks. The "old view" was that "by recognizing and accepting man's natural rights," people in this society found a fundamental basis of unity. The immigrant came here and became assimilated. But the "recent education of openness," with its celebration of diversity, is threatening the social contract that had defined the members of American society as individuals. During the civil rights movement of the 1960s, Black Power militants had aggressively affirmed a group identity. Invading college campuses, they

ald Takaki, *Iron Cages: Race and Culture in Nineteenth-Century America* (New York: Knopf, 1979).

3. Charles J. Sykes, *The Hollow Men: Politics and Corruption in Higher Education* (Washington, DC: Regnery Gateway, 1990); Dinesh D'Souza, *Illiberal Education: The Politics of Race and Sex on Campus* (New York: Free Press, 1991).

4. Allan Bloom, *The Closing of the American Mind: How Higher Education Has Failed Democracy and Impoverished the Souls of Today's Students* (New York: Simon & Schuster, 1987), pp. 19, 91-93, 340-41, 344.

demanded "respect for blacks as blacks, not as human beings simply," and began to "propagandize acceptance of different ways." This emphasis on ethnicity separated Americans from each other, shrouding their "essential humankindness." The black conception of a group identity provided the theoretical basis for a new policy, affirmative action, which opened the doors to the admission of unqualified students. Once on campus, many black students agitated for the establishment of black studies programs, which in turn contributed to academic incoherence, lack of synopsis, and the "decomposition of the university."[5]

Bloom's is a closed mind, unwilling to allow the curriculum to become more inclusive. Fortunately, many other educators have been acknowledging the need to teach students about the cultural diversity of American society. "Every student needs to know," former University of Wisconsin chancellor Donna Shalala has explained, "much more about the origins and history of the particular cultures which, as Americans, we will encounter during our lives."[6]

This need for cross-cultural understanding has been grimly highlighted by recent racial tensions and conflicts such as the black boycott of Korean stores, Jewish-black antagonism in Crown Heights, and especially the 1992 Los Angeles racial explosion. During the days of rage, Rodney King pleaded for calm: "Please, we can get along here. We all can get along. I mean, we're all stuck here for a while. Let's try to work it out." But how should "we" be defined?[7]

Earlier, the Watts riot had reflected a conflict between whites and blacks, but the fire this time in 1992 Los Angeles highlighted the multiracial reality of American society. Race includes Hispanics and Asian Americans. The old binary language of race relations between whites and blacks, *Newsweek* observed, is no longer descriptive of who we are as Americans. Our future will increasingly be multiethnic as the twenty-first century rushes toward us: the western edge of the continent called California constitutes the thin end of an entering new wedge, a brave new multicultural world of Calibans of many different races and ethnicities.[8]

If "we" must be more inclusive, how do we "work it out"? One crucial way would be for us to learn more about each other—not only whites about peoples of color, but also blacks about Koreans, and Hispanics about blacks. Our very diversity offers an intellectual invitation to teachers and scholars to reach for a more comprehensive understanding of American society. Here the debate over multiculturalism has gone beyond whether or not to be inclusive. The question has become, How do we develop and teach a more culturally diverse curriculum?

What has emerged are two perspectives, what Diane Ravitch has

5. Ibid., pp. 27, 29, 33, 35, 89, 90, 347.
6. *University of Wisconsin—Madison: The Madison Plan* (Madison: University of Wisconsin, 1988).

7. Rodney King's statement to the press; see *New York Times*, 2 May 1992, p. 6.
8. "Beyond Black and White," *Newsweek*, 18 May 1992, p. 28.

usefully described as "particularism" versus "pluralism." But, by regarding each as exclusive, even antagonistic, Ravitch fails to appreciate the validity of both viewpoints and the ways they complement each other.[9]

Actually, we need not be forced into an either-or situation. Currently, many universities offer courses that study a particular group, such as African Americans or Asian Americans. This focus enables students of a specific minority to learn about their history and community. These students are not necessarily seeking what has been slandered as self-esteem courses. Rather, they simply believe that they are entitled to learn how their communities fit into American history and society. My grandparents were Japanese immigrant laborers, and even after I finished college with a major in American history and completed a Ph.D. in this field, I had learned virtually nothing about why they had come to America and what had happened to them as well as other Japanese immigrants in this country. This history should have been available to me.

The particularistic perspective led me to write *Strangers from a Different Shore: A History of Asian Americans*. This focus on a specific group can also be found in Irving Howe's *World of Our Fathers: The Journey of the East European Jews to America*, Mario Garcia's *Desert Immigrants: The Mexicans of El Paso, 1880-1920*, Lawrence Levine's *Black Culture and Black Consciousness*, and Kerby Miller's *Emigrants and Exiles: Ire-*

land and the Irish Exodus to North America.[10]

Increasingly, educators and scholars are recognizing the need for us to step back from particularistic portraits in order to discern the rich and complex mosaic of our national pluralism. While group-specific courses have been in the curriculum for many years, courses offering a comparative and integrative approach have been introduced recently. In fact, the University of California at Berkeley has instituted an American cultures requirement for graduation. The purpose of this course is to give students an understanding of American society in terms of African Americans, Asian Americans, Latinos, Native Americans, and European Americans, especially the immigrant groups from places like Ireland, Italy, Greece, and Russia.

What such curricular innovations promise is not only the introduction of intellectually dynamic courses that study the crisscrossed paths of America's different groups but also the fostering of comparative multicultural scholarship. This pluralistic approach is illustrated by works like

9. Diane Ravitch, "Multiculturalism: E Pluribus Plures," *American Scholar*, 59(3):337-54 (Summer 1990).

10. Ronald Takaki, *Strangers from a Different Shore: A History of Asian Americans* (Boston: Little, Brown, 1989); Irving Howe, *World of Our Fathers: The Journey of the East European Jews to America and the Life They Found and Made* (New York: Simon & Schuster, 1976); Lawrence W. Levine, *Black Culture and Black Consciousness: Afro-American Folk Thought from Slavery to Freedom* (New York: Oxford University Press, 1977); Mario T. Garcia, *Desert Immigrants: The Mexicans of El Paso, 1880-1920* (New Haven, CT: Yale University Press, 1981); Kerby A. Miller, *Emigrants and Exiles: Ireland and the Irish Exodus to North America* (New York: Oxford University Press, 1985).

my *Different Mirror: A History of Multicultural America* as well as Gary Nash's *Red, White, and Black: The Peoples of Early America*, Ivan Light's *Ethnic Enterprise in America: Business and Welfare among Chinese, Japanese, and Blacks*, Reginald Horsman's *Race and Manifest Destiny: The Origins of American Racial Anglo-Saxonism*, and Benjamin Ringer's *"We the People" and Others: Duality and America's Treatment of Its Racial Minorities.*[11]

Even here, however, a battle is being fought over how America's diversity should be conceptualized. For example, Diane Ravitch avidly supports the pluralistic perspective, but she fears national division. Stressing the importance of national unity, Ravitch promotes the development of multiculturalism based on a strategy of adding on: to keep mainstream Anglo-American history and expand it by simply including information on racism as well as minority contributions to America's music, art, literature, food, clothing, sports, and holidays. The purpose behind this pluralism, for Ravitch, is to encourage students of "all racial and ethnic groups to believe that they are part

of this society and that they should develop their talents and minds to the fullest." By "fullest," she means for students to be inspired by learning about "men and women from diverse backgrounds who overcame poverty, discrimination, physical handicaps, and other obstacles to achieve success in a variety of fields." Ravitch is driven by a desire for universalism: she wants to affirm our common humanity by discouraging our specific group identities, especially those based on racial experiences. Ironically, Ravitch, a self-avowed proponent of pluralism, actually wants us to abandon our group ties and become individuals.[12]

This privileging of the "unum" over the "pluribus" has been advanced more aggressively by Arthur Schlesinger in *The Disuniting of America*.

In this jeremiad, Schlesinger denounces what he calls "the cult of ethnicity"—the shift from assimilation to group identity, from integration to separatism. The issue at stake, he argues, is the teaching of *"bad history under whatever ethnic banner."* After acknowledging that American history has long been written in the "interests of white Anglo-Saxon Protestant males," he describes the enslavement of Africans, the seizure of Indian lands, and the exploitation of Chinese railroad workers. But his discussion on racial oppression is perfunctory and parsimonious, and he devotes most of his attention to a defense of traditional history. "Anglocentric domination of schoolbooks

11. Ronald Takaki, *A Different Mirror: A History of Multicultural America* (New York: Little, Brown, 1993); Gary Nash, *Red, White, and Black: The Peoples of Early America* (Englewood Cliffs, NJ: Prentice-Hall, 1974); Ivan Light, *Ethnic Enterprise in America: Business and Welfare among Chinese, Japanese, and Blacks* (Berkeley: University of California Press, 1972); Reginald Horsman, *Race and Manifest Destiny: The Origins of American Racial Anglo-Saxonism* (Cambridge, MA: Harvard University Press, 1981); Benjamin Ringer, *"We the People" and Others: Duality and America's Treatment of Its Racial Minorities* (New York: Tavistock, 1983).

12. Ravitch, "Multiculturalism," pp. 341, 354.

was based in part on unassailable facts," Schlesinger declares. "For better or worse, American history has been shaped more than anything else by British tradition and culture." Like Bloom, Schlesinger utilizes the metaphor of eating. "To deny the essentially European origins of American culture is to falsify history," he explains. "Belief in one's own culture does not require disdain for other cultures. But one step at a time: no culture can hope to ingest other cultures all at once, certainly not before it ingests its own." Defensively claiming to be an inclusionist historian, Schlesinger presents his own credentials: "As for me, I was for a time a member of the executive council of the *Journal of Negro History.* . . . I have been a lifelong advocate of civil rights."[13]

But what happens when minority peoples try to define their civil rights in terms of cultural pluralism and group identities? They become targets of Schlesinger's scorn. This "exaggeration" of ethnic differences, he warns, only "drives ever deeper the awful wedges between races," leading to an "endgame" of self-pity and self-ghettoization. The culprits responsible for this divisiveness are the "multicultural zealots," especially the Afrocentrists. Schlesinger castigates them as campus bullies, distorting history and creating myths about the contributions of Africans.[14]

What Schlesinger refuses to admit or is unable to see clearly is how he himself is culpable of historical distortion: his own omissions in *The Age of Jackson* have erased what James Madison had described then as " 'the black race within our bosom' " and " 'the red on our borders.' " Both groups have been entirely left out of Schlesinger's study: they do not even have entries in the index. Moreover, there is not even a mention of two marker events, the Nat Turner insurrection and Indian Removal, which Andrew Jackson himself would have been surprised to find omitted from a history of his era. Unfortunately, Schlesinger fails to meet even his own standards of scholarship: "The historian's goals are accuracy, analysis, and objectivity in the reconstruction of the past."[15]

Behind Schlesinger's cant against multiculturalism is fear. What will happen to our national ideal of *"e pluribus unum?"* he worries. Will the center hold, or will the melting pot yield to the Tower of Babel? For answers, he looks abroad. "Today," he observes, "the nationalist fever encircles the globe." Angry and violent "tribalism" is exploding in India, the former Soviet Union, Indonesia, Guyana, and other countries around the world. "The ethnic upsurge in America, far from being unique, partakes of the global fever." Like Bloom and Ravitch, Schlesinger prescribes individualism as the cure. "Most Americans," he argues, "continue to see themselves primarily as individuals and only secondarily and trivially as

13. Arthur M. Schlesinger, Jr., *The Disuniting of America: Reflections on a Multicultural Society* (Knoxville, TN: Whittle Communications, 1991), pp. 2, 24, 14, 81-82.

14. Ibid., pp. 58, 66.

15. James Madison, quoted in Takaki, *Iron Cages*, p. 80; Arthur M. Schlesinger, Jr., *The Age of Jackson* (Boston: Little, Brown, 1945); idem, *Disuniting of America*, p. 20.

adherents of a group." The dividing of society into "fixed ethnicities nourishes a culture of victimization and a contagion of inflammable sensitivities." This danger threatens the "brittle bonds of national identity that hold this diverse and fractious society together." The Balkan present, Schlesinger warns, may be America's prologue.[16]

Are we limited to a choice between a "disuniting" multiculturalism and a common American culture, or can we transform the "culture war" into a meeting ground? The intellectual combats of this conflict, Gerald Graff suggests, have the potential to enrich American education. As universities become contested terrains of different points of view, gray and monotonous cloisters of Eurocentric knowledge can become brave new worlds, dynamic and multicultural. On these academic battlegrounds, scholars and students can engage each other in dialogue and debate, informed by the heat and light generated by the examination of opposing texts such as Joseph Conrad's *Heart of Darkness* and Chinua Achebe's *Things Fall Apart*. "Teaching the conflicts has nothing to do with relativism or denying the existence of truth," Graff contends. "The best way to make relativists of students is to expose them to an endless series of different positions which are *not* debated before their eyes." Graff turns the guns of the great books against Bloom. By viewing culture as a debate and by entering a process of intellectual clashes, students can search for truth,

as did Socrates "when he taught the conflicts two millennia ago."[17]

Like Graff, I welcome such debates in my teaching. One of my courses, "Racial Inequality in America: A Comparative Historical Perspective," studies the character of American society in relationship to our racial and ethnic diversity. My approach is captured in the phrase "from different shores." By "shores," I intend a double meaning. One is the shores from which the migrants departed, places such as Europe, Africa, and Asia. The second is the various and often conflicting perspectives or shores from which scholars have viewed the experiences of racial and ethnic groups.

By critically examining these different shores, students address complex comparative questions. How have the experiences of racial minorities such as African Americans been similar to and different from those of ethnic groups such as Irish Americans? Is race the same as ethnicity? For example, is the African American experience qualitatively or quantitatively different from the Jewish American experience? How have race relations been shaped by economic developments as well as by culture—moral values about how people think and behave as well as beliefs about human nature and society? To wrestle with these questions, students read Nathan Glazer's analysis of assimilationist patterns as well as Robert Blauner's theory of internal colonialism, Charles Murray on black welfare dependency as well as Wil-

16. Schlesinger, *Disuniting of America*, pp. 2, 21, 64.

17. Gerald Graff, *Beyond the Culture Wars: How Teaching the Conflicts Can Revitalize American Education* (New York: Norton, 1992), p. 15.

liam Julius Wilson on the economic structures creating the black underclass, and Thomas Sowell's explanation of Asian American success as well as my critique of the "myth of the Asian-American model minority."[18]

The need to open American minds to greater cultural diversity will not go away. Faculty can resist this imperative by ignoring the changing racial composition of student bodies and the larger society, or they can embrace this timely and exciting intellectual opportunity to revitalize the social sciences and humanities. "The study of the humanities," Henry Louis Gates observes, "is the study of the possibilities of human life in culture. It thrives on diversity. . . . The new [ethnic studies] scholarship has invigorated the traditional disciplines." What distinguishes the university from other battlegrounds, such as the media and politics, is that the university has a special commitment to the search for knowledge, one based on a process of intellectual openness and inquiry. Multiculturalism can stoke this critical spirit by transforming the university into a crucial meeting ground for different viewpoints. In the process, perhaps we will be able to discover what makes us an American people.[19]

Whether the university can realize this intellectual pursuit for collective self-knowledge is uncertain, especially during difficult economic times. As institutions of higher learning face budget cuts, calls for an expansion of the curriculum often encounter hostility from faculty in traditional departments determined to protect dwindling resources. Furthermore, the economic crisis has been fanning the fires of racism in society: Asian Americans have been bashed for the seeming invasion of Japanese cars, Hispanics accused of taking jobs away from Americans, and blacks attacked for their dependency on welfare and the special privileges of affirmative action.

This context of rising racial tensions has conditioned the culture war. Both the advocates and the critics of multiculturalism know that the conflict is not wholly academic; the debate over how America should be defined is related to power and privilege. Both sides agree that history is power. Society's collective memory determines the future. The battle is over what should be remembered and who should do the remembering.

Traditionally excluded from the curriculum, minorities are insisting that America does not belong to one group and neither does America's history. They are making their claim to the knowledge offered by the university, reminding us that Americans

18. Nathan Glazer, *Affirmative Discrimination: Ethnic Inequality and Public Policy* (New York: Basic Books, 1975); Robert Blauner, *Racial Oppression in America* (New York: Harper & Row, 1972); Charles Murray, *Losing Ground: American Social Policy, 1950-1980* (New York: Basic Books, 1984); William Julius Wilson, *The Truly Disadvantaged: The Inner City, the Underclass, and Public Policy* (Chicago: University of Chicago Press, 1987); Thomas Sowell, *Ethnic America: A History* (New York: Basic Books, 1981); Takaki, *Strangers from a Different Shore.* For an example of the debate format, see Ronald Takaki, *From Different Shores: Perspectives on Race and Ethnicity in America* (New York: Oxford University Press, 1987).

19. Henry Louis Gates, Jr., *Loose Canons: Notes on the Culture Wars* (New York: Oxford University Press, 1992), p. 114.

originated from many lands and that everyone here is entitled to dignity. "I hope this survey do a lot of good for Chinese people," an immigrant told an interviewer from Stanford in the 1920s. "Make American people realize that Chinese people are humans. I think very few American people really know anything about Chinese." As different groups find their voices, they tell and retell stories that liberate. By writing about the people on Mango Street, Sandra Cisneros explained, "the ghost does not ache so much." The place no longer holds her with "both arms. She sets [Cisneros] free." Indeed, stories may not be as innocent or simple as they might seem. They "aren't just entertainment," observed Native American novelist Leslie Marmon Silko.[20]

On the other side, the interests seeking to maintain the status quo also recognize that the contested terrain of ideas is related to social reality. No wonder conservative foundations like Coors and Olin have been financing projects to promote their own political agenda on campuses across the country, and the National Association of Scholars has been attacking multiculturalism by smearing it with a brush called "political correctness." Conservative critics like Bloom are the real campus bullies: they are the ones unwilling to open the debate and introduce students to different viewpoints. Under the banner of intellectual freedom

and excellence, these naysayers have been imposing their own intellectual orthodoxy by denouncing those who disagree with them as "the new barbarians," saluting Lynne Cheney, the former head of the National Endowment for the Humanities for defending traditional American culture, and employing McCarthyite tactics to brand ethnic studies as "un-American."[21]

How can the university become a meeting ground when the encounter of oppositional ideas is disparaged? What Susan Faludi has observed about the academic backlash against women's liberation can be applied to the reaction to multiculturalism. "The donnish robes of many of these backlash thinkers cloaked impulses that were less than scholarly," she wrote. "Some of them were academics who believed that feminists had cost them in advancement, tenure, and honors; they found the creation of women's studies not just professionally but personally disturbing and invasive, a trespasser trampling across *their* campus." Her observation applies to multiculturalism: all we need to do is to substitute "minority scholars" for "feminists," and "ethnic studies" for "women's studies." The intellectual backlashers are defending "their" campuses against the "other."[22]

20. Pany Lowe, interview, 1924, Survey of Race Relations, Hoover Institution Archives, Stanford, CA; Sandra Cisneros, *The House on Mango Street* (New York: Vintage, 1991), pp. 109-10; Leslie Marmon Silko, *Ceremony* (New York: New American Library, 1978), p. 2.

21. Dinesh D'Souza, "The Visigoths in Tweed," in *Beyond PC: Towards a Politics of Understanding*, ed. Patricia Aufderheide (St. Paul, MN: Graywolf Press, 1992), p. 11; George Will, "Literary Politics," *Newsweek*, 22 Apr. 1991, p. 72; Arthur Schlesinger, Jr., "When Ethnic Studies Are Un-American," *Wall Street Journal*, 23 Apr. 1990.

22. Susan Faludi, *Backlash: The Undeclared War against American Women* (New York: Doubleday, 1992), p. 282.

The campaign against multiculturalism reflects a larger social nervousness, a perplexity over the changing racial composition of American society. Here Faludi's insights may again be transferrable. The war against women, she notes, manifests an identity crisis for men: what does it mean to be a man? One response has been to reclaim masculinity through violence, to "kick ass," the expression George Bush used to describe his combat with Geraldine Ferraro in the 1984 vice-presidential debate. Eight years later, during the Persian Gulf war against Saddam Hussein, Bush as President demonstrated masculine power in Desert Storm. In a parallel way, it can be argued, the expanding multicultural reality of America is creating a racial identity crisis: what does it mean to be white?[23]

Demographic studies project that whites will become a minority of the total U.S. population some time during the twenty-first century. Already in major cities across the country, whites no longer predominate numerically. This expanding multicultural reality is challenging the traditional notion of America as white. What will it mean for American society to have a nonwhite majority? The significance of this future, *Time* observed, is related to our identity—our sense of individual self and nationhood, or what it means to be American. This demographic transformation has prompted E. D. Hirsch to worry that America is becoming a "Tower of Babel," and that this multiplicity of cultures is threatening to

tear the country's social fabric. Nostalgic for a more cohesive culture and a more homogeneous America, he contends, "If we *had* to make a choice between the *one* and the *many*, most Americans would choose the principle of unity, since we cannot function as a nation without it." The way to correct this fragmentization, Hirsch argues, is to promote the teaching of "shared symbols." In *Cultural Literacy: What Every American Needs to Know*, Hirsch offers an appendix of terms designed to create a sense of national identity and unity—a list that leaves out much of the histories and cultures of minorities.[24]

The escalating war against multiculturalism is being fueled by a fear of loss. " 'Backlash politics may be defined as the reaction by groups which are declining in a felt sense of importance, influence, and power,' " observed Seymour Martin Lipset and Earl Raab. Similarly, historian Richard Hofstadter described the impulses of progressive politics in the early twentieth century in terms of a "status revolution"—a widely shared frustration among middle-class professionals who had been displaced by a new class of elite businessmen. Hofstadter also detected a "paranoid style in American politics" practiced by certain groups such as nativists who suffered from lost prestige and felt besieged by complex new realities. Grieving for an America that had been taken away from them, they desperately fought to repossess their

23. Ibid., p. 65.

24. William A. Henry III, "Beyond the Melting Pot," *Time*, 9 Apr. 1990, pp. 28-31; E. D. Hirsch, Jr., *Cultural Literacy: What Every American Needs to Know* (Boston: Houghton, Mifflin, 1987), pp. xiii, xvii, 2, 18, 96, 152-215.

country and "prevent the final destructive act of subversion."[25]

A similar anxiety is growing in America today. One of the factors behind the backlash against multiculturalism is race, what Lawrence Auster calls "the forbidden topic." In an essay published in the *National Review*, he advocates the restriction of immigration for nonwhites. Auster condemns the white liberals for wanting to have it both ways—to have a common culture and also to promote racial diversity. They naively refuse to recognize the danger: when a "critical number" of people in this country are no longer from the West, then we will no longer be able to employ traditional reference points such as "our Western heritage" or speak of "our Founding Fathers." American culture as it has been known, Auster warns, is disappearing as "more and more minorities complain that they can't identify with American history because they 'don't see people who look like themselves' in that history." To preserve America as a Western society, Auster argues, America must continue to be composed mostly of people of European ancestry.[26]

What Auster presents is an extreme but logical extension of a view shared by both conservatives like Bloom and liberals like Schlesinger: they have bifurcated American society into "us" versus "them." This division locates whites at the center

and minorities at the margins of our national identity. "American," observed Toni Morrison, has been defined as "white." Such a dichotomization denies our wholeness as one people. " 'Everybody remembers,' " she explained, " 'the first time they were taught that part of the human race was Other. That's a trauma. It's as though I told you that your left hand is not part of your body.' "[27]

In their war against the denied parts of American society, the backlashers are our modern Captain Ahabs. In their pursuit of their version of the white whale, they are in command; like Ahab directing his chase from the deck of the *Pequod*, they steer the course of the university curriculum. Their exclusive definition of knowledge has rendered invisible and silent the swirling and rich diversity below deck. The workers of the *Pequod* represent a multicultural society—whites like Ishmael, Pacific Islanders like Queequeg, Africans like Daggoo, Asians like Fedallah, and American Indians like Tashtego. In Melville's powerful story, Ishmael and Queequeg find themselves strangers to each other at first. As they labor together, they are united by their need of mutual survival and cooperation. This connectedness is graphically illustrated by the monkey-rope. Lowered into the shark-infested water to secure the blubber hook into the dead whale, Queequeg is held by a rope tied to Ishmael. The process is

25. Lipset and Raab quoted in Faludi, *Backlash*, p. 231; Richard Hofstadter, *The Age of Reform: From Bryan to F.D.R.* (New York: Random House, 1955), pp. 131-73.

26. Lawrence Auster, "The Forbidden Topic," *National Review*, 27 Apr. 1992, pp. 42-44.

27. Toni Morrison, *Playing in the Dark: Whiteness in the Literary Imagination* (Cambridge, MA: Harvard University Press, 1992), p. 47; Bonnie Angelo, "The Pain of Being Black," *Time*, 22 May 1989, p. 121. Copyright © 1989 Time Inc. Reprinted by permission.

perilous for both men. "We two, for the time," Ishmael tells us, "were wedded; and should poor Queequeg sink to rise no more, then both usage and honor demanded that, instead of cutting the cord, it should drag me down in his wake." Though originally from different shores, the members of the crew share a noble class unity. Ahab, however, is able to charm them, his charisma drawing them into the delirium of his hunt. Driven by a monomanic mission, Ahab charts a course that ends in the destruction of everyone except Ishmael.[28]

On college campuses today, the voices of many students and faculty

28. Herman Melville, *Moby Dick* (Boston: Houghton Mifflin, 1956), pp. 182, 253, 322-23.

from below deck are challenging such hierarchical power. In their search for cross-cultural understandings, they are trying to re-vision America. But will we as Americans continue to perceive our past and peer into our future as through a glass darkly? In the telling and retelling of our particular stories, will we create communities of separate memories, or will we be able to connect our diverse selves to a larger national narrative? As we approach a new century dominated by ethnic and racial conflicts at home and throughout the world, we realize that the answers to such questions will depend largely on whether the university will be able to become both a battleground and a meeting ground of varied viewpoints.

ANNALS, *AAPSS*, **530**, November 1993

Is Assimilation Dead?

By NATHAN GLAZER

ABSTRACT: This article considers the decline in the positive attitude toward the term "assimilation" as an ideal for immigrant and minority groups in the United States, and it explores the period between World War I and the mid-1920s, during which assimilation moved from an ideal to a forceful policy, under the name "Americanization." During this period, attention was given almost exclusively to immigrants; blacks were totally ignored in the debate over assimilation and Americanization. Nevertheless, until the mid-1960s, the dominant black ideal for their future in the United States was assimilation. The failure of assimilation to work its effects on blacks as on immigrants, owing to the strength of American discriminatory and prejudiced attitudes and behavior toward blacks, has been responsible for throwing the entire assimilatory ideal and program into disrepute.

Nathan Glazer, professor of education and sociology at Harvard University, is the author or coauthor of Beyond the Melting Pot *(1963),* Affirmative Discrimination *(1975),* Ethnic Dilemmas *(1983), and* The Limits of Social Policy *(1989) and the author and editor of other works dealing with ethnicity and social policy. He is also coeditor of* The Public Interest.

"A SSIMILATION" is not today a popular term. Recently I asked a group of Harvard students taking a class on race and ethnicity in the United States what their attitude to the term "assimilation" was. The large majority had a negative reaction to it. Had I asked what they thought of the term "Americanization," the reaction, I am sure, would have been even more hostile. Indeed, in recent years it has been taken for granted that assimilation, as an expectation of how different ethnic and racial groups would respond to their common presence in one society or as an ideal regarding how the society should evolve or as the expected result of a sober social scientific analysis of the ultimate consequence of the meeting of people and races, is to be rejected. Our ethnic and racial reality, we are told, does not exhibit the effects of assimilation; our social science should not expect it; and as an ideal, it is somewhat disreputable, opposed to the reality of both individual and group difference and to the claims that such differences should be recognized and celebrated.

One might think there is nothing left to say. The idea that it would happen, that it should happen, has simply been discredited, and we live with a new reality. It was once called cultural pluralism, it is now called multiculturalism, and whatever the complications created by the term for educational policy, or for public policy in various other realms, that is what we must live with, and all of us must be ranged along a spectrum of greater or lesser enthusiasm and acceptance of the new reality. Even crit-

ics of the new multiculturalism take their place within this spectrum. Those who truly stand against it, the true advocates and prophets of a full assimilationism, are so minuscule in American public and intellectual life that they can scarcely be discerned in public discussion. One can point to the journal *Chronicles* and scarcely anything else. Neither liberals nor neoliberals, conservatives nor neoconservatives, have much good to say about assimilation, and only a branch of paleoconservatism can now be mustered in its defense. It is only they who would agree that even if it has not yet happened, it is something that, despite the reverses of the past thirty years, should have happened and should still happen.

My purpose is not to present a eulogy over a dead hope or demeaning concept. It is rather to argue that properly understood, assimilation is still the most powerful force affecting the ethnic and racial elements of the United States and that our problem in recognizing this has to do with one great failure of assimilation in American life, the incorporation of the Negro, a failure that has led in its turn to a more general counterattack on the ideology of assimilation.

THE HISTORY OF AN IDEA

But to go back: what was assimilation? It was the expectation that a new man would be born, was being born, in the United States. We can go back to that much quoted comment on what was the American, in Crèvecoeur's *Letters from an American Farmer* of 1782:

"What then is the American, this new man? He is either a European or the descendant of a European, hence that strange mixture of blood, which you will find in no other country. I could point out to you a family whose grandfather was an Englishman, whose wife was Dutch, whose son married a French woman, and whose present four sons have four wives of four different nations. *He* is an American, who, leaving behind him all his ancient prejudices and manners, receives new ones from the new mode of life he has embraced, the new government he obeys, and the new rank he holds."[1]

This passage, which Philip Gleason tells us "has probably been quoted more than any other in the history of immigration," has, of course, been generally cited to celebrate American diversity and the general acceptance of this diversity as forming the basis of a new nation, a new national identity, but in 1993 we will look at it with more critical eyes and note what it does not include as well as what it does: there is no reference to Africans, who then made up a fifth of the American population, or to American Indians, who were then still a vivid and meaningful, on occasion menacing, presence in the American world. In this article, I will refer to many other passages that to our contemporary eyes will express a similar surprising unconsciousness, or hypocrisy, or unawareness. Today we would cry out, "There are others there you are not talking about! What about them, and what place will they have in the making of the new American?"

The concept of assimilation looked toward Europe. It referred to the expected experience and fate of the stream of immigrants who were a permanent part of American life and consciousness from the time of the first settlements on the Atlantic seaboard to the 1920s, when it was thought—incorrectly—that we were now done with mass immigration of varied backgrounds to the United States.

There has been a good deal of discussion of a major characteristic of the emerging American national consciousness, or, we would say today, the emerging American identity. That is, that in many authoritative formulations, from the Declaration of Independence on, the American, the new nationality being formed here, is not defined ethnically, as deriving from an ancient common stock or stocks, as almost all other major modern nations define themselves. I may point out as an aside that while the term "identity" is almost essential in any discussion of this emerging American national character, it is a relative latecomer to the discussion. Philip Gleason tells us,

The term "identity" has become indispensable in the discussion of ethnic affairs. Yet it was hardly used at all until the 1950's. The father of the concept, Erik H. Erikson, remarked on its novelty in . . . *Childhood and Society* (1950): "We begin to conceptualize matters of identity . . . in a country which attempts to make a super-identity of all the identities imported by its constituent immigrants." In an autobiographical account published 20 years later, Erikson . . . quoted this passage and added that the terms "iden-

---

1. Michel Guillaume Jean de Crèvecoeur, *Letters from an American Farmer*, as quoted in Philip Gleason, "American Identity and Americanization," in *Harvard Encyclopedia of American Ethnic Groups* (Cambridge, MA: Harvard University Press, 1980), p. 33.

tity" and "identity crisis" seemed to grow out of "the experience of emigration, immigration, and Americanization."[2]

Many could be quoted on this surprising characteristic of American identity, its avoidance of explicit ethnic reference. Despite the fact that the American revolution was fought almost exclusively by men who traced their origins to the British Isles, and primarily to England, and that the signers of the Declaration of Independence and the framers of the Constitution were almost exclusively of this stock, they did not define their Americanness as an ethnic characteristic. They emphasized its dependence on adherence to ideals, to universal principles. Perhaps, as Gleason points out, this was because it was necessary for the rebels and revolutionaries to distinguish themselves from the ethnically identical country against which they were rebelling. But in any case, the ideological formulation of the definition of the American was there at the beginning. Years ago I quoted Hans Kohn, Yehoshua Arieli, and S. M. Lipset on this characteristic of American identity.[3] One could add other voices. As Gleason writes,

The ideological quality of American national identity was of decisive importance, vis-à-vis the question of immigration and ethnicity. To become an American a person did not have to be of any particular national, linguistic, religious, or ethnic background. All he had to do was to commit himself to the political ideology centered on the abstract ideals of liberty, equality, and republicanism. Thus the universalist ideological character of American nationality meant that it was open to anyone who willed to become an American.[4]

As anyone writing in 1980 must be, he is aware of the exclusions, not remarked on by the writers of those early ringing documents, perhaps exclusions of which they were not even aware, the blacks and Indians and, later, groups not in the beginning present in the new United States. Certainly, even if not specifically excluded, they were not intended to be included in these ringing affirmations of universality.

One could find here and there before the 1940s a few voices of significance who seem to make no exclusion. There was Emerson in 1845:

In this continent—asylum of all nations —the energy of Irish, Germans, Swedes, Poles, and Cossacks, and all the European tribes,—of the Africans, and of the Polynesians,—will construct a new race, a new religion, a new state, a new literature, which will be as vigorous as the new Europe which came out of the smelting-pot of the Dark Ages.[5]

There was Whitman. But one can ask even of Emerson, Did he mean it? What did he know of Polynesians, after all? And one can ask of the term he introduced to characterize the assimilation of the different elements, the "smelting pot," later to achieve fame in this discussion in the form of the "melting pot," Was that not too brutal, too strong, a metaphor for what was to be lost, to disappear, in

2. Gleason, "American Identity," p. 31.

3. Nathan Glazer, *Affirmative Discrimination* (New York: Basic Books, 1975).

4. Gleason, "American Identity," p. 32.

5. Harold J. Abramson, "Assimilation and Pluralism," in *Harvard Encyclopedia of American Ethnic Groups*, p. 152.

order to make this new race? The groups were to be more than melted, smelted, as in two or more metals becoming one (the Emerson passage begins with a reference to "Corinthian brass"). But for the moment ignoring the question of whether assimilation was too strong a demand, it is necessary to focus on who was to be assimilated.

FORGETTING THE BLACKS

In almost all the discussion of Americanization or assimilation until about World War II, the discussants had only Europeans in mind. This is true whether they favored or opposed assimilation and Americanization efforts. A reader today of the documents of the great Americanization drive of the second decade of this century will find no reference to blacks, then as now our largest minority. It is as if the turmoil of abolitionism, slavery, the Civil War, Reconstruction did not exist. All concern was with the "new" immigrants, that is, the mass immigration from Eastern and Southern Europe that brought enormous numbers of kinds of Europeans different from those the nation had become accustomed to. Admittedly, one could make the argument that "Americanization," the name of the assimilation movement of the time, could address only those who were not Americans, and were not blacks American-born and formally citizens? So, one could argue, this was the reason they were ignored in the great debate that finally degenerated into a resurgent Ku Klux Klan and the closing of the gates to the new immigrants.

Yet, when one looks at the aims of the Americanization movement, one asks, And why not blacks, too? The aims of the movement, in its earlier, benign form, were to make the newcomers citizens and encourage them to participate as individuals in politics (as against their domination by urban bosses), to teach them English (and here one main argument was to make them better and safer workers, in view of the huge toll of industrial accidents), to break up immigrant colonies ("distribution" it was called), and to teach American customs, which meant primarily sanitation and hygiene. All this would make the immigrants better Americans. One major motivation was concern that the new immigrants would not become good Americans, owing to lack of English, citizenship, and knowledge of American customs. With World War I, to this motivation was added fear of lack of patriotism or disloyalty. But the vigorous advocates of Americanization—social workers and businessmen, a strange mix that nevertheless characterized much of the progressivism of the time—were also trying to plead the case of the new immigrants against the arguments of their countrymen who increasingly favored immigration restriction. The social workers, we know, pled this case out of understanding and sympathy for the new immigrants; the businessmen, we may assume, out of self-interest, much as the *Wall Street Journal* of today argues for free immigration. But if these were the aims of the Americanization movement, why were not the blacks included?

Their exclusion is even more striking to the current reader in view of the language of the time, in which ethnic groups are referred to as "races" —but the first group that comes to mind when we speak of "race" today is not in the minds of these earnest and energetic advocates of assimilation and Americanization.

Consider one of the most authoritative statements of what was hoped for from Americanization, from Frances Kellor, a progressive woman social worker who was the heart and soul of the movement, indefatigably organizing committees, conventions, statements, programs.

Americanization is the science of racial relations in America, dealing with the assimilation and amalgamation of diverse races in equity into an integral part of the national life. By "assimilation" is meant the indistinguishable incorporation of the races into the substance of American life. By "amalgamation" is meant so perfect a blend that the absence or imperfection of any of the vital racial elements available, will impair the compound. By "an integral part" is meant that, once fused, separation of units is thereafter impossible. By "inequity" is meant impartiality among the races accepted into the blend with no imputations of inferiority and no bestowed favors.[6]

This is a late statement, made when the movement was taking on a harsher tone, and rather stronger than we would find from most advocates of Americanization, in particular in the emphasis on "amalgamation," which can only mean intermarriage to the point of the indistinguishability of

any distinct group. My concern here, however, is with the remarkable absence of the blacks, despite the continual emphasis on the word "race."

One of the early climaxes of the movement was a great meeting in Philadelphia, on 10 May 1915. Woodrow Wilson addressed a huge throng—5000 newly naturalized citizens, 8000 previously naturalized, a chorus of 5000 voices, and the like. He does not use the term "race" in his paean to the all-inclusiveness of America, but all races are clearly implied in his term "the people of the world":

This is the only country in the world which experiences this constant and repeated rebirth. Other countries depend upon the multiplication of their own native people. This country is constantly drinking strength out of new sources by the voluntary association with it of great bodies of strong men and forward-looking women out of other lands. . . . It is as if humanity had determined to see to it that this great Nation, founded for the benefit of humankind, should not lack for the allegiance of the people of the world.[7]

But we might again ask, Where were the blacks? Clearly, Wilson did not have them in mind.

This great meeting was the prelude to Americanization Day on 4 July 1915, when many meetings to welcome new citizens were held all over the country. One of them was in Faneuil Hall in Boston, addressed by Justice Louis Brandeis. He asserted that what was distinctly American was "inclusive brotherhood." Amer-

6. Frances A. Kellor, "What is Americanization?" *Yale Review* (Jan. 1919), as reprinted in Philip Davis, *Immigration and Americanization: Selected Readings* (Boston: Ginn, 1920), pp. 625-26.

7. Davis, *Immigration and Americanization*, p. 612; for a description of the meeting, see Edward George Hartman, *The Movement to Americanize the Immigrant* (New York: AMS Press, 1967), p. 11 n.

ica, as against other nations, "has always declared herself for equality of nationalities as well as for equality of individuals. It recognizes racial equality as an essential of full human liberty and true brotherhood. . . . It has, therefore, given like welcome to all the peoples of Europe."[8] He did not seem to have blacks in mind.

Most ironically, we find that one of the most active of the postwar Americanization groups was the Inter-Racial Council. We know what the name of the council would mean had it been used 20 years later. But in 1919 it struck no one as odd, apparently, that it did not refer to blacks and that it did not include blacks. Among a host of names of leading businessmen and bankers and political dignitaries we find some prominent immigrant names —Dr. Antonio Stella, M. I. Pupin, Gutzon Borglum, Jacob Schiff—but none belonging to blacks.[9]

As the Americanization movement began to shift from one befriending the immigrant, bringing him closer together to Americans, to one that seemed increasingly hostile, in which the generous offer of citizenship and full participation became the compulsory demand that the immigrant must learn the English language and American government, the Carnegie Corporation, trying to defend the earlier openness toward the immigrant, in the spirit of Jane Addams and Lillian Wald, sponsored a series of Americanization studies. Once again the language will surprise in its unconsciousness of the fact that "race"

might include other than Europeans. In James A. Gavit's *Americans by Choice*, on the issue of naturalization, we find again the argument with which we are familiar: that the American is not defined ethnically but by allegiance to an ideology. "The American Has No Racial Marks," one subtitle asserts. The text continues,

This absence of exclusive racial marks is the distinguishing physical characteristic of the American. True of him as of no other now or ever in the past is the fact that he is, broadly speaking, the product of *all* races. . . .

We are in the midst of the making of the "American." He does not yet appear what he shall be but one thing is certain, he is not to be of any particular racial type now distinguishable. Saxon, Teuton, Kelt, Latin and Slav—to say nothing of any appreciable contribution by yellow and brown races as yet negligible . . .—each of the races that we now know on this soil will have its share of "ancestorial" responsibility for the "typical American" that is to be.

The next heading reads, "Not Racial, But Cultural."[10]

Dealing as he does with naturalization, Gavit cannot, as more celebratory advocates of Americanization can, totally ignore the racial aspect: naturalization was racially limited. He does write:

It is not yet true—perhaps it will be very long before it can be true—that there is absolutely no bar to any person on account of race; for the law and its interpretations exclude from citizenship Chinese, Japanese, and certain people of India not regarded as "white"—although the blacks of Africa are expressly admitted. Nevertheless, it may be said broadly that

8. Davis, *Immigration and Americanization*, pp. 642-43.

9. Hartman, *Movement to Americanize the Immigrant*, pp. 220-21.

10. James A. Gavit, *Americans by Choice* (New York: Harper, 1922), pp. 10, 11-12.

regardless of race, the immigrant can come to America and win his way upon his own merits into the fellowship all the world calls "Americans."[11]

As we know, the Americanization movement lost its aspect of welcome and inclusion in the midst of the passions aroused by World War I and the postwar fear of Bolshevism and radicalism. It turned into something harsh and oppressive, in which the issue became less the opportunity to learn English than the insistence that nothing but English be learned; less the generous offer of citizenship than the widespread fear of subversion from aliens and naturalized citizens. Americanization developed a bad name among liberals. Insofar as there was still concern for the living and working conditions of immigrants, this became encompassed in a larger liberal movement for improving the conditions of working men, a movement that was easily capable of reconciling commitment to the cause of working people with opposition to further immigration. If the word "assimilation" now makes us suspicious, and "Americanization" even more so, among the older and more knowing it may be because of the excesses of the 1920s.

"Americanization" is no longer to be found in encyclopedias of the social sciences,[12] but it does appear in the first great *Encyclopedia of the Social Sciences* of 1930, and the comment we find there on the fate of Americanization will to some extent

explain to us why we do not hear much about it today:

This emphasis on the learning of English and naturalization, together with the unfortunate atmosphere of coercion and condescension in which so many war time Americanization efforts were conceived, had the effect of bringing the word into a disrepute from which it has never fully recovered. Contributing to the same result, in the period following the war, were the widely expressed fear and suspicion of the immigrant, his frequent indictment as a radical, attempts to suppress his newspapers and organizations, the ignoring of his own culture and aspirations, the charge that certain nationalities and races were inferior and unassimilable, and the use of intimidating slogans. Americanization work too frequently made the assumption that American culture was something already complete which the newcomer must adopt in its entirety. Such attitudes and activities were important factors in promoting restriction of immigration, but they did not advance the assimilation of the immigrants who were already in America.[13]

THE LIMITED VISION OF CULTURAL PLURALISM

But the point of this recital of the history of Americanization is not to add to the extensive literature that explores the neglect of and ignoring of the key question of the treatment of blacks in American society, nor to argue—although it is true—that immigrants were better treated and taken more seriously from the point of view of their inclusion in American society, nor to attack the Americanization movement for its excesses—all

11. Ibid., pp. 7-8.
12. Nor can we find what was once a key sociological concept, "assimilation," among the entries in the recent four-volume *Encyclopedia of Sociology* by C. F. Borgatta and M. L. Borgatta (New York: Macmillan, 1992).

13. Read Lewis, "Americanization," in *Encyclopedia of the Social Sciences* (New York: Macmillan, 1930), 2:33.

legitimate responses to it. It is to set the stage for something that has also received little attention: that the critics of Americanization and assimilation had little to say about blacks. However passionate in their defense of the contribution to American economy, culture, and politics of immigrants and immigrant groups, however strong in their resistance to the demand for assimilation, whatever arguments they raised in resistance to the expectation of assimilation, the critics—let us call them for convenience the "cultural pluralists," for it was they who raised the strongest objections—had little to say, indeed nothing to say, about adding blacks to the series of groups who they felt had every right to maintain their separate identity. Maybe they believed blacks should; maybe they never thought of them: they just never entered them into the argument.

There were, of course, critics of Americanization. There were fewer during its earlier, more benign form; more when it evolved under the pressures of war into an attack on "hyphenated Americanism," led by former President Theodore Roosevelt; more when it further evolved into the repression of the postwar years, through laws restricting aliens and imposing English, through administrative actions expelling aliens, through waves of public opinion against further mass immigration from Europe, and into the mass hysteria of the Ku Klux Klan and similar organizations. But those few voices of cultural pluralism that were then raised, and that we have in recent decades disinterred, had almost nothing to say about blacks in their

celebration of a possible "Transnational America," as in Randolph Bourne's phrase, in their attack on the critics of "hyphenated Americanism," in their insistence that each group, each "race," in the language of the time, had an inherent genius or character that should not be suppressed but allowed to flower, as in the argument of Horace Kallen. We search this modest literature in vain for any reference to black Americans.

Thus, when John Dewey spoke to the National Education Association in 1916 to defend the value of cultural pluralism, he did not seem to have blacks in mind. Of course, he was speaking in the context of an attack on the loyalty of Europeans. Nevertheless, one would have thought that America's largest minority might have entered into the discussion. Many groups were mentioned in his talk:

Such terms as Irish-American or Hebrew-American or German-American are false terms, because they seem to imply something which is already in existence called America, to which the other factors may be hitched on. The fact is, the genuine American, the typical American, is himself a hyphenated character. It does not mean he is part American and some foreign ingredient is added. It means that . . . he is international and interracial in his make-up. He is not American plus Pole or German. But the American is himself Pole-German-English-French-Spanish-Italian-Greek-Irish-Scandinavian-Bohemian-Jew—and so on.[14]

One searches Horace Kallen's *Culture and Democracy in the United States*, the fullest statement of the cultural-pluralist view of the time,

14. John Dewey, as quoted in Horace M. Kallen, *Culture and Democracy in the United States* (New York: Boni Liveright, 1924), pp. 131-32.

almost in vain for any reference to blacks. They cannot be fully escaped: after all, the introductory chapter is titled "Culture and the Ku Klux Klan," and Negroes are listed as among its targets. There are two other slightly fuller references. In speaking of the spirit of Know-Nothingism, he writes, "What differs from ourselves we spontaneously set upon a different level of value. If it seems to be strong it is called wicked and is feared; if it is regarded as weak, it is called brutish and exploited. Sometimes, as in the attitude toward the negro [sic], the emotions interpenetrate and become a sentiment focalizing the worst qualities of each." There is one more reference. Kallen is concerned in this passage with whether the current hysteria will wane, the integration of immigrants into American life under a liberal regime will continue (here "integration" clearly does not mean "assimilation"). But it may not happen. The immigrant may be fixed in the inferior economic position he now holds: "One need only cast an eye over the negro-white relations in the South to realize the limit that such a condition would, unchecked, engender."[15] Perhaps it is reading too much into very little, but one detects in this passage no expectation that there will be much change in this condition.

The significance of this episode in the history of American thinking about race and ethnicity is that the argument over assimilation and Americanization evoked by the mass immigration of the period 1880-1924 and by the pressures of World War I simply did not take blacks, let alone

15. Kallen, pp. 127, 165.

Mexican Americans or Asians, into account.

Thus the evolution of the argument did not take account of the groups that came in time to stand for both American minorities and immigrants. After World War II, Europeans did not stand for either. Discrimination against European groups declined rapidly after World War II. Thus they began to lose their status as minorities. Immigration, when it recovered after World War II, encompassed a rather modest stream of Europeans. When it grew, after 1965, into a volume rivaling that of earlier periods of mass immigration, it included very few Europeans: it became an immigration predominantly of Asians of varying nations, of Latin Americans of many nations, of Caribbean blacks of many nations. The European component was reduced to a small fraction.

Now blacks and others had to be included in the discussion. As something like cultural pluralism began to raise its head again with the coming of Hitler and the fear of a future war, the growing concern was no longer with European immigrants alone, as it was in the buildup to World War I. Americans generally and security agencies specifically were concerned about German American adherents of Nazism, with Italian adherents of Italian Fascism—many fewer than Nazi adherents—and most with Japanese Americans, who were the only group to be affected by a World War I-style hysteria. There was, then, a reprise to some extent of World War I concern with immigrant loyalty. Indeed, we even had a revival of something like the Americanization Day spectacles of the earlier period in the creation and brief history of "I Am an American Day." But the tone of the new movement was different in some key respects.

First, mass immigration had come to an end, and no one expected it to revive, whatever the needs of persecuted Jews and other groups harried by the Nazis. Perhaps this explains a greater degree of benignity.

But second, blacks and Hispanics and Asians were now definitely part of the story. Because we were fighting Hitler and his ideology of racial superiority, we had to take into account our own groups of racially defined second-class citizens, all suffering under a weight of legal as well as informal segregation, discrimination, and prejudice. Cultural pluralism, which had been in World War I and its aftermath only the evanescent hope of a few philosophers and journalists, became a sturdy growth, under a new name, intercultural education. The focus began to shift, from European immigrant groups to minorities of color. European immigrant groups were already well on the way to assimilation. In addition, Hitler had antagonized so many of them that disloyalty did not seem the great problem it had appeared in World War I; suspicion touched only the Japanese. And in fighting the ideology of race—physical race, biological race—how could we not be concerned with how we treated our racial minorities?

What was to be the fate of assimilation in this new dispensation? Whatever the new degree of tolerance for diversity, it was generally expected that assimilation would continue. Intercultural education was a far cry from a full-bodied cultural pluralism and presented no resistance to assimilation. It stood for tolerance, not for the maintenance of cultural difference and identity. Indeed, even if the term was not used, assimilation was what the advocates for our largest and most oppressed minority also wanted.[16]

WAS ASSIMILATION INEVITABLE?

The term "assimilation" was a key concept in the thinking of our most important sociologist of race and ethnicity, Robert E. Park, founder of the school of sociology at the University of Chicago, which went deeply into questions of race and ethnicity. Park and his colleagues had participated in the Carnegie Americanization studies I have referred to. Opponents of forceful Americanization, they nevertheless believed social trends were bringing an inevitable assimilation. They did not decry this; rather, they felt that this was the unavoidable result in time of the meeting of peoples. Park saw that the great problem in the way of assimilation was the blacks.

His 1930 article on assimilation in the *Encyclopedia of the Social Sciences* perceptively points to this as the stumbling block in the way of assimilation:

In a vast, varied and cosmopolitan society such as exists in America, the chief obstacle to assimilation seems to be not cultural differences but physical traits. . . .

16. For a characterization of the movement, see Nathan Glazer, *Ethnic Dilemmas, 1964-1982* (Cambridge, MA: Harvard University Press, 1983), pp. 104-8.

The Negro, during his three hundred years in this country, has not been assimilated. This is not because he has preserved in America a foreign culture and alien tradition. . . . no man is so entirely native to the soil. . . . To say the Negro is not assimilated means no more than to say that he is still regarded in some sense a stranger, a representative of an alien race. . . . This distinction which sets him apart from the rest of the population is real, but is not based upon cultural traits but upon physical and racial characteristics."

As for Europeans: "The ease and rapidity with which aliens have been able to take over American customs and manners have enabled the United States to digest every sort of normal human difference, with the exception of the purely external ones like that of the color of the skin."[17]

Park saw the key problem. Of course, he was not alone. Black intellectuals and leaders also saw where they stood. They were not even participants in the debate over assimilation and Americanization. Nevertheless, they strove for assimilation, or, rather, for the rights that they assumed would lead to assimilation. American liberals generally, supporters of black aims, saw no argument against assimilation in principle, for all groups. Park had set forth a scheme, which became quite influential in sociology, in which groups in contact moved through various phases, such as conflict and accommodation, ending in assimilation. Fifteen years ago, pondering the rise then of an earlier phase of multiculturalism, I noted this assimilationist stance of both sociologists who

17. Robert E. Park, "Assimilation," in Encyclopedia of the Social Sciences, 2:282.

studied race and ethnicity and black scholars and leaders.

Park and his leading students, I pointed out, while they did not put forth their preferences sharply, assumed assimilation was not only inevitable but would be all for the best. Thus

Louis Wirth, who was the chief successor to Park, made clear in The Ghetto that his preference was for assimilation: the Jew continued to exist only because of prejudice and discrimination; all the reactions of the Jew to this antagonism were humanly limiting; and assimilation, which to be sure required lowering the barriers to assimilation, was the desirable end result of the interaction of Jews and non-Jews in contemporary society.

The major works of E. Franklin Frazier on the black family went in the same direction. Insofar as the black family was stable and puritanical it was good—that was unquestioned. There was no hint, or scarcely any, that any distinctive cultural feature should survive as specifically Negro or black, or that there should be any effort to seek for such features.

This was not cultural arrogance or imperialism; instead, it was the point of view of the best-informed, most liberal, and most sympathetic analysts of the ethnic and racial scene. Assimilation was a desirable consequence of the reduction of prejudice and discrimination, while acculturation, that is, becoming more like the majority, would contribute to the reduction of discrimination and prejudice. This was the dominant liberal view until at least the 1950's.

It was also the view, insofar as a view could be discerned, of the representatives of racial and ethnic groups. The NAACP and the Urban League were clearly "assimilationist." Although it was clear that blacks could never because of race be indistinguishable from whites, it was desirable that they become culturally, socially, economically, and politically assimilated, that they be simply Americans with dark skins. All public agencies, including the government and the schools, and all private agencies that affected individual circumstances, including banks, businesses, housing producers, and landlords, were to be "color blind." In the 1950's the only legitimate form of differentiation proposed for American life was religious. . . .

Admittedly, in each group there were the maintainers and upholders of the ethnic conscience and consciousness, including schools, churches, philanthropic and civic organizations, networks of insurance societies, and social groups, but except by those whose direct interest was in maintaining them and the jobs they offered, these were regarded as survivals, fated to fall away as acculturation and assimilation progressed.

Acculturation and assimilation, if not the cruder "Americanization," were thus not simply the positions of the old Americans who were antagonistic to new immigrants and non-white races; they were also the positions of those who were most sympathetic to these groups and who understood them best, and even of the representatives of these groups.[18]

Of course, as we know, we are now very far from all this. The voices of opposition to integration burst out in the late 1960s and have gone through many permutations since. Bland intercultural education has succumbed to the rather more forceful multicultural education—though that too comes in all brands, from the mildest recognition of differences to a rather hysterical and irrational Afrocentrism. We even had, in the late 1960s

18. Glazer, *Ethnic Dilemmas*, pp. 100-101.

and 1970s, a brief explosion of revived ethnic assertiveness among white European ethnic groups, the heirs of the immigrants of the early decades of the century. It could not survive; assimilation had gone too far. We have a few modest programs in Italian American studies, and a sturdier growth of Jewish programs, which are able to draw not only on ethnic attachments that tend to be stronger than that for most white Europeans but also on religion, which creates a firmer body of institutions to parallel the purely ethnic and which has greater prestige and receives more tolerance in the American setting.

We come now to our question: is assimilation then dead? The word may be dead, the concept may be disreputable, but the reality continues to flourish. As so many observers in the past have noted, assimilation in the United States is not dependent on public ideology, on school curricula, on public approbation; factors in social and economic and cultural life foster it, and it proceeds apace. Read Lewis was right when, in his article on Americanization in the *Encyclopedia of the Social Sciences*, now more than sixty years old, he wrote:

Important as these conscious efforts are toward Americanization, they represent only a part of the social forces which play continuously upon the immigrant and determine the degree and rapidity of his assimilation. A conspicuous force which makes for adjustment is the urge to material success, which makes the immigrant adapt himself to American ways of work and business. This usually involves learning the English language as quickly as possible. Standardizing forces such as national advertisements, ten-cent store products, movies, radio and the tabloid press play also upon the immigrant.[19]

Correct for inflation, add television, baseball, football, basketball, and so on, and it is clear that the forces pressing assimilation have not lost power.

Call it "acculturation" if you will. But assimilation in its least deniable and strongest form, what was once called "amalgamation," also proceeds apace. The rates of intermarriage among all European ethnic groups is very high.[20] Even Jews, with their bar against intermarriage posed by religion, and who maintained a rather low rate of intermarriage through the 1940s, now show the very high rates at which individuals commonly marry outside their ethnic group, however defined. With these high rates in the postwar period, it is hardly clear what one's ethnic group is and how it is to be defined. Mary Waters, in *Ethnic Options*, shows how thin any sense of ethnicity among Americans of European origin has become.[21] But there is the great exception.

SEPARATENESS

If intermarriage is taken as key evidence for powerful assimilatory forces, then blacks are not subject to these forces to the same degree as others. Hispanic groups and Asian groups, despite the recency of the immigration of so many of them, and thus the greater power of family and group attachment, show rates of intermarriage approaching the levels of Europeans. Blacks stand apart, with very low rates of intermarriage, rising slowly. They stand apart, too, in the degree of residential segregation.[22] Thirty years of effort, public and private, assisted by antidiscrimination law and a substantial rise in black earnings, have made little impact on this pattern.

This is not the place to explain all this, but the apartness is real. And it is this that feeds multiculturalism. For one group, assimilation, by some key measures, has certainly failed. For others, multicultural education may be a matter of sentiment. But most black children do attend black-majority schools. Most live in black neighborhoods. Why should not multiculturalism, in the form of the examination of group history, characteristics, problems, become compelling as one way of understanding one's situation, perhaps overcoming it? The large statements of an American national ideal of inclusion, of assimilation, understandably ring false.

For Hispanics and Asian Americans, marked in varying degree by race, it is in large measure a matter of choice, their choice, just how they will define their place in American society. We see elements in these groups who, in their support of bilingual education and other foreign-language rights, want to establish or preserve an institutional base for a separate identity that may maintain some resistance to the forces of assimilation. For blacks, too, there are

19. Lewis, "Americanization," p. 34.

20. Stanley Lieberson and Mary Waters, *From Many Strands: Ethnic and Radical Groups in Contemporary America* (New York: Russell Sage Foundation, 1988).

21. *Ethnic Options* (Berkeley: University of California Press, 1990).

22. Douglas S. Massey and Nancy A. Denton, *American Apartheid* (Cambridge, MA: Harvard University Press, 1993).

choices—we see the existence of choices in the writings of black intellectuals who oppose the stronger tendencies of multiculturalism. But the difference that separates blacks from whites, and even from other groups "of color" that have a history of discrimination and prejudice in this country, is not to be denied. It is this that is the most powerful force arguing for multiculturalism and for resistance to the assimilatory trend of American culture and of American society.

Living Proof:
Is Hawaii the Answer?

By GLEN GRANT and DENNIS M. OGAWA

ABSTRACT: Hawaii has often been heralded for its relatively harmonious race relations, which encompass a great diversity of Asian and Pacific cultures. As the national concern with respect to multiculturalism escalates into a debate over the merits of ethnicity versus amalgamation into the American melting pot, an understanding of Hawaii's social and racial systems may demand greater scrutiny. The living proof that the islands' people offer is not racial bliss or perfect equality but an example of how the perpetuation of ethnic identities can actually enhance race relations within the limits of a social setting marked by (1) the historical development of diverse ethnic groups without the presence of a racial or cultural majority; (2) the adherence to the values of tolerance represented in the Polynesian concept of *aloha kanaka*, an open love for human beings; and (3) the integration of Pacific, Asian, European, and Anglo-American groups into a new local culture.

Glen Grant is director of American studies at Tokai International College, where he also coordinates a program on Hawaiian multicultural studies. The author of numerous works on Hawaii, Dr. Grant has been a Foreign Research Fellow at the National Institute of Multimedia Education in Tokyo, Japan.

Dennis M. Ogawa is professor of American studies at the University of Hawaii and a former East West Center senior fellow. His books include Jan Ken Po *and* Kodomo No Tame Ni. *He was recently honored as one of Hawaii's Distinguished Historians by the Hawaiian Historical Society.*

"MULTICULTURALISM" has in recent years emerged as a buzzword in a variety of social arenas, from marketing to corporate management, from tourism to academia, as a controversial new redefinition of what constitutes the American character. While ethnic diversity within the national melting pot or cultural salad bowl has long been recognized as a salient feature of American life and has long been heralded as the creation of "this new race," the recent interest in the unmeltable aspects of ethnicity has raised certain concerns about the prospects of the United States' being able to survive balkanization along racial, ethnic, and other minority group lines. With an increasing recognition that in the near future the traditional Caucasian majority will be demographically challenged in their position of power and cultural dominance by a rising tide of new Hispanic and Asian immigrants and a new generation of Afrocentrically educated African Americans, social philosophers are reexamining the sinew that holds America's diverse people together and questioning the merits of a multicultural society.

The most articulate arguments urging caution with respect to this rising tide of ethnicity have been presented by Arthur M. Schlesinger, Jr., in his lively and thought-provoking *Disuniting of America: Reflections on a Multicultural Society*. "The new ethnic gospel," explains Schlesinger,

rejects the unifying vision of individuals from all nations melted into a new race. Its underlying philosophy is that America is not a nation of individuals at all but a nation of groups, that ethnicity is the defining experience for most Americans, that ethnic ties are permanent and indelible, and that division into ethnic communities establishes the basic structure of American society and the basic meaning of American history.[1]

Citing numerous examples of ethnic and racial division in the "Soviet Union, Yugoslavia, India, South Africa, Sri Lanka, Cyprus, Somalia, Nigeria, Liberia, Angola, Sudan, Zaire, Guyana, Trinidad—you name it," where separatist tendencies have led to fragmentation, resegregation, or tribalization, Schlesinger cautions that "our national heterogeneity makes the quest for unifying ideals and a common culture all the more urgent."[2]

Schlesinger's reflections on a multicultural society, embracing examples of societies from around the world where such diversity often leads to a breakdown of national cohesion, curiously neglects to even mention in passing fashion America's one truly multiethnic state, Hawaii. With a population of over 1.1 million people, who represent nearly forty different ethnic and racial groups, none of which is a majority, the eight major Hawaiian islands have been home to a remarkable experiment in human cooperation and cultural interaction that has been widely acclaimed as the "melting pot of the Pacific," a "crossroads of East and West" in a social setting imbued with the Polynesian spirit of *aloha*.

While the Hawai'i Visitors Bureau has attempted to market that cooper-

1. Arthur M. Schlesinger, Jr., *The Disuniting of America: Reflections on a Multicultural Society* (New York: Norton, 1992), p. 16.
2. Ibid., pp. 10, 18-20.

ative spirit as a drawing card of tourism, and while the palm tree, sand, surf, and "genial natives" called by novelist James Michener the Golden Men[3] have led nonislanders to view Hawaii as an aberration not to be taken seriously, the deeper social and cultural forces working on the islands' ethnic diversity may actually have critical implications for a nation rapidly being transformed to resemble the island racial mosaic. If legal and illegal immigrants continue to enter the United States at the current estimated rate of about 1 million a year, then within thirty years the American population will be characterized by a new ethnic mix of Third World, Pacific, and Asian newcomers. Characterized by demographer Leon Bouvier as the "Pacific invasions,"[4] this new infusion of non-Western immigration will accelerate the process of de-WASPing America. The Caucasian race in 1960 represented 88.6 percent of the U.S. population; by 1990, that number had dropped to 75.6 percent, a decline that Bouvier has projected will reach 61 percent by 2020. Most tellingly, he suggests that among children under age 15, ethnic and racial minority groups could now be approaching the point of becoming the majority. The composition of the nation's immigrant flow will also be a dramatic break from the Euro-oriented past, if recent trends are an indication: 85 percent of the immigrants entering the United States between 1971 and 1990 were predomi-

nantly from the Third World, with 44 percent from Latin America and the Caribbean, 36 percent from Asia, and 20 percent from Mexico.[5] If these trends are accurate, then the island truism that "in Hawaii no one race is a majority" is going to be applicable to the entire United States. Instead of looking to Beirut, the Balkans, or Bosnia-Herzegovina for doomsday examples of how multicultural societies become tribalized and then dissolve into violence, an examination of the ethnic dynamics of Hawaii's people may be far more relevant to American communities seeking a positive model of how diverse ethnicities can live in relative harmony while still contributing to the commonweal.

Is Hawaii living proof that a community composed of minority groups that maintain a sense of ethnic pride and cultural distinctiveness can still peacefully develop a unifying common culture required to prevent a Tower of Babel? While avoiding the intellectual snare of setting up Hawaii's race relations as a model of how diverse people can learn to live together in harmony or falsely promoting the islands as a society without racial tensions or inequities, the dynamics of how people of all ethnicities interact with one another in Hawaii illustrate that under certain conditions, multiculturalism can be a viable social reality that enhances interethnic cooperation instead of internecine rivalry. Modern island multiculturalism, however, needs to be understood in the context of the

3. James Michener, *Hawaii* (New York: Fawcett Crest Books, 1959), p. 1130.

4. Leon Bouvier, *Pacific Invasions: Immigration and Changing America* (Lanham, MD: University Press of America, 1992).

5. Quoted in Peter Brimelow, "Time to Rethink Immigration? The Decline of the Americanization of Immigrants," *National Review*, 22 June 1992, p. 30.

unique peopling of the islands under well-defined racial structures—a historical process that created diverse ethnic communities without the presence of a racial or cultural majority, promoted *aloha* (spirit of racial tolerance), and encouraged an amalgamation of Pacific, Asian, European, and Anglo-American cultures into a new local brand of behavior, language, folklore, racial attitude, and interracial marriages best characterized in the island slogan, "Lucky You Live in Hawaii."

HAWAII: A LIVING RACIAL LABORATORY?

The academic interest in the multicultural dimensions of what was heralded in the 1920s as Hawaii's living laboratory of race relations first began with a group of mainland-trained sociologists at the University of Hawaii that included Andrew Lind, Bernhard Hormann, and Romanzo Adams. Influenced by Robert E. Park's pioneering work in race relations at the University of Chicago, these sociologists found the islands a fascinating example of cultural assimilation and consequently encouraged their students to do fieldwork in their own ethnic communities. These early ethnographic observations—often conducted by second-generation Asian Americans who were attending the college—provided invaluable insights into the first stages of immigrant assimilation in the islands and were regularly published by the Sociology Department in *Social Process in Hawaii* and as major studies in Romanzo Adams's *Peoples of Hawaii* and *Interracial Marriage*

in Hawaii[6] and Andrew Lind's *Island Community, Hawaii's People*, and *Hawaii: Last of the Magic Isles*.[7] While Lind continually cautioned racially torn outsiders against making the "unwarranted assumption that Hawaii possesses some peculiar magic that might be exported to exorcise the evils of racism elsewhere,"[8] his assertion that the islands were curiously free from overt racial violence lent substance to the widely held sentiment that in Hawaii, *aloha* prevailed.

Adams, Lind, and Hormann began to examine Hawaii's multicultural environment three decades after it was dramatically altered as a result of shifting racial and socioeconomic patterns. Since the *kanaka maoli* population—the indigenous people of the islands—had willingly opened the doors to *haole* immigration—to foreign immigrants—following the first visit of Captain James Cook in 1778, the numerical dominance of the indigenous people had tragically declined as a result of rising death rates and plummeting birthrates brought on by foreign diseases. While the size of the native population at the time of Captain Cook's arrival has been

6. Romanzo C. Adams, *The Peoples of Hawaii* (Honolulu: American Council, Institute of Pacific Relations, 1933); idem, *Interracial Marriage in Hawaii: A Study of the Mutually Conditioned Processes of Acculturation and Amalgamation* (Montclair, NJ: Patterson Smith, 1968).
7. Andrew Lind, *An Island Community: Ecological Succession in Hawaii* (Chicago: University of Chicago Press, 1938); idem, *Hawaii's People* (Honolulu: University of Hawaii Press, 1955); idem, *Hawaii: The Last of the Magic Isles* (New York: Institute of Peace Relations, 1969).
8. Lind, *Hawaii's People*, p. x.

disputed as being from as low as 200,000 to as high as 1 million people,[9] the first uncontested census figures in the 1830s reveal the shocking consequences of Euro-American contact on Pacific islanders—the American missionary census estimated the *kanaka maoli* population to have fallen to about 130,000 men, women, and children. By the time of the Hawaiian Kingdom's census of 1853, that number had declined to 70,000. Thirty years later, what seemed like an irreversible decline continued until the number of indigenous people in Hawaii would drop to its lowest ebb of 40,000, 49.1 percent of the total island population.[10] Having become a minority in their own homeland, the *kanaka maoli* would also witness the erosion of their communal land system; it would be replaced by a Euro-American concept of fee-simple rights of property ownership and a large-scale agricultural industry of sugar cultivation controlled by a small minority of largely American planters.[11]

9. For many years, Captain Cook's estimate of the population in 1778 as being between 350,000 and 400,000 was commonly accepted by historians, anthropologists, and popular lore. David Stannard of the American Studies Department at the University of Hawaii has recently challenged the validity of these figures, sparking a new, sometimes heated debate over what the actual size of the Native Hawaiian population was at the time of contact with the West. See David Stannard, *Before the Horror: The Population of Hawaii on the Eve of Western Contact* (Honolulu: University of Hawaii, Social Science Research Institute, 1989); Eleanor C. Nordyke, *The Peopling of Hawaii* (Honolulu: University of Hawaii Press, 1977).

10. Lind, *Hawaii's People*, p. 20.

11. See Lily Kameeleihiwa, *Native Land and Foreign Desires: How Shall We Live in*

Despite the efforts of Hawaiian monarchs to maintain their sovereignty through a balance of power between Great Britain, France, and the United States, as the size of the native population waned, the Americans on the islands emerged, early in the nineteenth century, as the most influential foreign community. American sandalwood merchants and later the whaling fleets dominated the cash economy of the islands from as early as the 1810s through the introduction of King Sugar in the 1860s. Following the boost given to Hawaiian sugar during the American Civil War, when Northern consumers looked to new sources for sweetener, an explosion of sugar productivity took place on the islands, with capital investment flowing in from the newly settled West Coast. Further reinforcing the cultural influence of the United States over Hawaii were the extensive activities of the American Protestant missionaries who, since their arrival in 1820, had promoted Hawaiian literacy, public education, Christian religion, American lifestyles, and Euro-American laws and government. By the time of the overthrow of the Hawaiian monarchy on 17 January 1893, the American population living on the islands represented less than 5 percent of the total population but had been able in only two generations to assume complete

Harmony? (Honolulu: Bishop Museum Press, 1992), for a contemporary Native Hawaiian historian's interpretation of how conflicting cultural and economic values between the new foreign community and the traditional *kanaka maoli* resulted in the dispossession of native lands.

political, economic, and cultural control over the archipelago.[12]

The Anglo-American oligarchy had long recognized that the rapid demographic decline of the native population had undermined the primary source of labor for the exponentially expanding sugar plantations. While Hawaiian monarchs had earlier hoped that immigration of single males of so-called cognate races from Asia would rejuvenate the part-Hawaiian population, the sugar planters essentially were concerned about importing cheap laborers. Recruited from China, Japan, Okinawa, Korea, Puerto Rico, the Philippines, Portugal, Russia, the South Pacific, and even from among African American sharecroppers in the American South, tens of thousands of foreign laborers were brought to the Hawaiian islands to work on sugar plantations under three-year contracts at minimal wages. For the indigenous population, the impact of this repeopling of the islands must have been overwhelming. In just two decades, from 1880 to 1900, 27,000 Chinese and over 67,000 Japanese contract laborers came to work in the sugar fields, an in-migration that nearly doubled the total population of Hawaii during that time period. A total of over 336,800 Asian, Portuguese, and

Puerto Rican immigrants would settle in the islands between 1885 and 1929.[13]

In most cases, the Asian immigrants were single male sojourners who had expected to make a fortune and then return to their homelands. Many immigrants, however, eventually renewed their plantation contracts or moved on to the few opportunities open to them as independent farmers or small entrepreneurs. As the years passed, return to the homeland seemed an increasingly unlikely prospect as the immigrants settled into life on the islands through the establishment of families. Although some intermarriages took place between Asian immigrants and native women in these early years, for groups such as the Japanese the acquisition of a wife from the homeland was essential. As a result, the practice of "picture bride," or arranged marriage, became widespread, slowly equalizing the gender ratio within that ethnic community and promoting the permanent establishment of ethnic communities.

By the 1930s, when Adams, Lind, and Hormann were first assessing the islands' racial dynamics, the ethnic breakdown of Hawaii had become a true mosaic of Asian and Pacific people living under an American sugar oligarchy that was controlled by the *kama'aina haole*, or long-term resident Caucasians, who were frequently descendants of early merchants and missionaries. Organized into the five large economic conglomerates of Alexander and Baldwin, Castle and Cooke, Theo Davies, American Fac-

12. With the 100th anniversary of the overthrow of the Hawaiian monarchy being remembered on 17 January 1993, several new popular histories have promoted a conspiratorial theory of history, viewing the annexation of the islands as a long-planned scheme of missionaries and merchants. See Michael Dougherty, *To Steal a Kingdom* (Waimanalo, HI: Island Press, 1992); Rich Budnick, *Stolen Kingdom: An American Conspiracy* (Honolulu: Aloha Press, 1992).

13. Lind, *Hawaii's People*, pp. 32-34.

tors, and C. Brewer—the Big Five—the Anglo-Americans' minority control of the islands was protected through their interlocking directorates. Board members of one island firm frequently had genealogical ties to members of the other company boards, breeding a new form of monarchy in a supposedly democratic American territory. The virtually unchallenged economic power of the Big Five was complemented by their tight control over the reins of the territorial legislature. As one social historian has noted, "The use of the government apparatus as an instrument of class domination was never more in evidence than during the mature plantation stage of Hawaii's development."[14]

The only real challenge to this economic and political hegemony was the muscle of the U.S. military, which, especially in the 1930s, increasingly saw Hawaii's multiculturalism and provincial oligarchic rule as an uncertain threat to national security. By 1941, 37.3 percent of the population was of Japanese ancestry, 23.0 percent Portuguese and Anglo, 15.2 percent Hawaiian and part-Hawaiian, 12.4 percent Filipino, 6.8 percent Chinese, 2.0 percent Puerto Rican, 1.6 percent Korean, and 0.2 percent other ethnicities. These exotic ethnicities may have added a certain charm to the tropical setting, but from the viewpoint of an increasingly anxious and sabotage-conscious military establishment, the unmixed races of Hawaii prompted the sentiment in the United States Congress that the territory was too un-American to become a full-fledged state in the Union.

In many ways, the early congressional hearings on Hawaiian statehood accurately observed that the nature of race relations on the islands and the continuation of ethnic affinities among immigrants and, to a lesser degree, among their children were indeed unlike the "American melting pot" that was absorbing immigrants from Europe.[15] For while new immigrants to urban centers of the northeastern United States at the turn of the century frequently faced intense Americanization campaigns to weaken the use of homeland languages and dissolve ethnic boundaries, in Hawaii the opposite was often true. The Anglo-American minority who had created and maintained control over the sugar plantation society had devised a divide-and-rule management policy that encouraged ethnic separateness not for the sake of promoting cultural integrity but to prevent a united labor force. By encouraging the natural prejudices that already existed between the ethnic groups and by remaining aloof from the actual daily operations of the plantation, the oligarchy could preserve their racial superiority within island society while legitimizing their position through extensive paternalism.

14. Noel Kent, *Hawaii: Islands under the Influence* (New York: Monthly Review Press, 1983), p. 77.

15. For a review of the arguments against statehood status for Hawaii due to the large number of Asian Americans, who could turn against the United States in time of war, see Hawaii Equal Rights Commission, *Statehood for Hawaii and the Visit to the Islands of the 1932 Joint Congressional Committee on Hawaii* (Honolulu: Hawaii Equal Rights Commission, 1937), pp. 12-13.

The process of keeping the races apart began even before the immigrant set sail for the islands; in many of the early labor contracts, the insistence that a Japanese worker would not be housed near Chinese or made to work alongside Filipinos was specifically stipulated. The physical design of the plantation camps such as Waialua or Ewa on Oahu, Haiku or Puunene on Maui, Olaa or Papaikou on Hawaii, or Hanapepe on Kauai were uniform.[16] The *haole* owners usually kept a residence on the plantation in the cool higher elevations, where the "big house"—invariably painted white—was remotely visible. The managers—also *haole*—who controlled the field, mill, and accounting operations, were segregated into Haole Camp, a beautifully landscaped and manicured area conveniently located near the company office, the plantation store, the recreation center, tennis courts, and the train depot. The rank of the manager often determined the size of his house and its location, and admittance to Haole Camp was frequently restricted by race.

The field and mill workers lived in camps separated by ethnicity. The housing, food, and medical needs of the plantation workers were taken care of by the company; each worker was assigned a *bango*, or a number that was pressed into a metal tag and that was used to identify him or her at work, in the store, or at other plantation facilities. The homes and bar-

16. For a map of "an island plantation community" that clearly delineates the racially segregated camps, see Lind, *Island Community*, facing p. 308.

racks within the various camps, sometimes physically separated by a cane field, belonged to the plantation and were thus loaned to the workers, who occupied them as long as their work for the company was satisfactory. Eviction—stemming from infraction of the company rules, immorality, labor disputes, or strikes—was quickly enforced by Hawaiian and part-Hawaiian plantation police. Place names such as Spanish Camp, Verona Camp, Japan Camp, or Alabama Camp—the latter housing African American sharecroppers in the 1880s—on the modern map of Hawaii are stark indications of the racial segregation that defined island society after the appearance of King Sugar.

Buffering the non-Caucasian laborers from the *haole* managers and owners were the *luna*, the foremen who in the early years of the plantation often enforced work productivity with whips. While some foremen were selected from among the laborers to serve as the boss, more likely they were Portuguese who, since their immigration to the islands from the Azores and Madeira Islands in the 1880s, had been utilized as *luna*. Their hulking size in comparison to the Asians, their European language base, and their Caucasian features associated them with the power elite, while their dark complexions and non-Anglo customs linked them to a working immigrant class. In their role as supervisors, the Portuguese *luna* maintained daily contact with the laborers and enforced plantation rules and regulations. Thus, while the Anglo remained separate and aloof from the workers, assuming a status accorded racially based deference symbolized in their sometimes being known as "Father" and "Mother" to the workers, the Portuguese *luna* took the brunt of hostility, resentment, and rebellion. It is interesting to note that in contemporary Hawaii, ethnic humor still frequently targets the "Portogee" for being "stupid, talkative, and filled with themselves," characteristics usually reserved for supervisors.

The perpetuation of these ethnic enclaves and divisions also meant that the immigrants were not encouraged to form the common bonds of American language, customs, and values that immigrants to other states frequently experienced. While American Protestants in Honolulu may have riled against their cousins' evident tolerance of religion, economic and racial necessity required that Buddhist temples, Shinto shrines, Catholic churches, and other ethnic expressions of faith be not only allowed but supported. A company set aside land for the various ethnic groups to erect their separate houses of worship, and it allowed Chinese and Japanese language schools to be opened on plantation property so that the homeland language could be taught to the second generation. Special religious holiday observances—for example, New Year's celebrations for the Chinese and Japanese immigrants—were allowed, as were foreign language newspapers and movies, exotic foods, and native dress and customs.[17]

In the 1920s, Americanization efforts were initiated by some Christian groups such as the YMCA and YWCA, and the public schools effectively promulgated among the second generation the English language and basic American values of democracy, individualism, and patriotism. Without, however, a dominant Anglo-American community to serve as a daily role model, separated by thousands of miles from a white majority, these Americanization efforts were mild compared to those experienced by immigrant groups in the continental United States.[18]

The trump card of the sugar oligarchy to ensure ethnic separatism on the plantation was the establishment of a staggered wage based upon ethnic seniority. In other words, those ethnic groups who had been working on the plantation longer received a higher wage for exactly the same menial work that more recent arrivals were doing. In 1901, for example, a Scottish blacksmith would have made $4.16 a day, compared to $2.94 for a part-Hawaiian blacksmith, $2.37 for a Portuguese, and

17. For a multicultural perspective on plantation work, recreation, and lifestyles, see Ronald Takaki, *Pau Hana: Plantation Life and Labor in Hawaii, 1835-1920* (Honolulu: University of Hawaii Press, 1983).

18. Despite Americanization pressures on Hawaii's plantation laborers, ethnic cohesion was an equally powerful political and cultural force. The fact that an activist Japanese journalist such as Fred Makino could rally the Japanese community to defy the attempts of the territorial legislature to shut down the Japanese language schools in the 1920s speaks more strongly of the continuance of ethnic pride and maintenance of cultural integrity than the weak efforts of others to promote Americanism. See Dennis M. Ogawa, *Kodomo No Tame Ni (For the Sake of the Children): The Japanese American Experience in Hawaii* (Honolulu: University of Hawaii Press, 1977), pp. 145-49.

$1.50 for a Japanese.[19] A field laborer could expect to earn 47 cents a day if he was Japanese, more if he was Chinese, and less if he was Filipino. Ethnic jealousies and feelings of superiority, even outbursts of violence, were not uncommon on the early-twentieth-century plantation. However, from the planters' point of view, promotion of racial animosity meant that a collective labor union cutting across ethnic lines was an impossibility. When Japanese laborers struck on several Oahu plantations in 1909, shutting down the island's sugar production, Japanese labor leaders refused to solicit or receive support from Filipino workers. As a result, the strike was broken through the importation of Filipino scabs. The 1920 sugar strike was a Japanese labor movement similarly doomed to failure; again, the movement's spirit of ethnic separateness prevailed, thereby causing the disappointing results.

The divide-and-rule engineered plantation society thus worked in an immediate sense to prevent ethnic groups from realizing that a small racial minority wielded enormous economic clout over the non-Anglo-American majority. Ironically, moreover, the lack of a powerful Americanization movement, the tolerance and even encouragement of ethnic diversity, allowed immigrants to perpetuate their cultural baggage in relative isolation. American socioeconomic and political systems may have been entrenched in the islands in the prewar decades, but from the plantation-dominated rural districts to downtown

Honolulu, the languages, lifestyles, customs, and foods of part-Hawaiians and Hawaiians; Chinese, Japanese, Filipino, and Portuguese immigrants; and the *kama'aina haole* were everywhere evident. The British novelist W. Somerset Maugham visited Honolulu in 1916 and described a common downtown street scene that was bustling with multiculturalism:

Along the streets crowd an unimaginable assortment of people. The Americans, ignoring the climate, wear black coats and high, starched collars, straw hats, soft hats and bowlers. The Kanakas, pale brown, . . . have nothing on but a shirt and a pair of trousers; but the half-breeds are very smart with flaring ties and patent-leather boots. The Japanese, with their obsequious smile, are neat and trim in white duck, while their women walk a step or two behind them, in native dress with a baby on their backs. The Japanese children, in bright-colored frocks, their little heads shaven, look like quaint dolls. Then there are the Chinese. The men, fat and prosperous, wear their American cloths oddly, but the women are enchanting with their tightly-dressed black hair, so neat that you feel it can never be disarranged. . . . Lastly there are the Filipinos, the men in huge straw hats, the women in bright yellow muslin with great puffed sleeves.

It is the meeting place of East and West. The very new rubs shoulders with the immeasurably old.[20]

ALOHA KANAKA: THE
NATIVE HAWAIIAN
LEGACY OF TOLERANCE

With such a strong sense of unmelting ethnicity institutionally

19. Lawrence Fuchs, *Hawaii Pono: A Social History* (New York: Harcourt, Brace & World, 1961), p. 55.

20. W. Somerset Maugham, *The Trembling of a Leaf* (Garden City, NY: Garden City Publishing, 1921), pp. 207-8.

structured in island society based upon racial segregation, to what degree did historical ethnic animosities and racial prejudices erupt into overt violence? Several times in the twentieth century individuals from the *haole* and non-*haole* ethnic groups committed murders that nearly escalated into open racial warfare. When a distinguished *kama'aina haole*, S. Edward Damon, was senselessly murdered outside of Honolulu one night in 1904 by Jose Miranda, a Puerto Rican laborer, sentiments against the immigrant laborers from Puerto Rico reached a point where lynch mobs were openly threatened, although they were never organized.[21] Similarly, the kidnapping of a *haole* child from an exclusive Caucasian school in 1928 and his subsequent murder by a disturbed Japanese youth was the occasion for large public vigilante meetings at which Japanese immigrants were railed against, but the threats were never acted on.[22] When, in 1932, Navy Lieutenant Thomas Massie was found guilty of manslaughter in the shooting of a Hawaiian who had been accused of raping the officer's wife, the power of the Caucasian military authorities was used to reduce the sentence of 10 years at hard labor to one hour under police custody. It was feared that the Hawaiian community would lash out violently at this bla-

tant racist exercise of power, but, except for a few fist fights between locals and military personnel in island bars, no such race riot materialized.[23]

Why had the islands been spared such racial divisiveness? Certainly, as a tiny minority, the Caucasian race relied primarily on law enforcement agencies and their control over socioeconomic and governmental institutions to protect their interests— open violence against any one race was ultimately suicidal. For the non-Caucasian ethnic groups, the paternal nature of plantation society meant that one's economic survival depended fully upon the oligarchy. Public protests and mass meetings may vent internal community unrest, but on an island where opportunities are limited, one quickly tempers rage in light of basic needs.

In addition, under the earlier influences of the Hawaiian monarchy, there was a Polynesian disavowal of conventional racial prejudices, as defined in Euro-American terms, in social and legal relationships. The value of *aloha kanaka*, the love of one's fellow human beings, often translated into public policy. For example, early African American residents on the islands, some of them escaped slaves turned seamen or whalers, found employment, native wives, and social acceptance among the nineteenth-century *kanaka maoli*. Many early American merchants were no doubt surprised to find one of the influential foreigners in Honolulu in the 1820s to be a former slave, Anthony Allen, living with two native wives in Waikiki on several acres of

21. For the history of Puerto Ricans on the islands, see Norma Carr, "Puerto Ricans in Hawaii: 1900-1958" (Ph.D. diss., University of Hawaii, 1989).

22. Dennis M. Ogawa, *Jan Ken Po: The World of the Japanese Americans of Hawaii* (Honolulu: Japanese American Research Center, 1973), pp. 113-49.

23. See Theon Wright, *Rape in Paradise* (Honolulu: Mutual Publishing, 1990).

land offered to him by King Kamehameha I, a close friend and associate.[24] When, in his youth, King
Kamehameha IV visited Washington, D.C., and was called a "nigger"
by a trolley conductor who forced him
to ride in a separate section of the car,
the young monarch was shocked and
disgusted with what he viewed as
American racial discrimination.[25] Indeed, it was not until the overthrow
of the Hawaiian monarchy in 1893
and the prominence of American attitudes that the census listed groups
by race, not nationality.

The open sexual frontier of race
relations no doubt added also to the
perpetuation of *aloha* in the dealings
of the races. With a shortage of white
women residing on the islands, interracial marriages quickly became acceptable for foreigners living in Hawaii. After much discussion and
hand-wringing, American Protestant
missionaries agreed to sanction all
marriages between Native Hawaiian
women and foreign men whether or
not the bride or groom was Christian.
Chinese merchants similarly married Hawaiian women even though
many of them also had a wife in their
homeland. No miscegenation laws,
which were common in the United
States for a time, ever existed in the
Hawaiian islands.

The cumulative effect of these hos-
pitable Hawaiian attitudes toward

race and intermarriage curtailed the
natural dislikes and prejudices of di-
vergent foreign immigrants. The result was what Andrew Lind called the
"policy of racial unorthodoxy," in
which overt discrimination and hostility need to be submerged but are
sublimated through covert deeds of
rudeness, gossiping, derision, interpersonal aloofness, or outright nasti-
ness.[26] Thus it is not uncommon to
hear an islander speak in glowing
terms about the special *aloha* spirit
of Hawaii while in the same breath
complaining about the "damn *haole*"
or "uppity Jap" or "lazy *kanaka*" who
lives next door. Newcomers are be-
wildered and often angered by the
seeming incongruity between the racial harmony that is professed everywhere and the everyday reality that
race awareness, ethnic separateness,
and covert discrimination are also
prevalent.

LOCAL IDENTITY:
THE EMERGENCE OF
MULTICULTURAL LIFESTYLES

Another force that helped to
weaken the impact of ethnic prejudice was the emergence of multicultural lifestyles that were subtly
acquired through the generations.
While Hawaii's immigrant generation may have been able to cling to
the bonds of their distinct ethnicity,
the second generation were involved
in the public schools and on the playgrounds in an even more fascinating
and complex process of cultural interaction. The outcome of this cultural
blending—this process by which chil-

24. Marc Scruggs, "Anthony D. Allen: A
Prosperous American of African Descent in
Early 19th Century Hawaii," *Journal of Hawaiian History* 26:55-94 (1992).
25. For a discussion of Kamehameha IV's
dislike of American manners and attitudes, see
Ralph S. Kuykendall, *The Hawaiian Kingdom,
1854-1874* (Honolulu: University of Hawaii
Press, 1953), p. 35.

26. For a full discussion of the policy of
racial unorthodoxy, see Lind, *Hawaii*.

dren of Native Hawaiian and immigrant groups living under the plantation system created a multicultural lifestyle—has been what Bernhard L. Hormann called the "pidgin culture."[27] Incorporating on its surface the plethora of ethnic foods and customs commonly associated with being local—from taking one's shoes off before entering someone's house to eating a plate lunch filled with Japanese sushi rice, Chinese chow fun noodles, Korean kimchee pickled cabbage, Portuguese sweet bread, Filipino lumpia spring rolls, washed down with American beer—this pidgin culture is the basis for a powerful self-perception of islanders that they are uniquely multicultural in their lifestyles. John Kirkpatrick has correctly noted that "local identity" has allowed Hawaii's people to "draw on ethnic traditions to support particular identities and to oppose forms of discrimination, but they can also transcend the limits of particularistic traditions without renouncing ethnic identities."[28] Indeed, islanders of all races who have been born and raised in Hawaii are quick to note that, when they go to the continental United States, they often experience culture shock. In the reverse, *haole* newcomers to the islands—*malihini*—have

27. Hormann's pidgin culture is discussed in John F. McDermott, Jr., "Toward an Interethnic Society," in *People and Cultures of Hawaii: A Psychocultural Profile*, ed. John F. McDermott, Jr., Wen-Shing Tseng, and Thomas W. Maretzki (Honolulu: John A. Burns School of Medicine and University of Hawaii Press, 1980), p. 228.

28. John Kirkpatrick, "Ethnic Antagonism and Innovation in Hawaii," in *Ethnic Conflict: International Perspectives*, ed. J. Boucher and D. Landis (Beverly Hills, CA: Sage, 1987), pp. 298-99.

expressed similar culture shock when attempting to assimilate the local lifestyles, including the problem of trying to understand the intonations and connotations of pidgin English. One Honolulu community college even went so far recently as to offer a series of classes on local culture in an effort to ease the adjustments of new residents to the sometimes subtle nuances of island multiculturalism.[29]

For the Standard English-speaking newcomers to the islands, one of the major shocks encountered is the complexity of island dialect, or pidgin, as it is spoken in Hawaii. The language used by immigrants on the plantation was not Standard English but a unique Hawaiian-English patois with a growing vocabulary of words contributed by the various immigrants. Termed "pidgin English," this lively lingo of work, play, and daily intercourse could hardly represent a force of Americanization—indeed, American educators were horrified at its widespread, pervasive influence not only on the language of the immigrant but on the second generation as well. Despite the establishment of Standard English schools to segregate the proper users of English from the incorrigible pidgin speakers, and intermittent campaigns to stamp out pidgin English,

29. In 1988-90, Kapi'olani Community College in Honolulu offered several workshops under the title "The Island Way: An Introduction to Hawai'i's Multicultural Lifestyles," taught by Glen Grant through the Office of Community Services. Enrolled in the workshops were not only newcomers to Hawaii but also long-term *haole* residents and military personnel attempting to unravel the local style of behavior.

the dialect has survived in the islands because of its social function as a language of affiliation. Even the most articulate speakers of the King's English will revert to island dialect when letting down their guard with local friends.

The blending process that took place among Hawaii's children within the plantation society, schoolrooms, and playgrounds went beyond the swapping of language, food, and customs. A more substantive negotiation of what have been called "points of commonality" was also taking place as deeper values stemming from agrarian, communal social networks found comfortable expression among children of Pacific, European, and Asian cultural backgrounds. Within the maze of culture through which human beings negotiate their lives, points of commonality are found that provide a common ground of understanding. In essence, the cultural history of the Hawaiian islands in the last century has been a continuous process of finding points of commonality, negotiating the ties by which diversity can be maintained while acting together with mutual reward and comfort.[30]

One of the major points of commonality on which the children of immigrants and Native Hawaiians found ready understanding was the extensive role that the extended family played in their lives. Whether their parents were from Japan, China, the Philippines, Portugal, or the rural villages of Hawaii, island children had been adapted to a world

of extended family relationships that transcended specific ethnic groups. What anthropologists examining the Native Hawaiian community have called "the mini-max principle" was not unfamiliar to children who had been raised in Asian homes—the maximization of family and kinship affiliations required a minimization of self-interest. In the child-rearing practices of these island modified extended families, all with rural backgrounds, the children learned reliance on group interdependency, reciprocal obligations, an open attitude toward sharing, and a reluctance to engage in self-promotion or aggression. The avoidance of open conflict and restraint in acting in one's personal interest were behaviors learned within the ethnic home, and children quickly discovered that these were points of commonality with others outside on the playground.

Another coping strategy developed on the playground was symbolized in the expression "ain't no big thing," the self-effacing response one usually gives to a personal slight or problem between friends or cousins.[31] Translated into a social tactic of resolving personal or group differences, the self-effacement surfaces in the form of ethnic humor in both personal conversation and social entertainment. Outsiders often respond to the open ethnic stereotyping and joke telling of Hawaii entertainers as repulsive— a flashback to localized *Amos 'n Andy*

30. See Glen Grant, "Race Relations in the Hawaiian School: The *Haole* Newcomer," in *Kodomo No Tame Ni*, by Ogawa, pp. 588-96.

31. For a discussion of the Native Hawaiian cultural paradigm of mini-max affiliations and coping strategies, see Alan Howard, *Ain't No Big Thing: Coping Strategies in a Hawaiian-American Community* (Honolulu: University Press of Hawaii, 1974).

or *Charlie Chan* caricatures told without evident compunction. Underlying this ethnic humor, which is regularly greeted by local audiences with uproarious laughter, is the "ain't no big thing" syndrome at work—"In Hawaii," the message says, "we get along so well that we have all learned to laugh at ourselves, our foibles, and our self-importance." It is important, as local humorist Frank DeLima always stresses, that whoever enters the realm of ethnic jokes starts the joking by making fun of his or her own ethnicity first. "Here in Hawaii," DeLima has written,

we laugh at ourselves more than most people do in other places. Hawaii is a chop suey nation—Portagee, Pake, Buddha Head, Sole, Yobo, Kanaka, Haole, all mixed up. Nobody is in the majority here. We are all part of at least one minority group. Some of us are part of several minority groups. And we all laugh at ourselves. This is healthy.[32]

Flowing from these family, kinship, and group values and coping strategies, then, "pidgin culture," as described by Hormann, constitutes "a new 'mixed' ethnic group . . . with only quasi-ethnocentrism. The Asian cultures retained focal points of their identity—ceremonies, temples, language schools—but otherwise began to absorb new influences. Some believe that this allowed a peaceful, gradual merging of individual ethnic identity with a common one."[33] When an islander is asked, "What are you?"

by another islander—a very common question during a first-time encounter in multiethnic Hawaii—it is not uncommon for the respondent to list all of his or her racial ancestral roots. When asked the same question by a tourist, however, the simple, proud response is, "Local."

While points of commonality served to draw various ethnicities into a powerful local identity, rising interracial marriage rates among the second, third, and fourth generation have further diluted the tendencies toward racial hostility. In the period 1912-13, 13 percent of the marriages were interracial. Twenty years later, by 1931-32, the rates had increased to 32 percent, and during World War II, when military personnel and construction workers from the continental United States inundated Hawaii, the interracial marriage rate climbed to 38.5 percent.[34] The continued widespread acceptance of interracial marriage in Hawaii was reflected in the fact that over 45.9 percent of all marriages in 1991 were between individuals of different races.[35] In light of the national rate of marriage between Caucasians and African Americans, one-third of 1 percent,[36] the Hawaiian experience is unique. Multiculturalism is not an intellectual ambiguity in Hawaii but a living reality where, within a single indi-

32. Frank DeLima, *Frank DeLima's Joke Book*, ed. Jerry Hopkins (Honolulu: Bess Press, 1991), p. v.

33. McDermott, Tseng, and Maretzki, eds., *People and Cultures of Hawaii*, p. 228.

34. Lind, *Hawaii's People*, pp. 112-13.

35. State of Hawaii, Department of Business and Economic Development and Tourism, *The State of Hawaii Data Book 1991: A Statistical Abstract* (Honolulu: Department of Business and Economic Development, 1991), p. 82.

36. Thomas F. Pettigrew, "Integration and Pluralism," in *Eliminating Racism: Profiles in Controversy*, ed. Phyllis A. Katz and Dolmas A. Taylor (New York: Plenum Press, 1988), p. 26.

vidual, it is not uncommon to find eight distinct ethnic heritages.

THE EMERGENCE OF MODERN HAWAII: THE MULTICULTURAL STATE

The plantation society that was instrumental in the perpetuation of ethnic distinctiveness also, therefore, created the setting where, through the evolution of multicultural lifestyles, language, points of commonality, and interracial marriages, a local identity could be created. The decades since the 1940s have witnessed the breaking down of the racial barriers defining one's island caste and the continuing maturation of a more equitable multiethnic society. World War II shattered the idyllic calm of the "sugar-coated fortress," opening the islands up to a new breed of *haole*—the middle-class Anglo-American who, without wealth, prestige, or status, rubbed shoulders with islanders who for half a century viewed Caucasians with deference. Seeing the *haole* as mechanics, soldiers, ditch diggers, waitresses, and even prostitutes humanized and demystified what had been the paternal elite.

The social upheaval of Hawaii under military control was followed in the postwar era by the rapid growth of the International Longshoremen's and Warehousemen's Union, which was finally able to draw together a multiethnic labor force as a successful challenge to the power of the old oligarchy. Concurrent with the economic challenges of the union to the Big Five was the changing political scene of the 1950s as American-born, second-generation island-ers initiated what was called a "bloodless revolution" in the territorial legislature. Reorganizing the nearly defunct Democratic Party as a vehicle of change, a coalition of Japanese American war veterans and young politicians of mixed ethnicity, under the political leadership of a *haole* former policeman named John Burns, captured a majority in both houses of the legislature, initiating a network of leadership that would propel Daniel Inouye into the United States Senate and Burns into the Office of Governor. Statehood in 1959 and the introduction of the commercial jet airliner further weakened the grip of the plantation society on modern Hawaii as tourism replaced sugar as the single most important industry on the islands. Since the advent of King Tourism, Hawaii has witnessed a spiraling growth of population, in-migration from the continental United States, urban sprawl, and resort developments in what had once been pristine rural areas.

Although the plantation way of life that once dominated island culture is fading into nostalgia, the ethnic distinctiveness that this racial setting helped create remains a potent force in race relations, especially the minority status of all groups. When former Governor John Burns was asked by a reporter what one situation he could foresee as posing a serious danger to the harmony of the races in Hawaii, he responded by simply jotting down on a piece of paper, "51 percent." If any single race were to dominate on the islands as a majority, he explained, the political, social, and cultural balance of the islands would be turned topsy-turvy. One race would be in a position where it could dominate an election or set public policy for the others, generating racial jealousy and animosity to a degree unseen on the islands.

Is Hawaii at risk of either becoming dominated by a single ethnic group or succumbing to ethnic divisions that could unravel what has been promoted as the "living laboratory of race relations"? The danger that would result from the emergence of a racial majority still seems remote. The largest racial group has become the Caucasians, with 33 percent of the population, followed by Japanese Americans, 22 percent; Filipinos, 15 percent; Hawaiians and part-Hawaiians, 13 percent; with Spanish-origins, Chinese, African Americans, Koreans, Vietnamese, Native American Indians, Samoans, and other Asian and Pacific islanders composing the remaining 17 percent of the population.[37] With the continued high rates of interracial marriage, however, it seems more likely that the islands will continue to be increasingly cosmopolitan, with mixed race ancestry, instead of single racial identification, the norm.

In terms of racial equality in the context of political and economic power, the islands still have a long way to go before breaking down the glass ceilings that are institutionally supported barriers to some ethnic groups. The tourist industry, for example, has to a large degree quietly replicated the older plantation system, although without any of the

plantation system's paternalism. Owned by multinational corporations headquartered in the mainland United States or Japan, a typical Waikiki hotel is managed at the top level by Caucasians from outside of Hawaii, while middle management is recruited from the local population, many of them graduates from the Travel Industry Management School at the University of Hawaii. Most of the frontline service jobs, however, are performed largely by either part-Hawaiians or immigrants from the Philippines. The nature of occupations may be vastly different and the racial divide-and-rule policy unarticulated, but the ethnic stratification is obvious nevertheless to anyone who enters the back offices of most large visitor industry businesses. At the University of Hawaii, where over 60 percent of the student body is Asian American in ancestry, it is interesting to note that 75 percent of the faculty is Caucasian[38]—another indication that racial imbalances are to be found in some of the critical arenas of policymaking.

Socioeconomically, this situation has led to racial inequalities in terms of income. The per capita income of islanders illustrates how Japanese and Chinese Americans have been able to attain higher levels of economic security and higher occupational status while the Hawaiian, part-Hawaiian, and Filipino communities have been disproportionately

37. State of Hawaii, Department of Business and Economic Development, *Data Book*, p. 42.

38. This statistic is based upon a work in progress on the racial structures at the University of Hawaii, conducted by Dr. Virgie Chatterg, director of the Center for Multicultural Higher Education Studies, University of Hawaii at Manoa.

represented in the lower income ranges.[39] Most important, in a study of economic and occupational trends among Hawaii's people conducted over a 10-year period, Jonathan Okamura stresses that the evidence shows very little change in the relative status of ethnic groups. "The social structure in Hawaii that ultimately emerges is of a stratification system that is very resistant to change, to the detriment of more than one-third of its population," he concludes.[40]

This situation, however, may not seem as static as Okamura portends. As the Filipino community of Hawaii continues to become localized through the establishment of modified extended families, the political arena is becoming an important platform to voice the Filipinos' need for economic and political reform. Election to high office in Hawaii requires a broad multicultural appeal to ensure a majority vote, and, with the political ascendancy of Lieutenant Governor Ben Cayetano, more political players will no doubt be emerging from the Filipino community. If the example of the Japanese American community is any indicator, then political leverage will precede assimilation into the economic and educational structures of island society.

The rising political consciousness of the Native Hawaiian community will further complicate the political arena with exciting prospects for re-adjusting the socioeconomic status of island ethnic groups. The 100th anniversary on 17 January 1993 of the overthrow of the Hawaiian monarchy initiated a statewide effort by dozens of Hawaiian groups to seek redress for past injustices and the establishment of a land base over which native sovereign rights can be exercised. Within the next few years, the Native Hawaiian sovereignty movement will dramatically affect not only politics but also the economic, cultural, and racial life of the islands as islanders of all ethnic backgrounds are forced to face the historical facts surrounding the overthrow of the monarchy in 1893 and its lasting consequences for the cultural well-being of the islands' indigenous people.

While the ethnic problems suggested here perhaps dismiss Hawaii as a social model of race relations, the dynamics of ethnicity understood in the island context is not without importance to those seeking a justification of the value of multiculturalism. The process by which ethnic values and identity have been perpetuated on the islands without wholly diluting them and forcing them into an American mold dominated by Anglo-American culture illustrates that the maintenance of ethnicity does not necessarily lead to the disuniting of a society that the critics of multiculturalism have feared. Indeed, in the absence of a single racial majority, the result has been the creation of a new culture that reflects the legacy of *aloha* and points of commonality—a truly diverse community that binds Asian, Pacific, European, and American heritages into a lifestyle shared across the boundaries of race.

39. Lind, *Hawaii's People*, pp. 84-90.

40. Jonathan Y. Okamura, "Ethnicity and Stratification in Hawaii," in *Operation Manong Resource Papers No. 1* (Honolulu: University of Hawaii, Operation Manong Program, 1980), p. 11.

ANNALS, *AAPSS*, **530**, November 1993

Recrafting the Common Good: Immigration and Community

By ROBERT L. BACH

ABSTRACT: Recent urban unrest has rekindled interest in the impacts of immigration on established U.S. communities. Yet little is known about the ways in which newcomers and established residents interact. Popular journalists emphasize only incidents of conflict and turmoil. This article examines the current portrayal of conflicts between immigrants and established residents. Immigrants and established residents live in social worlds divided institutionally and residentially. Although their separation maintains a degree of order, it creates pressures on those occasions when newcomers and established residents interact, including interactions in workplaces, stores, schools, and parks. The article also explores how both groups are working together to face common problems after two decades of profound economic restructuring. New demands on immigration and community policies must mobilize the voluntary sector to generate new resources and to articulate the values derived from their diverse communities. Voluntary organizations face challenges to adjust their established practices and to redefine their membership. These efforts are fundamental for recrafting the common good.

Robert L. Bach is an associate professor of sociology and director of the Institute for Research on Multiculturalism and International Labor at Binghamton University, New York. He has written extensively on a variety of migration-related issues, including labor flows, refugees, community change, regional integration, and state policies. His current research focuses on Cuban, Vietnamese, and Chinese migration to the United States; voluntary sector participation in settlement activities; human rights, refugees, and North-South relations; and immigrants' legal needs in the United States.

C ERTAIN events characterize their times. The Watts riots in the 1960s, the hostage crisis in the late 1970s, the Mariel boatlift in 1980, and certainly the fall of the Berlin Wall in 1989 all left indelible images of their social and political contexts. The events themselves were not historically decisive, but they remain the anchor of memories, emotions, and opinions about the problems they represent.

The 1992 Los Angeles riots may be a similar event for the current decade. After years of neglect, they symbolize a renewed interest in the well-being of urban communities. But they have also rekindled concern about the impact of immigration. The aftermath of the riots has changed public discourse about the last two decades of high levels of immigration to the United States. After years of positive reporting on immigrants' economic contributions, national media such as the *Wall Street Journal* and *Business Week* have refocused on the growing social and cultural impact of immigrants. Rhetoric about riots and rioters has returned to popular discourse and, this time, included immigrants. Perhaps the most graphic reaction included these warnings about the role of immigration in Los Angeles's decay: "When the barbarians sacked Rome in 410, the Romans thought it was the end of civilization. You smile—but what followed was the Dark Ages."[1]

This new popular voice goes beyond efforts of organizations such as the Federation for American Immigration Reform that have long sup-

ported more limited immigration. It includes growing segments of the environmental movement and fragments of the conservative coalition that throughout the 1980s supported large-scale immigration. A split in the conservative ranks became most visible during the presidential primaries as David Duke, Patrick Buchanan, and California Governor Pete Wilson campaigned against newcomers. Most of this new conservative opposition to immigration rests on its alleged social and cultural impacts.[2]

Much of the scholarly literature on immigration is ill prepared to respond to this current popular assault on the impact of newcomers on established communities. Most immigration research has focused primarily on individual and group differences in rates of assimilation or on structural barriers to economic advancement. Policy discussions have focused almost exclusively on questions about the volume and criteria for admissions. Questions about group advancement, ethnic identity, and empowerment obviously are critical issues for understanding the unequal patterns of immigrant incorporation in the United States. Still, these approaches are limited in their understanding of the full recomposition of community life that has resulted from the political and economic restructuring of the 1980s and the new cultural diversity that large-scale immigration has created.[3]

1. Jack Miles, "Black-Brown Relations," *Atlantic Monthly*, p. 42 (Oct. 1992).

2. Peter Brimelow, "Time to Rethink Immigration?" *National Review*, 22 June 1992, pp. 30-46. See also the exchange in "Why Control the Borders?" *National Review*, 1 Feb. 1993, pp. 27-34.

3. Robert L. Bach, "Immigration: Issues of Ethnicity, Class, and Public Policy in the United States," *The Annals* of the American

REDIRECTING IMMIGRATION RESEARCH

Refocusing immigration research to include community transformation as a whole requires attention to three primary issues. First, attention to broad social transformations challenges ethnic categories that have become well entrenched in both scholarly and public policy discussions. The new immigration, with all its ethnic, class, linguistic, and religious variations, has changed the composition and relationships between members of groups in urban communities. Class divisions within immigrant groups are now at least as great as between established residents. Immigrants often share more with members of other ethnic or racial groups within their social strata than with individuals of different strata within their own national-origin groups.

Within-group heterogeneity also complicates ethnic identification. One result of the multiplication of national origins of new immigrants throughout the 1970s and 1980s is that newcomers often have little in common with those with whom they are categorized. For instance, the ethnic label "Hispanic" obscures the ways in which immigrants from El Salvador differ significantly from waves of Mexican immigrants who settled before them.[4] Popular media also continue to reduce much of this new social complexity to simple spinoffs of black and white differences. *Time*

Academy of Political and Social Science, 485:139-52 (May 1986).

4. Nestor P. Rodriguez, "Undocumented Central Americans in Houston: Diverse Populations," *International Migration Review*, 21:4-26 (Spring 1987).

magazine, for instance, has treated the intertwining of ethnic, linguistic, national, and cultural differences as merely a middle ground between black and white, not quite black and not quite white. Preoccupation with racial differences, of course, is understandable; it still remains the American dilemma. Yet ethnic and racial diversity has changed qualitatively from the concerns established during the civil rights movement, when group-conscious empowerment strategies and identities became well established.

Second, immigration research neglects established communities. The focus on characteristics of different immigrant groups and their structural positions systematically ignores relationships that newcomers form with established residents within certain social spheres. Research often overstates the extent to which sources of change and lack of advancement are due to characteristics of immigrant groups and differences between them, rather than to broad political and economic restructuring that affects all groups. Very little research has taken as its point of departure the "commonality between immigrants and minorities in the U.S. economy"[5] and the difficulties that immigrants share with established residents living in the same or neighboring communities. General conditions in local communities, whether related to housing, jobs, schools, crime, or recreational facilities, constrain not only how immigrants are able to adapt to their host community but also how communities respond to newcomers.

5. Bach, "Immigration."

Research also understates the extent of change in many established communities. For many immigrants who live in communities in which the primary, dominant group is Chicano or African American, Anglo conformity, long considered the reference point for assimilation, is simply no longer salient. African Americans now face large numbers of racially similar Haitian immigrants, who bring a different language, culture, and class background. Latino communities, long dominated by residents of either Mexican or Puerto Rican heritage, now find as much difference between groups that speak Spanish as between Spanish speakers and long-established, English-speaking residents. In Miami, for instance, Haitian immigrants enter and adapt to predominantly African American schools, while in San Diego, Mexican immigrants and Southeast Asian refugees face well-established Chicano communities. Immigrants' adjustments to U.S. life are adaptations to the dominant subcultural patterns in local schools and neighborhoods and to the perception of the place of minorities in U.S. society as a whole.

Ironically, even the Anglo reference point has changed. Turn-of-the-century European immigration was as heterogeneous and contentious as the contemporary influx. Settlement often created social tensions that took on an ethnic character. As historian Arthur Schlesinger points out, European immigration "itself palpitated with internal hostilities, everyone at everybody else's throats."[6]

6. Arthur Schlesinger, Jr., *The Disuniting of America: Reflections on a Multicultural So-*

Only the distortions of historical hindsight and the lens of contemporary politics have blurred and transformed these differences and vibrant diversity into a mythical homogeneous Euro-ancestry.

Third, the theoretical foundations of much immigration research miss opportunities to identify cooperative efforts between newcomers and established residents, especially those that lead to communitywide activities. Little attention is given to the everyday activities, organized and unorganized, that bring people together and form the foundations for community stability and change. When the popular media turned to ask why communities were in conflict, few studies could offer evidence of common interests and shared activities amid the social and cultural diversity within urban areas. Unchallenged, the media report pervasive images of intergroup conflict.

In the mid-1980s, a similar flurry of media reports about conflict between immigrants and established residents, primarily between Korean shopkeepers and African American customers, stimulated the creation of a nationwide project to explore the character of relations between newcomers and established residents.[7]

---

ciety (Knoxville, TN: Whittle Communications, 1991), pp. 70-71.

7. The Changing Relations Project was developed in 1986, organized in 1987, and carried out from 1988 to 1991. A national board organized the research, which involved ethnographic fieldwork by six teams of over 50 researchers working in Philadelphia, Miami, Chicago, Garden City (Kansas), Houston, and Monterey Park (California). For the board's final report, see National Project Board, *Changing Relations: Newcomers and Established Residents in*

Among other things, the project sought to determine the extent to which newspaper accounts about conflicts between immigrants and established residents reflected the true character of community relations. What was happening in the quiet, day-to-day activities that the media never examined? Who was at work bringing people together? Was the nation fragmenting and polarizing, or were there possibilities for democracy and community?

Overall, the project's results show a much more complex and subtle story than that reported by the press. Tensions certainly exist between immigrants and established residents. Korean shopkeepers and their African American neighbors are not the only examples. Still, in the communities studied, the incidence of conflict is much less than the media report. Rather, communities contain myriad everyday encounters that bring about coexistence, accommodation, and change in quiet but stark contrast to the dramatic portraits of conflict. Possibilities also exist for converting pervasive social tensions into creative strategies of accommodation, working together to reconstruct community. The National Project Board concludes that

there is a common experience of crisis in many of America's communities which limits interactions and possibilities for cooperation [between immigrants and established residents]. Yet, these same problems also create shared interests and compatible goals. Many of the most promising signs of leadership and intergroup organization focus on local issues of com-

U.S. Communities (New York: Ford Foundation, 1993).

munity standards, including the availability, cost, and value of housing, social services, schools, education, law enforcement, and safety.[8]

This study and others[9] offer potential, promising responses to the growing concern about relations between new immigrants and established residents and the viability of urban communities. They direct attention to two critical questions. What are the conditions and activities that create social tensions and conflicts and ultimately threaten communities, and what are the social and human bonds that hold people and places together?

IMMIGRATION, DIVERSITY,
AND SOCIAL CONFLICT

The new diversity of major U.S. cities now divides groups along lines of language, race, culture, identity, and history. Demography and economic restructuring have combined to drive whites into suburbs, blacks into separate neighborhoods, and, now, new, diverse immigrants in among them. In these areas, immigrants and established residents live in socially divided worlds. Residential and institutional separation, of course, is not new in the United States or to newcomers. African American novelist Richard Wright described his discovery of an earlier etiquette of intergroup relations as he, too, crossed a border—that from

8. National Project Board, *Changing Relations: Newcomers and Established Residents in U.S. Communities*, technical report (New York: Ford Foundation, 1991), pp. 23-24.

9. For example, see Lawrence Fuchs, *The American Kaleidoscope: Race, Ethnicity, and the Civic Culture* (Hanover, NH: University Press of New England, Wesleyan University Press, 1991).

the black South to the white North: black and white were " 'each seemingly intent upon his private mission. There was no racial fear. Indeed, each person acted as though no one existed but himself.' "[10]

Many immigrants and established residents have carved out distinct social arenas, including the differential use of service agencies, businesses, and community organizations. Labor markets have become sharply separated. In the office buildings of many large cities, the daytime white and black work force gives way to a nighttime immigrant, and often undocumented, service corp. This social distance is so clear and well defined that some groups find it easy to claim ownership over particular areas and activities. In Houston, researchers recorded two examples: "When blacks were asked why they did not participate in other general education classes [in which Latinas participated], the usual response was 'those classes are for Mexicans' or 'everyone speaks Spanish in those classes.' " Another informant said that "Blacks expect Mexicans to go to LULAC while Blacks go to the NAACP."[11] The impact of assertions of cultural ownership, of course, is to dominate activities in a way that blocks the participation of other groups from potentially shared projects.

Paradoxically, it is this segregation and separation that create tensions when and where groups come

into contact. Groups interact in only a few special places, including schools, workplaces, churches, and playing fields. These are rare places, and each faces the excessive strain of absorbing and responding to the demographic diversity that characterizes America's communities. Few of them are capable of continuously withstanding the strain.

Still, social tensions do not simply explode as the summer heat rises or the number of newcomers grows or the volume of rock music increases. Riots, such as those that followed the Rodney King verdict in Los Angeles, do not happen just because of economic decline, intergroup tensions, and social neglect, although these, of course, are essential ingredients. Rather, tensions ignite into conflict through abuse and opposition; someone or something makes them happen. In the 1960s, various national commissions concluded that many civil disorders resulted from "police riots." Recent disorders involving immigrant communities in Miami, Washington, D.C., and Los Angeles also resulted from clear miscarriages of justice.

Conflict also results when established groups and leaders resist change and take a hard-line approach to traditional community standards. For example, in Monterey Park, a suburb of Los Angeles, negative reactions to immigrants resulted from English-only advocates' attempts to ban Chinese shopkeepers from using both English and Chinese

10. Quoted in James R. Grossman, *Land of Hope: Chicago, Black Southerners and the Great Migration* (Chicago: University of Chicago Press, 1989).

11. Houston Research Team, as reported in *Changing Relations*, by National Project Board (1991).

12. Monterey Park Research Team, as reported in *Changing Relations*, by National Project Board (1991).

characters on their signs.[12] The signs posed no safety hazards, and they clearly met acceptable community norms. Opposition to them created hostility where there could have been receptiveness, and resentment when there should have been cooperation.

Much less dramatic social tensions than the all-too-familiar hate crimes and abuses that plague contemporary U.S. life can also lead to conflict. Today's demography creates a social context for misinterpretation of even the most routine interpersonal tensions by turning clashes between individuals into intergroup conflict. The greater the mix of groups, the more likely it is that normal tensions and conflicts will express, by numerical chance, intergroup antagonisms. The rise in conflict between different minority groups, for instance, may result as much from the increase in the number of opportunities to have these encounters as from a significant increase in motivations to harm each other. Under the new demographic diversity, the same number of interpersonal incidents as before can produce a greater number of incidents between different groups.

The response and interpretation of interpersonal and intergroup tensions can themselves become sources of conflict. Professional mediators or the media often mistakenly represent interpersonal incidents as intergroup conflict. Community dispute resolution efforts can bring into a neighborhood mediators who work with models of group membership that force residents to seek out appropriate group representatives to satisfy the required rules of formal negotiations. This representational model trans-

forms neighborly disputes into conflicting claims about distributive justice among groups. When mediators are not present, social tensions are often worked out between the individuals involved.[13]

ECONOMIC RESTRUCTURING

The primary source of social separation and the tensions that it fosters lie deeply rooted in the restructuring of the U.S. economy. After all, it is the economy that brings immigrants to the United States and distributes the resources to settle in new communities. Economic demand brings groups together, but it also pushes them apart. It changes the ways in which established residents as well as immigrants have learned to accommodate to each other and adds uncertainty and competition to their perceptions of each other.

The increase in social inequality and the general weakness of the U.S. economy in the 1980s had strong consequences for both immigrants and established residents. It rekindled the central debate between economic growth and social fairness that haunts much of democratic politics in America. In the last decade, market-based competition and antigovernment rhetoric supported efforts to promote unfettered, aggregate economic growth, lower taxes, and increased corporate flexibility.[14] The

13. Sally Engle Merry, *Urban Danger: Life in a Neighborhood of Strangers* (Philadelphia: Temple University Press, 1981).

14. Ralf Dahrendorf, *The Modern Social Conflict: An Essay on the Politics of Liberty* (London: Weidenfeld & Nicolson, 1988).

emphasis on aggregate growth, however, ignored or obscured the underlying issues of fairness and an awareness of persistent poverty and marginalization. Excessive privatization also undermined civic participation, leaving many with a strong sense of decline. Neglect made many problems seem even more intractable than before.

Higher levels of immigration and less regulated use of newcomer and established labor were inextricable parts of these national trends.[15] Yet political attention to the legislative battle over the levels of admissions misrepresented the interplay of immigration with these general conditions. Economic restructuring accounts for one of the most misunderstood issues of contemporary relations between immigrants and established residents —the extent to which immigrants compete with and displace U.S. workers. Historically, the workplace was one of the most important locations for interactions between newcomers and established residents and for creation of shared interests and goals. After two decades of the decline of unions, the collapse of large-scale manufacturing and, with them, large production facilities, and the growth of service industries, the work force is fragmented. Individual workers are isolated, laboring away in smaller service-oriented firms or connected only by new technologies designed to make the exchange between humans faster and more efficient but less personal. Much of this separation corresponds to deep divisions in the work force by race, ethnicity, and gender.

Although many observers have tried to dismiss it, the connection between this economic restructuring and the perception and experience of job loss is real enough.[16] Typical reactions from communities throughout the nation are reflected in these observations recorded by researchers from Houston: "The same is true for Blacks who used to work at the ship channel. Many Blacks lost their jobs because of mechanization and also as a result of the downturn in the economy in the 1980s . . . if you go to the channel today you won't see many Blacks but you will see a number of Latinos. It is believed, by the people inside and outside the community, that racism has prevented many Blacks from being rehired at the channel." "Many Blacks in the city note that at one time you could see black women standing at bus stops around the River Oaks area waiting to go home; now one sees Latino immigrant females at these stops."[17] Similar experiences of restructuring and loss are not limited to African Americans. They can be recorded among whites who have witnessed the movement of wealthy Taiwanese into Monterey Park and among Anglos watching the influx of Cubans to Miami.[18]

The problem in understanding the nature of economic relations between

15. Julian Simon, *The Economic Consequences of Immigration* (New York: Basil Blackwell, 1989).

16. George Borjas, *Friends or Strangers: The Impact of Immigrants on the U.S. Economy* (New York: Basic Books, 1990).

17. Houston Research Team, as reported in *Changing Relations*, by National Project Board (1991).

18. National Project Board, *Changing Relations* (1993).

immigrant and established groups is that restructuring, by definition, creates new job openings while destroying others. The openings and closings do not occur in an orderly manner, and there is often little displacement because there is little competition. New workers, including immigrants, often fill the opening jobs precisely because employers seek additional workers as they expand. During much of the 1980s, the business cycle drew many new workers into the labor force. But, as the economy faltered and firms were moved or closed, established residents watched as the jobs they held disappeared and those employing immigrants remained.

This continuous fluctuation within the labor market leads simultaneously to two apparently contradictory conclusions. As various studies have shown, the net result of immigration in a dynamic economy is virtually zero.[19] But the gross movements of workers within the labor market, with some established workers losing jobs while others gain, have the consequence of creating abundant experiences and accurate accounts of job displacement due to immigration. Communities do not live in the aggregate, nor do people perceive net or balanced outcomes. The continual neglect of the large gains and losses in the labor market leads to an excessively benign account of the impact of economic restructuring on workers in general and, in some cases, of immigration on established residents.

LINGUISTIC DIVERSITY

Intergroup tensions also result from the use of different languages in the same social activities. Political battles over bilingualism in the last two decades polarized the debate about language usage and distorted its importance to everyday encounters in local communities. Communities throughout the nation continue to demonstrate the need for active pursuit of language training and protection from forced loss of native, non-English languages, a loss that harms educational progress and adjustment in general. They also demonstrate a pervasive desire among immigrants to learn English.

Yet language is a complex and contradictory force in social relations. Sharing a language binds some people together while separating others. The use of several languages in a shared social arena, such as in neighborhoods, playgrounds, and community meetings, can create clear intergroup tensions.[20] The reasons, though, are complex. For example, the Philadelphia team of the Changing Relations Project reported instances in which the militant push for Spanish-English bilingual programs was resented and opposed by Korean and Polish groups moving into the same area.[21] Immigration has produced many more of these multilingual communities than is generally realized. For instance, the 1990 U.S. census revealed that Los

---

19. Richard Freeman, *Immigration and the Work Force: Economic Consequences for the United States and Source Areas* (Chicago: University of Chicago Press, 1992).

20. National Project Board, *Changing Relations* (1993).

21. Philadelphia Research Team, as reported in *Changing Relations*, by National Project Board (1991).

Angeles County has at least ten languages spoken by significantly large numbers of people within its borders.[22] In these new diverse communities, older models of English-Spanish bilingual programs, like traditional models of race relations based solely on black-white interactions, no longer remain applicable.

Language use also means something very different depending on the class and power of each group. For low-wage immigrants, speaking a language other than English means survival. On the other hand, learning English is a necessary route to upward mobility. Yet, for upper-class Cuban or Chinese immigrants, language use can be a source and symbol of power, and the social clash a test of who dominates a community. For elite non-English-speaking groups, public and private demands to use English are often interpreted as a threat to their privilege and status, a loss for those who are used to commanding their own social worlds.

CRAFTING A NEW PLURALISM

Unquestionably, intergroup tensions are rooted in deeply entrenched social, economic, and political trends that separate and divide. Yet efforts to cross these dividing lines are made daily. Newcomers and established residents do not coexist simply by avoiding each other. Active, conscious decisions to organize around common issues—not just for the sake of integration but when diverse people perceive similar interests—exist throughout U.S. cities. Today's failures to recognize and build upon them grow more out of an inability to craft ways to work together than from overwhelming resistance among either established residents or newcomers.

Over a century ago, observers noted that efforts to continuously reinvent democracy in the United States begin with the "little associations" of voluntary participation. Voluntary associations, organized formally or informally, provide the energy, resources, and direction for community building. They mobilize private and group values into community standards, obligations, and responsibilities and are especially important in shaping culture and discourse. Even as early as Tocqueville's travels, observers recognized that voluntary associations reinforced the value of diverse interests to community life.[23]

Most theoretical perspectives on community change predict that government monopolization of social policy and community programs inevitably diminishes the role of the voluntary sector. Historically, however, the voluntary sector expands during periods of increased immigration. Voluntary organizations serve as critical intermediaries between immigrants and established residents. They form the basis of association and social trust that cement local relationships, then become the foundation for participation in regional and

22. U.S., Department of Commerce, Bureau of the Census, *1990 Census of Population and Housing Summary Tape File 3A, Los Angeles County*.

23. Robert Wuthnow, "The Voluntary Sector: Legacy of the Past, Hope for the Future?" in *Between States and Markets: The Voluntary Sector in Comparative Perspective*, ed. Robert Wuthnow (Princeton, NJ: Princeton University Press, 1991), pp. 3-29.

national political, social, and economic life.

In the last two decades, expansion of government activities has coincided with an increase in voluntary sector activities, including those serving immigrants. As one observer has remarked, "What is new is that [growth in] both immigrant and ethnic associations [has taken] place in countries with large institutionalized social welfare programs and professional social work bureaucracies."[24] Youth organizations, informal business and commercial groups, community-improvement leagues, immigrant associations, and charitable associations, among others, have all proliferated. Their activities include assistance offered by established residents to help resettle newcomers, neighborhood cleanups that involve both newcomers and established residents, expansion of selections in community libraries to provide learning space for all groups, and youth sports clubs that bring together both children and their parents. The persistence and even revival of these voluntary associations and activities challenge the value of both bureaucratized programs and laissez-faire, market-oriented policies toward immigrant settlement.

Voluntary associations also provide a context for crafting informal social rules that organize and ultimately control community problems when they arise. For instance, part of the problem that arises between Korean shopkeepers and African American consumers is that employers draw only from family and friends for their workers. They establish few connections to the people in the neighborhood who at some time shop in their stores. The result is that no one in the store has the trust or informal authority forged through familiarity and extensive social connections to negotiate and confine a misunderstanding before it becomes a larger social conflict.[25]

MOVING FORWARD

The voluntary sector faces two profound challenges in responding to the contemporary settlement of immigrants and the renewal of interest in community reconstruction. During the 1980s, voluntary organizations adopted an increasingly direct role as primary agents of immigrant and refugee settlement. Voluntary organizations expanded and shifted their programs to serve newcomers in large part because of the rapid increase in the availability of federal resources through the Refugee Act of 1980 and the State Legalization Impact Assistance Grants (SLIAG) that accompanied the 1986 Immigration Reform and Control Act. By the late 1980s, though, the government had reduced its commitment to new immigrants and the communities in which they settle. The Immigration Act of 1990, which is only now becoming operational, expands the number of new immigrants and their geographical

24. Shirley Jenkins, "Introduction: Immigration, Ethnic Associations, and Social Services," in *Ethnic Associations and the Welfare State: Services to Immigrants in Five Countries*, ed. Shirley Jenkins (New York: Columbia University Press, 1988), p. 2.

25. An example is provided by the Chicago Research Team in *Changing Relations*, by National Research Board (1991).

and occupational backgrounds. Yet the act offers no significant government resources to respond to the new volume or composition.

Similar reductions in funding for refugee resettlement have created problems for voluntary agencies serving local communities. After a decade of increasing refugee admissions, substantial declines in per capita support for resettlement finally resulted in such a deep cut in available funds that it required fundamental restructuring of the federal program. Privatization became a rallying call and a mechanism for disinvesting the federal government from refugee resettlement and responsibility for its immigration policy. Proposed changes shift greater control and authority over settlement activities to local voluntary agencies. But, unless the Clinton administration reverses course, these changes leave local areas and organizations without a matching increase in resources.

The Refugee and SLIAG programs, however, are part of a general crisis in the relations between different branches of government that has resulted in huge gaps between federal authority and local capacities. In a March 1993 speech at the Kennedy School of Government, Governor Ann Richards of Texas characterized this crisis of federalism as an "adversarial combat between different levels of government: between state and local governments and the Federal Government. The power to mandate," she emphasized, "has become separated from the power to pay." One way to respond to this crisis, of course, is to increase the financial resources available to local governments to pay for federally mandated programs. To a large extent, this is the aim of a new lobbying effort that seeks to gain additional federal resources by constructing an immigrant policy for the United States. The idea borrows heavily from the 1980s model of refugee resettlement and its structure of reimbursing states for federally mandated programs in local communities.

The problem with this strategy is that the adversarial battle that Governor Richards identified requires, by way of counterattack, a restructuring that is not completely acceptable to those advocating a national immigrant policy. By following federal dollars, an immigrant policy could undermine community efforts at reform and, through targeting newcomers as a separate, special group, further reinforce community divisions. Such a policy could also promote exactly what anti-immigrant groups charge—that immigrants have needs that require special programs because there are too many of them for communities to absorb.

An alternative strategy of local mobilization begins with the recognition that the problems most immigrants face are shared by the entire community. Just as immigrants are not to blame for community problems, neither should they become an excuse for state and local governments to seek federal money to solve general fiscal woes. Voluntary agencies that work at the community level will, by their nature, be the fuel for the fire that energizes a new push for restructuring local programs. Established programs themselves must change to incorporate immigrants' and refugees' needs by changing established methods of defining priorities, recruiting members, and providing assistance. Local activities and coalitions need a degree of independence from government mandates, especially those that target only particular groups, to craft programs that work in the interests of everyone in the community.

The voluntary sector's second profound challenge results from its indirect involvement in newcomer settlement activities. Many established community organizations face a potential mismatch in their ability to respond to the needs and diversity of new immigrants. The ethnic and racial diversity of recent immigration has posed an especially difficult dilemma for established organizations initially organized around group rights and empowerment. The need to promote group solidarity and identity remains, especially at a time when attempts to overturn previous gains have increased. Yet some of these organizations have now become sources of separation and exclusion. Their group-based empowerment strategies may not be organizationally effective, and attempts to reach out may conflict with immigrants' own political strategies.

Tensions between groups in a period of large-scale settlement are not new. Still, established groups and institutions may not be well suited to respond to these new demands. Historically, trade unions were a primary mechanism for integrating diverse newcomers into a common work force. Yet these same unions also excluded women, African Americans, and unskilled workers. In addition, although unions have been his-

torically one of the most important voluntary sector organizations in receiving new immigrants, the recent decline in membership and the impact of government reforms have weakened their capacities to respond to diverse newcomers. Immigration reform in the last four or five years has driven a wedge between the interests of many immigrant advocacy groups and unionized workers, pitting groups whose political focus is employment standards and social protections against those seeking larger numbers of immigrants.[26] Yet, when local unions, such as those representing maintenance workers and hotel employees, alter existing practices to respond to the language issues and health needs of immigrants, they can succeed in effectively encouraging the participation of both their established and newcomer members.[27]

One of the new challenges of this local diversity involves civil rights groups. Especially in cities in which the white majority is no longer numerically or politically dominant, the axis of group interactions has shifted. Increasingly, interracial, interethnic tensions and conflicts are between "minority" groups all seeking access and participation in the city's established institutions.

These organizations have not necessarily excluded anyone from membership. Rather, as ethnic and racial

26. Robert L. Bach, "Settlement Policies in the United States," in *Australian and U.S. Immigration Policies*, ed. J. Jupp and G. Freedman (New York: Oxford University Press, 1992).

27. Robert L. Bach and Howard Brill, *Impact of IRCA on the U.S. Labor Market and Economy*, final report to the U.S. Department of Labor, 1991.

diversity expands, the appeal of established civil rights groups for reform and assistance often refers to increasingly narrow definitions of constituents and their interests. By simply maintaining an established membership and focus while community issues and composition have diversified, these groups represent less of the local population. Community members who experience these changes often mention the need for more flexibility for existing community organizations to respond to newcomers. For other observers, the problem lies in the redirection of public resources or in simply not being responsive to the changing diversity. For example, in Miami, the public resources claimed by a growing immigrant population challenged American-born blacks and strengthened resistance to Haitian newcomers.[28] Ironically, some observers in Miami are also concerned that "as Cubans come to dominate elite institutions, they may emulate the earlier exclusionary practices of established residents, particularly with regard to minorities. This became dramatically evident when the Cuban American Bar Association decided to exclude a Mexican from its ranks."[29]

Many of the groups and organizations that were born during the civil rights movement are now established community institutions. The new challenge is to organize civil rights, empowerment-based strategies, and the desire of many new immigrant groups to forge their own community associations into efforts that expand cooperation and search for shared goals that redefine the public order and common good.

TAKING UP THE
GLOBAL CHALLENGE

Concern about the social implications of immigration reflects a familiar response to urban unrest. Twenty-five years ago, former Vice President Hubert Humphrey voiced similar worries about riots, conflicts, and commitment to community. When announcing his campaign for the presidency, he said, "Either we turn backward into a continually increasing polarizing of the nation and a widening spiral of fear—or we continue to go forward into a new day of justice and order. Which way: Apartheid or democracy? Separation or community? A society of ordered liberty or a society of fear and repression?"[30]

After the Los Angeles riots of 1992, the new discourse about immigration and community renewal is fundamentally rooted in a revival of discussions about the common good and a clear shift away from the assimilation of individual immigrants and distribution of benefits to separate groups. Yet recent commentators have noted generally that efforts to define and articulate the common good have become increasingly difficult. Some have even suggested that the United States has lost its civic culture,[31] including the core values

28. Miami Research Team, as reported in *Changing Relations*, by National Project Board (1991).
29. National Project Board, *Changing Relations* (1993), p. 68.

30. Speech before B'nai B'rith, New York City, 1968.
31. Daniel Kemmis, *Community and the Politics of Place* (Norman: University of Okla-

that have been essential for forging a national culture out of successive waves of diverse immigrants.[32]

The rise and dominance of government, the argument goes, may have created alternative ways of thinking about public responsibility. Rather than feeling personally responsible for neighbors and communities, individuals turn to centralized agencies, and to the professionals employed by these agencies, as a more effective means of addressing complex problems. The market ideology of the 1980s also carried negative implications for the spirit of voluntarism. As social service agencies adopted market-based principles of assessing outcomes, paid professionals were more likely to make decisions according to financial considerations than according to the traditional values of caring and helping embodied in volunteer work.

Despite these changes, recent public opinion studies show that altruism and the spirit of voluntarism remain high in the U.S. population. Voluntary associations remain actively engaged as contributors to the new debates about local culture. They often serve as the fundamental building blocks of public debate about social standards. They are, as Berger and Neuhaus have described them, "important laboratories of innovation in social services . . . [that] sustain the expression of the rich pluralism of American life."[33] They work on a

daily basis with programs in schools, churches, youth and recreational groups, and employer and worker organizations and certainly among direct service providers. Many local associations have consciously recrafted their membership and programs to mirror the full diversity of local ethnic residents. This strategy creates and reinforces new visions of the nation's culture, a grassroots multiculturalism, that may be emerging from efforts to respond to the incredible ethnic diversity of many of the communities in which immigrants have settled.

These social, cultural, and political pressures on established communities that accompany immigration are not unique to the United States.[34] The internationalization of U.S. communities is part of a global shift that involves closer integration among diverse peoples. Regional economic integration, free trade, and common markets are establishing and expanding bonds between peoples of the world that further encourage large-scale immigration. Family connections, even transnational communities, have emerged that now fuel self-propelled, large-scale immigration.

This is also a period of dramatic disintegration of established communities and the making of new political entities. Disintegrating pressures are closely connected to migration is-

homa Press, 1990); Harry C. Boyte, *Commonwealth: A Return to Citizen Politics* (New York: Free Press, 1989).

32. Fuchs, *American Kaleidoscope*.

33. Peter L. Berger and Richard John Neuhaus, *To Empower People: The Role of Mediat-*

ing Structures in Public Policy (Washington, DC: American Enterprise Institute for Public Policy Research, 1977), p. 36.

34. Frank Bovenkerk, Robert Miles, and Gilles Verbunt, "Racism, Migration and the State in Western Europe: A Case for Comparative Analysis," *International Sociology*, 5(4): 475-90 (Dec. 1990).

sues that seem to lead to an endless string of crises. The images are all too familiar: Kurdish rebels in Iraq, Haitian boat people, Hong Kong detention camps, asylum seekers attacked in Marseilles and Berlin, and ethnic cleansing in Yugoslavia. Now, according to some, Los Angeles, Washington Heights, Mt. Pleasant, and Liberty City join the list of communities at risk where immigrants have settled in large numbers.

Public reactions to the Los Angeles riots are not the first or last time that calls to curb immigration will be offered as an antidote to America's social ills. Taking care of one's own is a natural response to difficult times. But millions of immigrants are already a settled part of hundreds of communities throughout the United States. They reflect the nation's success and commitment to shared values of family reunion and humanitarian spirit.

Community renewal in those areas in which immigrants have settled requires a fundamental shift in perspective among the popular media, policymakers, and researchers. A new focus is called for that examines community and national transformation. An initial conceptual step is to recognize that immigrants are neither strangers nor outsiders to their new communities. The nation frequently forgets its responsibility for immigration. Migration to the United States occurs primarily by invitation. What most established Americans have never fully understood, but which immigrants never forget, is that America is deeply implicated in the migration flow and its destiny. U.S. employers fuel the immigration, U.S. foreign policy embraces it, and U.S. family values maintain it.[35]

35. Rephrased from National Project Board, *Changing Relations* (1993), p. 21.

ANNALS, *AAPSS*, **530**, November 1993

An Agenda for Tomorrow:
Immigration Policy and Ethnic Policies

By LAWRENCE H. FUCHS

ABSTRACT: Since 1980, the Congress of the United States and three Presidents have vastly expanded immigration, mostly from Asia and Latin America. The expansion, having come as a result of policies enacted in 1980, 1986, and 1990, has stimulated a growing movement for immigration restriction. Even if that movement is partly success-ful, immigration is likely to continue at high levels, and it is important to pay attention to public policies that will help unify immigrants and their children as Americans. A civic unity policy agenda is suggested for the new Clinton administration that will promote civic unity while protecting ethnic diversity.

Lawrence H. Fuchs, the Meyer and Walter Jaffe Professor of American Civilization and Politics at Brandeis University, is the author of several books on immigration and ethnic studies, including The American Kaleidoscope: Race, Ethnicity, and the Civic Culture *(1991), the recipient of the J. H. Franklin Award for the year's best book in American studies and the T. Saloutos Award for the year's best book in immigrant history. Professor Fuchs, who is now a member of the U.S. Commission on Immigration Reform, served as executive director of the Select Commission on Immigration and Refugee Policy (1978-81).*

O NE startling fact in these times of high immigration is how little attention has been paid to the impact of immigration on policies that affect relations between ethnic groups and the polity as a whole. Immigration policy has received attention at dozens of congressional hearings over the last two decades, through internal research and analysis by Republican and Democratic administrations from the presidency of Gerald Ford through that of George Bush, and by extensive public hearings and research conducted from 1978 to 1981 by the Select Commission on Immigration and Refugee Policy, whose more than 100 recommendations received substantial attention in the press.

A DECADE OF CONSENSUS ON IMMIGRATION POLICY AND INCREASED IMMIGRATION

As a result of these efforts, a bipartisan consensus developed around five major propositions leading to the passage of the Refugee Act of 1980, the Immigration Reform and Control Act of 1986, and the Immigration Act of 1990:

1. As the world's most powerful advocate of human rights, the United States should accept its fair share of refugees and asylees.

2. As a nation that prides itself on living by the rule of law, the United States should not encourage or wink at illegal migration and should take steps to curtail it.

3. As a nation committed to a civil rights vision that all persons who live and work in the United States lawfully should be guaranteed the Four-

teenth Amendment's promise of equal protection of the laws, the United States should not import foreign nationals in a large-scale guest-worker program that would make invidious distinctions between them and U.S. citizens and resident aliens.

4. As a nation whose interest is well served by substantial levels of immigration, the United States should modestly increase the number of immigrants lawfully admitted.

5. As a nation that believes its national identity is rooted in its commitment to democratic ideals and values available to all without regard to national ancestry, religion, or color, the United States should admit immigrants without reference to those characteristics.[1]

1. For a detailed explication of the recommendations of the Select Commission on Immigration and Refugee Policy, see *U.S. Immigration Policy and the National Interest: Staff Report of the Select Commission on Immigration and Refugee Policy, April 10, 1981* (Washington, DC: Government Printing Office, 1981). For editorial and newspaper comment on the Select Commission, see *U.S. Immigration Policy and the National Interest, Appendix H to the Staff Report of the Select Commission on Immigration and Refugee Policy, Public Information Supplement* (Washington, DC: Government Printing Office, 1981), pp. 663-701. See also Peter H. Schuck, "The Emerging Political Consensus on Immigration Law," *Georgetown Immigration Law Journal*, 5(1) (Winter 1991). See also idem, "The Politics of Rapid Legal Change: Immigration Policy in the 1980s," *Studies in American Political Development*, vol. 6 (Spring 1992). For other reviews of the events that contributed to the building of that consensus and the passage of legislation, see Lawrence H. Fuchs, "Immigration Reform in 1911 and 1981: The Role of Select Commissions," *Journal of American Ethnic History*, 3(1) (Fall 1983); idem, "The Search for a Sound Immigration Policy," in *Clamor at the Gates*, ed. Nathan Glazer (New York: Institute for

The premise underlying this last conclusion is that the success of immigrants in adapting to American society and acquiring loyalty to the American nation depends in large measure on public policies that, while permitting and protecting the maintenance of old-country languages and cultural values, do not distribute rewards or penalties on the basis of race, religion, or nationality. Despite that premise, little thought has been given by the Congress or the executive branch to the implications of immigration policy for ethnic policies concerning language and affirmative action in contracting, employment, education, and political representation.

The decade's sweeping immigration legislation began in 1980 when Congress created a separate category of admissions for refugees and asylees and continued in 1986 with an attempt to curtail flows of illegal aliens by applying sanctions to employers who hire them. The 1986 law also repudiated proposals for a large temporary guest-worker program and legalized slightly more than 3 million illegal aliens, adjusted the status of nearly 100,000 special entrants who had come from Cuba and Haiti in the early 1980s to that of permanent resident alien, and updated the registry provision in the

Contemporary Studies, 1985); idem, "The Corpse That Would Not Die: The Immigration Reform and Control Act of 1984," *Revue européenne de migration internationale*, 6(1) (1990); idem, "Thinking about Immigration and Ethnicity in the United States," in *Immigrants in Two Democracies: French and American Experience*, ed. Donald L. Horowitz and Gerard Noiriel (New York: New York University Press, 1992).

Immigration and Nationality Act from 1948 to 1972 to allow illegal aliens who could show more or less continuous residence since that date to receive permanent residency. Two years later, Congress and the President expanded immigration further. An Amerasian category was created to allow the admission of children fathered by U.S. servicemen in Vietnam and their families—essentially meaning mothers and other children—giving 37,658 such persons immigrant status from 1989 through 1991.

Finally, in 1990, during a time of extreme economic uncertainty and with the nation about to enter a prolonged recession and war in the Persian Gulf, Congress provided for a slight expansion of family-reunification immigration and almost tripled the number of immigrants chosen for their skills independent of family ties from 54,000, including the immediate families of the principal beneficiaries. Another provision established a safe haven for those already in the United States fleeing civil war and natural disasters and was made applicable immediately to Salvadorans for a minimum of 18 months; this provision has since been renewed. Other pro-immigration measures included an expansion of visas for persons from Hong Kong, establishing a transitional diversity program, and allowing 40,000 visas a year for nationals of 33 countries that had low rates of immigration in recent years.

Under these laws, the total number of persons to be awarded permanent resident status—including refugees and asylees who adjust their status—will average at least 700,000 a year through the rest of the 1990s.

An additional 100,000 refugees and asylees probably will double the annual yearly average of newcomers compared to the twenty years between 1961 and 1980. Changes in the composition of immigrants have been even more dramatic. In 1964, the year before the passage of legislation ending discrimination against immigrants from Asia and Eastern Europe, there were more French nationals admitted than Koreans, more than twice as many Germans as Filipinos, and eight times as many Italians as immigrants from India. In 1991, those three Asian countries accounted for almost ten times as many immigrants as from the three European countries: 108,169 compared to 11,578, respectively.

THE OPPOSITION TO EXPANDED IMMIGRATION

Missing from the debate over immigration policy in the 1980s was the traditional opposition to expanded immigration from labor unions and African Americans. Organized labor lobbied for curbs on illegal migration but was not unsympathetic to the Select Commission's recommendations on legal immigration. Most black leaders, particularly those in the Congressional Black Caucus, allied themselves with the expansive immigration views of Mexican American leaders in an effort to build a broader coalition on other issues of mutual concern, even to the point of opposing the application of sanctions on employers who knowingly and willfully hired illegal aliens.[2]

2. Lawrence H. Fuchs, "The Reaction of Black Americans to Immigration," in *Immigra-*

Also almost entirely absent from the debates over the 1986 and 1990 immigration acts were the xenophobic arguments of the past. One exception came from Claire Booth Luce, a former member of Congress, former ambassador to Italy, the author of plays and novels, and the wife of the founder of *Time* and *Life* magazines. She told an interviewer that since earlier immigrants were white, they could be assimilated more easily than newcomers who come to the United States and start families in order to gain citizenship and take advantage of the welfare system.[3]

Her comments were supported by William F. Buckley, Jr., the founder and head of the conservative journal the *National Review*. It was not racist, he argued, to prefer the ways of one's own culture and not to want to be deluged by those who do not live by Western customs and values. Buckley, who did not acknowledge the earlier history of opposition to Irish and German immigrants on much the same ground on which Mrs. Luce found Asian and Latino immigrants objectionable, endorsed her view that earlier immigrants could adjust to democratic values and learn English quickly, compared to more recent immigrants. Alone among the leading cultural conservatives of the period, Buckley emphasized how difficult it would be to teach American values to the Latin Americans who

tion Reconsidered, ed. Virginia Yans-McLaughlin (New York: Oxford University Press, 1990).

3. For an account of the interview with Claire Booth Luce, see William Raspberry, "Mrs. Luce: An Awful Interview," *Washington Post*, 15 Sept. 1982.

come to the United States in ever increasing numbers.[4]

But Buckley was no match for other cultural and economic conservatives, led by President Reagan, who were cheerleaders for expanded immigration and ethnic diversity. Reagan, who, with the leadership of Congress, after receiving the final report of the Select Commission, reinforced the commission's emphasis on immigration as a source of American strength and presided over a series of feel-good events like the celebration of the centennial of the Statue of Liberty that stressed the virtues of diversity. The President, and most of his culturally and economically conservative supporters, such as Jeane Kirkpatrick, George Bush, and George Will, lauded immigration and immigrants as proof that the American dream still lived.[5] Only a few years after Buckley's article, the President again spoke of the " 'golden door' " that continued to welcome new immigrants from all over the world. Praising the fact that Americans carried the blood lines of over 140 countries, Reagan enthusiastically proclaimed, " 'That's America.' "[6] Like traditional economic conservatives, the President also was a major spokesman for free-market economists, the *Wall Street Journal*, the United States Chamber of Commerce, the National

Bureau of Economic Research, and others who believed that immigration was good for the economy.[7]

The main opposition to expanded immigration in the 1980s came from a cluster of persons concerned with its potential effects on population growth, the environment, and American workers. The principal organizations working for immigration restriction were the Federation for American Immigration Reform (FAIR), established in 1979, the older Zero Population Growth, and, later, the Center for Immigration Studies, a Washington think tank on immigration. Following passage of the 1990 Immigration Act, FAIR and the Center for Immigration Studies returned to the debate with a new sense of urgency. They pointed to the failure of employer sanctions under the 1986 act to sharply curtail illegal immigration. Indeed, illegal aliens in 1992 were acquiring authorizations to work at a rate of half a million a year (many were temporary worker authorizations given to illegal aliens already working and on their way to obtaining permanent residency). The restrictionists also tried to alert Americans to the fact that the United States granted a larger number of immigrant visas in 1990 and 1991 than in any two years in its history (a temporary situation because of the

---

4. William F. Buckley, Jr.'s column in *Washington Post*, 1 Oct. 1982.

5. Lawrence H. Fuchs, *The American Kaleidoscope: Race, Ethnicity, and the Civic Culture* (Hanover, NH: Wesleyan University Press and the University Press of New England, 1991), pp. 365-71.

6. President Reagan is quoted in Fuchs, *American Kaleidoscope*, p. 367.

7. The best-known proponent of immigration as a strong economic good, almost without cost, was Julian L. Simon. See his *Economic Consequences of Immigration* (Cambridge, MA: Basil Blackwell and the Cato Institute, 1989). See also the National Bureau of Economic Research summary report, *Immigration, Trade, and the Labor Market*, ed. Richard B. Freeman (Washington, DC: National Bureau of Economic Research, 1988).

newly legalized aliens adjusting their status to that of immigrant).

Probably the most troublesome of the restrictionists' charges is that immigration is particularly harmful to black and Latino citizens. "The pervasive effects of ethnic network recruiting and the spread of non-English languages in the work place has in effect locked many blacks out of occupations where they once predominated," concluded Frank Morris, the dean of the graduate school at Morgan State.[8] Labor economist Vernon Briggs, Jr., of Cornell University, and demographer Leon F. Bouvier, formerly a vice president of the Population Reference Bureau and a member of the staff of the Select Commission, also argued that American blacks particularly are harmed by mass immigration into the cities of the North and West, where, he maintained, they lose out in competition, not just for jobs and training opportunities but for services and housing, too.[9]

Unskilled and poorly educated illegal aliens unquestionably compete with some unskilled and poorly educated Americans, who are disproportionately black and Latino. But the restrictionists of the 1990s, often relying on the work of economist George Borjas, also assert that an increasing proportion of lawfully admitted immigrants are relatively unskilled and less educated than they used to be. Assuming that Borjas's methodology is sound and his conclusions persuasive, one could still argue against numerical restriction but call for the United States to choose immigrants based on educational and skill criteria instead of family relationships.[10] The question as to whether lawfully admitted immigrants serve mainly as substitutes for American workers and depress wages and standards for American workers or as complements who help to stimulate an economy through their own skills, hard work, savings, and investment is one that will be examined closely by the Commission

8. Frank Morris, statement before the House Judiciary Subcommittee on Immigration, Refugees, and International Law and the House Labor Committee Immigration Task Force, 13 Mar. 1990, reported in *Immigration 2000: The Century of the New American Sweatshop* (Washington, DC: Federation for American Immigration Reform, 1992), p. 3.

9. *Immigration 2000*, pp. 5-23. Bouvier, who wrote four data-laden books published by the Center for Immigration Studies in 1991 and 1992, has been especially concerned about the impact of immigration on the ability of different ethnic groups to get along. See his *Peaceful Invasions: Immigration and Changing America* (Washington, DC: Center for Immigration Studies, 1991); Leon F. Bouvier and Bob Weller, *Florida in the Twenty-First Century: The Challenge of Population Growth* (Washington, DC: Center for Immigration Studies, 1992); Leon F. Bouvier and Dudley L. Poston, Jr., *Thirty Million Texans?* (Washing-

ton, DC: Center for Immigration Studies, 1992); Leon F. Bouvier, *Fifty Million Californians?* (Washington, DC: Center for Immigration Studies, 1992).

10. See George Borjas, *Friends or Strangers* (New York: Basic Books, 1990). There is no question that low-skilled immigrants, whether legal or illegal, place extra demands on the services of localities, sometimes at considerable cost. See "Impact of Undocumented Persons and Other Immigrants on Costs, Revenues and Services in Los Angeles County" (Report prepared for the Los Angeles County Board of Supervisors, 6 Nov. 1992). Many scholars continue to reject Borjas's interpretation of the negative economic impacts of immigrants. A recent entry in the debate is Thomas Muller, *Immigrants and the American City* (New York: New York University Press, 1993).

on Immigration Reform, created by
the 1990 Immigration Act to evaluate
its effects. But the restrictionists are
obviously correct in asserting that
immigration, legal and illegal, at
high levels generates tension in the
major cities in which immigrants settle. An article by Jack Miles entitled
"Blacks v. Browns" in the October
1992 issue of the *Atlantic Monthly*,
widely distributed by FAIR and the
Center for Immigration Studies,
pointed out that more than half of
those arrested in the wake of the Los
Angeles riots were Latinos and that
40 percent of them already had criminal records. Miles presented a litany
of harsh facts concerning the struggle
over power and services that have
comparable examples in other cities.
Black social service workers were let
go to make room for bilingual speakers. A janitorial service in downtown
Los Angeles has been taken over by
nonunionized immigrants, who replaced unionized black workers.[11]

Success in substantially reducing
illegal migration in the 1990s depends in large part on the willingness
of Congress to adopt a secure, reliable system of identifying employees
eligible to work. Although the present system is not effective and probably has created some discrimination
against foreign-sounding and -look-
ing citizens, the argument remains
fierce as to whether a new and secure
system to verify job applicants as au-
thorized to work can be phased in and
made effective enough to cut back
substantially on the migration of illegal aliens, particularly as an un-

known and perhaps large proportion
of them work in an ethnic cash economy where they may not be asked for
identification. A staff report from the
Select Commission argued in the affirmative, as did a 1993 report from
the Commission on Agricultural
Workers, and many experts at hearings and consultations throughout
the last decade have as well. The
major problem is essentially political
and not technical. Despite public
opinion polls that have consistently
shown a large majority of Americans—including Hispanics—supportive of efforts to curtail the flow of
unauthorized workers into the
United States, a combination of Mexican American advocacy group leaders in coalition with the Black Congressional Caucus, civil liberties
advocates, and lobbyists for agricultural and other employers have been
able to frustrate any attempt to make
the system more effective.[12]

11. Jack Miles, "Blacks v. Browns: The
Struggle for the Bottom Rung," *Atlantic
Monthly*, p. 41 (Oct. 1992).

12. Rosanna Perotti, "IRCA's Anti-Dis-
crimination Provisions: What Went Wrong?"
International Migration Review, 26(3):732-53
(Fall 1992). On the relative ineffectiveness of
employer sanctions, see U.S., Department of
Labor, Bureau of International Labor Affairs,
"Employer Sanctions and U.S. Labor Markets:
First Report," 1991; on the utilization of em-
ployee eligibility systems, see U.S., Congress,
Senate, Committee on the Judiciary, Subcom-
mittee on Immigration and Refugee Policy,
*Systems to Verify Authorization to Work in the
United States*, Hearing, 97th Cong., 1st sess.,
October 2, 1981 (Washington: U.S. Government Printing Office, 1982); "Options for a
New Employment Verification" (Staff report
prepared for the use of the Subcommittee on
Immigration and Refugee Affairs, Committee
on the Judiciary, U.S. Senate, 102d Cong., 2d
sess., 1992). On the question of discrimination,
the U.S. General Accounting Office, as provided for by the Immigration Reform and Control Act, gave Congress a report in March 1990

IMMIGRATION TO CONTINUE AT HIGH LEVELS

Whether or not progress is made in strengthening measures to curtail illegal migration, the restrictionists are not likely to have much success in substantially reducing the scale of legal immigration. It will be difficult for them to convince Congress to make such cuts before the Commission on Immigration Reform submits its final report on 1 September 1997. The only obvious target for reduction would come from the approximately 465,000 family reunification immigrants set for annual admissions beginning in fiscal year 1995.[13] Virtually untouchable within that category are the immediate relatives of U.S. citizens—spouses, children, and parents—of whom 237,103 were admitted in fiscal year 1991, a number almost certain to increase by 1995. That leaves as a target the 226,000 numerically restricted visas set aside for all other family reunification preferences, the most vulnerable of which are the preference for the spouses and unmarried children of lawful permanent residents and especially the preference for brothers and sisters of U.S. citizens. The 1990 act sets aside 114,200 visas for the first group, with a minimum of 77 percent allocated to the spouses and minor children of legal permanent residents without regard to per-country

that concluded that "many employers discriminated because the law's verification system does not provide a simple or reliable method to verify job applicants' eligibility to work." See U.S., General Accounting Office, *Immigration Reform: Employer Sanctions and the Question of Discrimination*, Mar. 1990, p. 4.

13. The number actually admitted is likely to be slightly higher.

ceilings, following the recommendation of the Select Commission. Congress is not likely to vote to prevent hardworking, taxpaying, citizenship-bound permanent resident aliens from having their spouses and minor children join them legally. A stronger case can be made for cutting the maximum 26,226 visas set aside for adult unmarried sons and daughters of resident aliens (subject to country ceilings), based on the argument that such persons, even if unmarried, should wait until their petitioner parents become citizens and should try in the meantime to be admitted as employment-based immigrants. But even if that argument is persuasive to Congress, the reduction in immigration would be tiny.

The most likely target for any reduction in lawful immigration is in the U.S. citizens' sibling preference. Sixty-five thousand visas, plus unused visas from earlier preferences if there are any, were provided in the 1990 act for brothers and sisters of U.S. citizens. This preference has been attacked for more than a decade, based on two arguments. The first is that the growth in visa demand is peculiarly exponential. A citizen brother petitions for a noncitizen sister and several years later she comes with a husband and several children. She and the husband become citizens in five years, and he then petitions for a sister or brother and family.

The second argument, already alluded to, is that brothers and sisters are not sufficiently close relatives to justify a categorical preference. That position has been consistently opposed by Italian, Jewish, Asian, and

Hispanic groups on the ground that brothers and sisters are just as or almost as important to family in many cultures as sons, daughters, spouses, and parents. Several members of the Select Commission tried to confine the brother-sister category to never-married brothers and sisters, reasoning that those who had married in the source country had established their own families there. But not one of the four Democrats from Congress on the commission voted for the change.[14]

Restrictionists also argue that the number of refugees admitted should be sharply reduced from its recent current annual average of around 120,000. FAIR makes the case that current refugee policy is driven to a large extent by domestic politics and foreign policy, a conclusion with which few would disagree. FAIR also points out that it is much less expensive for the United States to help support refugees in other countries than it is to admit them.[15] Perhaps the obligation to take large numbers from the former Soviet Union and Southeast Asia will lessen in the 1990s; they accounted for more than half of those adjusting their status in 1991. But in a world where the United States is attempting to encourage other countries to accept the oppressed victims of ethnic and tribal strife, it is not in a position to make substantial cuts in refugee admissions. Mounting pressures on Europeans to admit refugees from Bosnia-Herzogovina, Azerbaijan, Georgia, Iraq, Iran, and other killing fields will keep the pressure on the United States to accept its fair share. In a world of tremendous uncertainty and resurgent violent nationalisms, it is highly unlikely that the United States will reduce refugee admissions below the 50,000 normal annual flow contemplated by the Refugee Act of 1980. In the meantime, recent refugee admissions dictate that for the next six or seven years, the number of those already in the United States who adjust their status to that of immigrant will average at least 100,000.

Unless there is a new surge of xenophobia in the nation generally, immigration from all over the world will continue at high numbers. Except for Pat Buchanan, no major political figure has made the xenophobic argument that newcomers from Asia and Spanish-speaking countries are less capable of becoming Americans than European immigrants were in the past.

14. After extensive hearings and discussions on the subject, 7 members of the 16-member Select Commission actually voted for a change to admit only unmarried brothers and sisters. They were the Attorney General of the United States, Benjamin Civiletti; Father Theodore Hesburgh, Chairman of the Select Commission; Secretary of Labor Ray Marshall; Senators Alan Simpson (R-Wyoming) and Charles Mathias, Jr. (R-Maryland); and Representatives Hamilton Fish, Jr. (R-New York) and Robert McClory (R-Illinois). Except for Civiletti and Marshall, no other Democrat on the commission—the Secretary of State, the Secretary of Health and Human Services, all eight members of Congress, and three public members—voted for change. See *U.S. Immigration Policy and the National Interest, Appendix I to the Staff Report of the Select Commission on Immigration and Refugee Policy: Summary of Commission Recommendations and the Votes, Supplement to the Final Report* (Washington, DC: Government Printing Office, 1981), p. 79.

15. Federation for American Immigration Reform, *The 1991 Federation for American Immigration Reform World Refugee Report,* (Washington, DC: Federation for American Immigration Reform, 1992).

But Peter Brimelow, a senior editor of *Forbes* magazine, recently revived the argument made by William F. Buckley, Jr., in 1982 that American unity was threatened by the immigration of Asians and Latinos. In an article that, not surprisingly, appeared in the *National Review*, he complained that Americans were being urged to abandon "the bonds of a common ethnicity and instead to trust entirely to ideology to hold together their state [polity]." Maintaining that American identity was related to the fact that a majority of Americans are Christian and white, he cited President Calvin Coolidge approvingly for stating unflinchingly at the time of the passage of the national origins immigration quotas in 1924 that " 'America must be kept American.' " Brimelow commented, "Everyone knew what he meant."[16]

THE NEED TO CHANGE ETHNIC POLICIES

There is no dispute as to what Coolidge meant; the only issue is what does it mean to be an American. As suggested earlier, the pro-immigration policies of the last 12 years were based on the premise that the children of newcomers from Laos or Bangladesh can acculturate to an American system of government and laws based on individual rights and liberties—the unifying principle of the civic culture—just as easily as the children of newcomers from Germany or Scotland. The premise that Americans are unified by an idea and

the institutions, symbols, and rituals that express it is one with which President Clinton seems to agree. When he expressed horror about ethnic hatred and killing in Bosnia at a news conference shortly before his inauguration, he added a modest note of pride in the United States by saying, "I know we've got a lot of problems in this country . . . I know the tensions, for example, in Los Angeles . . . but Lord of Mercy, there's 150 different racial and ethnic groups in Los Angeles County. I mean, we are at least making an effort to go forward . . . I know that ethnic divisions are one of the strongest impulses in all of society, all over the world. But we've got to take a stand against it."[17]

There is considerable evidence to support the conclusion that recent immigrants, and especially their children, are adapting to the American civic culture.[18] President Clinton surely is right in asserting that Los Angeles is not Bosnia. But civic unity and ethnic peace cannot be taken for granted, and he and his administration should begin a careful analysis of which immigration and ethnic policies contribute to civic unity and which do not. Of course, civic unity, like health care and environmental protection, will be enhanced by a renewal of the American economy. But whether or not the United States achieves economic growth, it would

16. Peter Brimelow, "Time to Rethink Immigration?" *National Review*, 22 June 1992, pp. 34-35, 44.

17. Account of press conference with President-Elect Bill Clinton, *New York Times International Edition*, 14 Jan. 1993, p. A-8.

18. For a demonstration of the success that American society still has in acculturating immigrants, see Fuchs, *American Kaleidoscope*, chap. 18.

be desirable if the President could persuade the country and Congress to reexamine policies that now promote ethnic division. He should begin that process of persuasion with a major speech on immigration and ethnic policies. It is unlikely that his large policy agenda and his political situation would enable him to make such a speech before 1995, but he should make it as soon as he can. It would go something like this:

"My fellow Americans,

"Tonight I want to speak to you about ethnic conflict in our great country. We live in a world torn by ethnic and religious hatred. Here at home we have racial and ethnic strife, but nothing like that which afflicts peoples in Europe, Asia, and Africa. That is not just a matter of our luck. It is because we are a nation whose unifying idea, proclaimed in our Declaration of Independence, is that all men and women are created equal in dignity regardless of their race, religion, or national ancestry.

"We did not follow that principle through most of our history, and we do not always follow it today. But it is my guiding star. It is the principle that forbids our government from favoring one church over another. It is the principle that guarantees your freedom to express the cultural values and traditions of your ancestors without interference by the state as long as you respect that freedom for others. It is the principle that informs the Fourteenth Amendment promise to all persons within our boundaries that they will receive equal protection of the law. And it is the same principle that enables us to accept as potential Americans immigrants from all over the world, whether they are brown, white, yellow, or black, whether they are Muslims, Christians, Buddhists, Jews, or members of any other religious group or none at all.

"Accepting large numbers of immigrants from vastly different backgrounds—most of whom are related to some of us already here—makes it more important than ever that they and their children learn about America's first principle of respect for the equal dignity of others regardless of race, religion, or national background. That requires all of us to reexamine policies that, no matter how well intended, are having the effect of undermining the principle for which our nation stands and on which its unity and civic peace depend.

"When we welcome lawfully admitted immigrants, we should say to them that our nation will try hard to help them learn English so they can participate fully in our society; we should make it clear that our nation will respect their religious and cultural traditions but will not use tax dollars to support them. We should promise that we will do our best to protect them against any form of discrimination based on race, religion, or national origin but that no government will set aside contracts, jobs, or places at universities and colleges for them based on their ethnicity. And we should encourage them to learn as quickly as possible about the principles, institutions, rituals, holidays, and heros and heroines of this democracy.

"Let me say a few words about what I intend to do to help immigrants and refugees learn these lessons about their new country.

"We should do much more to help immigrants and especially their children learn to read, write, and speak English effectively without compromising in any way the right of their families and communities to encourage them to maintain the language and culture of their ancestors. The main reason that English acquisition is so important, especially for the children, as the vast majority of immigrants already realize, is that competence in English will help them to achieve economic success.

"Most U.S.-born Latinos and Asians actually use English as their primary language,[19] but we are not doing a good enough job with English-language-deficient youngsters in school now. Cities are stretched beyond capacity in their ability to provide English-language training for both adults and children. Compounding that problem is the fact that local school districts are limited in choosing the pedagogical methods that they believe are best suited to help schools teach newcomer children English. Most federal funds are earmarked for bilingual programs, some of which may not be as effective as other methods of teaching English. President Reagan tried, and partly succeeded, to free federal dollars to support the English-language-training decisions made by local educators, a policy that I now endorse. The federal government has no business to be directing local governments as to what educational pedagogies work best to help youngsters learn English, although it does have a strong responsibility to call for and monitor results.[20]

"It is also time to reevaluate many policies that go under the heading of affirmative action. Such policies have come into being with the best of intentions to correct a historical record in which Americans departed from the principles of equal human dignity and equality before the law. Many immigrant-ethnic groups—Irish, Jews, Italians, East Europeans, Asians, and Latinos—were treated with harsh discrimination and sometimes brutality. In the case of Asians and Latinos, those actions were backed with the force of law.

"We are especially ashamed of the history of land grabbing and violence against Native Americans and the enslavement of and systematic segregation and discrimination against African Americans. In the 1960s and early 1970s, we began to deal more honestly and equitably in our national policy toward Native American nations. That is a special relationship based on treaty and other obligations that must always be honored.

"In an effort to remedy the continuing effects of racism against African

19. See Rodolfo De La Garza et al., *Latino Voices: Mexican, Puerto Rican, and Cuban Perspectives on American Politics* (Boulder, CO: Westview Press, 1992). De La Garza's data also revealed that most Hispanics do not think of themselves as either Hispanic or Latino. They prefer to be identified, as do immigrants from Europe or Asia, by their country of origin.

20. For what has gone wrong with bilingual education in the United States, see Rosalie Pedalino Porter, *Forked Tongue: The Politics of Bilingual Education* (New York: Basic Books, 1990). See also Joseph Berger, "School Programs Assailed as Bilingual Bureaucracy," *New York Times*, 4 Jan. 1993. On the importance of English to the global economy, see "English: Out to Conquer the World," *U.S. News and World Report*, 18 Feb. 1985, pp. 49-57.

Americans, we began programs of affirmative action under President Lyndon Johnson to enlarge their opportunities. It was not intended at first that other groups would be designated as the beneficiaries of such programs, but federal and state governments soon began to designate Asians and Hispanics, among all immigrant-ethnic groups, as minorities for purposes of affirmative action. The intention was to make American society as open and inclusive as possible for members of nonwhite groups, since they were the ones who had been denied equal opportunity one way or another under the force of law. But affirmative action for immigrant-ethnic groups cannot be justified by a theory of past discrimination because immigrants to the United States now and in recent years—more than three quarters of whom are Asian and Latino—are not the descendants of those who suffered discrimination at the hands of Americans in the past. Nor can affirmative action be justified for such groups by any theory of competitive disadvantage, since many immigrants have relatively high skills and levels of education and a majority of those who are disadvantaged by poverty and other factors are native-born white Americans.

"There are many instances where affirmative action programs are pitting one group against another, setting in motion ethnic competition and divisiveness that is harmful to all of us. To expand economic opportunity through affirmative action for those who have traditionally been excluded is good. To enforce proportionality according to some population formula in the letting of contracts, hiring of workers, and admission of students to colleges and universities is bad.[21] We should not encourage Americans, including immigrants who are citizens-to-be, to believe that the only way they can obtain benefits is to identify themselves ethnically. But that is what some well-intentioned laws and regulations do. One example is the Voting Rights Act, as amended in 1982, which obliges the gerrymander of political jurisdictions to promote the election of ethnic candidates. There is nothing un-American about members of ethnic groups wanting to choose representatives of their own kind. And any action to limit voters in making that choice imposed by gerrymandering or other

21. A recent example of how hard affirmative action programs pit one group against another came when Republican Governor George Voinovich of Ohio decided to award minority set-aside contracts to companies owned by immigrants from India, 19 of which received contracts under the state minority program. African American elected officials immediately protested that the action was illegal because the Asian Indian businessmen did not constitute an economically disadvantaged group. But one of the Indian businessmen countered that the black-owned firms continue to get, in his words, "all the work." See Gerard Lim, "Asian Indians Recognized as Legitimate Minority in Ohio," *Asian Week*, 22 Jan. 1993, p. 3. Another example of bad public policy recommendations is in the report of the U.S. Commission on Civil Rights in the form of the commission's frequent support of charges of discrimination against Latinos by the authorities in Washington, D.C. The commission called for more Latinos in the District's governing bodies to make up for alleged discrimination against them. But its attempt at some kind of proportional representation did not take into account that many Hispanics are illegal aliens and that most Latinos in the city are recent immigrants with a limited command of English. Its recommendations could lead to discrimination against qualified blacks.

election rules constitutes discrimination, which must be stopped. But our laws should not be used through gerrymander or in any other way to encourage immigrants and others to believe that the only way they can achieve fair representation in the American political system is through ethnic representation.[22] Unfortunately, that is what the law does now. It is a mistake for our government to push voters to believe that all of their interests—as women, men, parents, workers, business persons, Californians, and the like—are to be represented only or even best on an ethnic basis. Pushed to its logical extreme, Vietnamese will want Vietnamese representatives only, Dominicans will want Dominicans, and so on.

"We must hold fast to the principle that individuals should be judged on merit regardless of ethnic background. Of course, the reality is that discrimination occurs in housing, employment,

---

22. For an early and still the most trenchant analysis of the damaging effects of the 1982 Voting Rights Act amendments that oblige gerrymandering on ethnic and racial grounds, see Abigail M. Thernstrom, *Whose Votes Count? Affirmative Action and Minority Voting Rights* (Cambridge, MA: Harvard University Press, 1987). In many jurisdictions, the Republican Party has developed a strategy of heavily packing black voters into inner-city districts, leaving nearby suburban jurisdictions more Republican than when they were racially mixed. Federal courts have not overruled the legislative justification for racial and ethnic gerrymandering, which is that the votes of blacks and Latinos are somehow diluted unless districts are gerrymandered to promote the election of blacks and Latinos. Of course, the main provisions of the Voting Rights Act are superb and should be enforced thoroughly, as they have been. See Linda Greenhouse, "Court Backs Minority Voting Districts," *New York Times*, 3 Mar. 1993.

contracting, police protection, and other aspects of public life, particularly against African Americans, and it happens every day. Race has always been the most important dividing line in our society, and we live today with the legacy of government-protected slavery and segregation. Immigrants and new Americans should understand that this nation owes a deep debt to the descendants of American slaves, and it is for them that the key programs of affirmative action were initiated.

"Even affirmative action programs for African Americans were never intended to last forever. There is considerable evidence that many of them have been helpful in giving chances to African Americans who would have been shut out from some opportunities without them. It should be a matter of pride to all Americans that we have so many black leaders who have taken advantage of those opportunities in all walks of life, including the United States Congress. They have overcome enormous obstacles and proven that hard work and ability will win out when people are given the chance.[23] And we still need affirmative action to recruit African Americans for jobs from which they have been excluded. But we should recognize that most affirmative action programs do not get at the problems of poverty, bad schooling, drugs, and competition for low-wage go-nowhere jobs that plague the inner cities of our nation, problems that sometimes are intensified by illegal immigration. Problems of ethnic conflict are not

---

23. For a more detailed analysis of the costs and benefits of affirmative action, see Fuchs, *American Kaleidoscope*, chaps. 22 and 23.

limited to the major cities, but it is in them that such tensions are palpable.

"We need a five-part attack on the problems that impede ethnic harmony and American unity, and I will appoint task forces made up of civic leaders from many aspects of American life and from different backgrounds to recommend legislation based on my guidelines.

"First, I want to know the most effective method of linking sanctions against employers who knowingly hire illegal aliens to a reliable system of identifying employees eligible to work. I am convinced that a system consistent with civil liberty protections for all Americans can be developed and phased in over a period of five to ten years to curtail illegal migration. Most illegal aliens are good, ambitious people seeking to improve their lives, but that is not the issue. Not every such person in the world can be admitted to the United States. We admit 700,000 to 800,000 immigrants a year and more than 100,000 refugees legally. We decide to do this to reunify families and in the interests of our nation. But it is not in the national interest to wink at illegal migration. We don't need a back door for low-wage, exploitable workers. We don't need or want to have a class of workers unprotected by the law. We don't want to build fences on our borders or interdict boats at sea or have periodic roundups of aliens on buses, street corners, or at places of business. The best way to prevent those things from happening is to have an effective means of identifying those who are eligible to work in the country when they apply for a new job. If the system is effective—

and the one we have now is not—it will penalize employers who knowingly hire illegal aliens and cut back the flow of illegal migrants to a much smaller number.

"Second, I will appoint a task force to recommend how we can most efficiently spend federal dollars to speed the effective learning of English by immigrants, especially the youngsters, so they will not be closed out of opportunities in a continental and global economy that relies increasingly on the effective use of English.

"Third, I will appoint a task force to provide a plan that will show how we can phase out government-enforced affirmative action programs that rely heavily on numbers as a measure of success in expanding opportunities for nonwhites while retaining and improving programs that emphasize recruitment and training to expand opportunities for all disadvantaged Americans. I will ask that task force to include in its plan the phasing out of proportionality-based affirmative action for all groups except American-born African Americans by the year 2000 and to have such programs eliminated entirely by the year 2010.

"Fourth, I want a plan for stepped-up vigorous enforcement of all anti-discrimination legislation, including enforcement of constitutionally sanctioned legislation against hate crimes. I want to know how best to coordinate the activities of federal, state, and local agencies in preventing and punishing discrimination in housing, banking, education, and employment. Housing discrimination leading to segregation may be the reason for the worst of inner-city problems, and we must do everything we can to try to end it.[24] I want a plan to end the segregation that has been imposed on African Americans, Puerto Ricans, and dark-skinned Americans in our inner cities. In the meantime, we must provide more police protection, better education, and better health care and, most important of all, we must work to create decent jobs that make choices real for Americans who now believe they are without choices. The task force with these responsibilities should also make recommendations as to how best to guarantee that police authorities will not abuse their power in dealing with African Americans, Latinos, Asians, and Native Americans.

"Fifth, I will appoint a task force to provide recommendations that will help our states and localities emphasize a civic education in all schools that respects diversity and most em-

phatically stresses those aspects of American history, principles, and law that make us a nation based on the ideal of individual rights regardless of race, religion, or national background. I want to promote a civic education that makes clear this nation's repudiation of the old European model of ethnic group rights that seems to lead to never ending strife.

"My fellow Americans, diversity is an American strength, but unless we protect the central principle of individual rights that makes diversity possible, we will drift toward racial and ethnic separatism. This administration will not allow that drift to take place. We will respect and cherish the great diversity that comes to America now from almost every country in the world, even as we enact policies that help all who live and work lawfully in this country to have genuine equality of opportunity and to unify as Americans.

"I count on your help in fulfilling this great American dream."

24. Douglas S. Massey and Nancy A. Denton make that case persuasively in a brilliantly argued book, *American Apartheid: Segregation and the Making of the Underclass* (Cambridge, MA: Harvard University Press, 1993).

ANNALS, *AAPSS*, **530**, November 1993

"Of Every Hue and Caste": Race, Immigration, and Perceptions of Pluralism

By PETER I. ROSE

ABSTRACT: Taking its title from Walt Whitman's *Song of Myself*, this article reconsiders the conceptualization of "pluralism" in light of an ongoing debate about race and ethnicity in what the poet called this "Nation of many nations." While focused mainly on white and black aspects of identity politics, the issues reviewed have implications for all Americans. These include the nature and meaning of minority status and the responses of those so designated to their situations and to each other. It is suggested that many of the concerns expressed today about challenges posed by Americans who wish to assert the uniqueness of their heritages and to encourage others to recognize them are but variations on an old theme—save for one crucial factor. This time those most vigorously touting the importance of such pride in diversity are representatives of black and other racial minorities.

Peter I. Rose, Sophia Smith Professor and director of the American Studies Diploma Program at Smith College, is currently a visiting fellow of St. Catherine's College, Oxford. He is the author of They and We; The Subject Is Race; Strangers in Their Midst; *and* Mainstream and Margins. *In addition to this issue of* The Annals, *he is editor of* The Study of Society; The Ghetto and Beyond; Nation of Nations; Americans from Africa; Seeing Ourselves; Views from Abroad; Working with Refugees; *and, with S. Rothman and W. J. Wilson,* Through Different Eyes.

NOT long ago, after years of refurbishing, the immigration facility at Ellis Island was rededicated. In one celebration after another, Americans of different backgrounds —European, African, Asian, and Latino—paid homage to all those things that that portal to America was said to represent: shelter, opportunity, liberty, justice. One person after another extolled the wonders of "the world's oldest democracy"; "this haven in a stormy sea"; "our Nation of Nations"; "the house that we call Freedom."

Yet some who attended the festivities and many more who heard the speeches on radio or television found it all a bit disingenuous. While acknowledging the fact that there had been remarkable advances in intergroup relations in the century that had just passed, especially the integration of the children and grandchildren of the "tired and poor and tempest-tost" who came through Ellis Island in the years between 1892 and 1954, and great successes in the realm of civil rights for all citizens, especially during the last three decades, they knew that just across the harbor—and throughout the land— there were struggles that belied the lofty rhetoric of acceptance, inclusion, and unity. There still are.

Wretched slums not all that different from those that existed when the reception center was first dedicated still pock the cityscape. These days, however, instead of the babble of German, Italian, Polish, Yiddish, and brogue-heavy English, so confusing and offensive to the ears of many old Americans who felt they were being overrun with "queer and repulsive"[1] alien elements, the urban centers resound in Spanish, Chinese, Korean, Vietnamese, and Black English. These days the voices of the ghetto poor are more often than not those of people whose skins are considerably darker than those of the "swarthy" Italians, Poles, Slavs, and Jews who came in great numbers in the late nineteenth and early twentieth century. But what many face—poverty, alienation, rivalry with others in similar straits, and envy for those who have managed to escape—has a depressing familiarity, particularly to those close at hand.

City councilors, police authorities, social workers, schoolteachers, factory managers, storekeepers, journalists, bail bondsmen, welfare mothers, gang members, local residents, and nearby neighbors are the real experts in urban sociology. They know that the melting pots are seething caldrons of competition and intergroup tension, and, to paraphrase Bob Dylan, they do not need outside pundits to tell them that they are boiling over. Consider the headlines: "FROM KILLING FIELDS TO MEAN STREETS"; "BLACKS VS. BROWNS"; "LATIN MASS"; "BONFIRE IN CROWN HEIGHTS"; "DANGEROUS LIAISONS"; "THE NEW POLITICS OF RACE." The last phrase suggests that something is different in the ways various groups interact with one another.

Dramatic changes have occurred, especially in the relativity of poverty,

1. Hutchins Hapgood, *The Spirit of the Ghetto* (New York: Funk & Wagnalls, 1902), p. 5.

the deterioration of communal structures, the intensity of the violence, and the technology of intergroup combat in the inner-city areas, but, in certain ways, it may be said *plus ça change, plus c'est la même chose*—the more things change, the more they stay the same. At bottom, what is called the new politics of race is more a variation on an old theme, one that has been heard since the earliest days of nationhood.

THE OLD POLITICS OF RACE

Alexis de Tocqueville, a great admirer of American democracy, predicted that, even with the emancipation of the slaves, the racial situation in the United States would be a continuing source of domestic unrest. Writing in the 1830s, Tocqueville expressed the fear that the majority of whites would never overcome their views of the innateness of their own superiority and that the majority of blacks would never lose their enmity for the humiliation and suffering they had experienced.[2] Tocqueville claimed that what we now call "racism" would "perpetually haunt the imagination of Americans, like a painful dream."[3]

Nearly a century and a half after Tocqueville's famous visit to America, another Frenchman, the sociologist Raymond Aron, offered another assessment.

"As far as I am concerned, the greatest achievement of American society is to have drawn millions of people from the lower classes of Europe and made them into good American citizens. That is an extraordinary performance, an unprecedented marvel of acculturation. But you didn't do it without paying a heavy price. ... You have permanently un-integrated fringe, consisting chiefly of blacks and Puerto-Ricans. .... You did very well in assimilating national minorities, but not nearly as well with racial minorities."[4]

Aron, highlighting the dramatic demographic changes that had occurred between the 1830s and the then-present day, made specific reference to the fact that America had long ago ceased to be a society whose principal groups were an Anglo-American majority and a black minority. It had become "a nation of immigrants."[5]

Despite the poetic ring to the expression, historians of the period point to the fact that not all or even most of the newcomers, including those millions of "lower-class" Europeans, were welcomed with equanimity. Once in the United States, they

2. See Peter I. Rose, introduction to *Through Different Eyes: Black and White Perspectives on American Race Relations*, ed. Peter I. Rose, Stanley Rothman, and William J. Wilson (New York: Oxford University Press, 1973), p. v.

3. Alexis de Tocqueville, *Democracy in America*, Henry Reeve text revised by Francis Bowen (New York: Vintage Books, 1945), 2:391-92.

4. Quoted from "Talk with a 'Reasonable Man,' " by Milton Viorst. Originally appeared in the *New York Times Magazine*, 19 Apr. 1970, p. 96. Copyright © 1970 by Milton Viorst.

5. For recent assessments, see Ellis Cose, *A Nation of Strangers: Prejudice, Politics and the Populating of America* (New York: Morrow, 1992); Lawrence H. Fuchs, *The American Kaleidoscope: Race, Ethnicity and the Civic Culture* (Hanover, NH: Wesleyan University Press, 1990); Roger Daniels, *Coming to America* (New York: Harper, 1990); Walter Nugent, *Crossings: The Great Transatlantic Migrations, 1870-1941* (Bloomington: Indiana University Press, 1992).

often found themselves ranked and treated according to a congeries of criteria that determined their collective as well as individual place in a hierarchy of acceptability and acceptance. Time of arrival, region of origin, cultural attributes, religious preferences, and physical appearance were among the factors that determined how they were greeted and how they were treated. It was already an old story.[6]

When this country was established, the new nation, like the original colonies, was overwhelmingly white and Protestant, and most citizens hoped it would stay that way. There was great resistance by the Anglo-Americans—who came to call themselves "native Americans"— when émigrés from poverty-ridden Ireland sought refuge in this country. Their presence triggered the first major attempt to restrict immigration, but no formal, specifically targeted restriction against the Irish or any single "nationality" was imposed. That dubious distinction came in 1882, when the Chinese Exclusion Act was enacted. Not long afterward, renewed fear of foreign agitators combined with deeply rooted sentiments against certain groups led to the formation of the Immigration Restriction League. Founded in 1894, it lobbied against those regarded by many as members of "unassimilable races."

In his classic lament, *The Passing of the Great Race*, published in 1916, Madison Grant called for the exclu-

sion of members of "inferior" races, specifically the "Alpine, Mediterranean and Jewish breeds."[7] Grant's views were echoed by many contemporaries. Several years later, for example, John Rowland, in an essay entitled "A Connecticut Yankee Speaks His Mind," saw the "Nordic stock in America . . . doomed to extinction in competition with the ancient, generalized stocks from southeastern Europe and Asia minor." He suggested that, to avoid further contamination of people like himself, "the one thing that we can do right now is to lock and bar the gate."[8]

Rowland's xenophobic essay was published in 1924, the same year that the most restrictive immigration law in American history was passed, a law that effectively closed the already heavily guarded gates, keeping millions of immigrants and would-be refugees, most especially the very groups singled out by the likes of Grant and Roberts and Rowland, from entering the United States. By 1929, when the Reed-Johnson National Origins Act of 1924 was fully operative, a total of 165,000 persons were allowed to enter in any given year; 82 percent of those eligible were to come from countries of Northern and Western Europe, 16 percent from Southern and Eastern Europe, and only 2 percent from the rest of the world.

6. See Ronald Takaki, *Iron Cages: Race and Culture in Nineteenth-Century America* (New York: Knopf, 1979).

7. Madison Grant, *The Passing of the Great Race* (New York: Scribner, 1916), pp. 88-92 passim.

8. John Rowland, "A Connecticut Yankee Speaks His Mind," *Outlook*, 136:478-80 (March 1924). See also Kenneth Roberts, *Why Europe Leaves Home* (Indianapolis: Bobbs Merrill, 1922).

Those who had managed to enter before the heavily biased Quota Law was implemented had hardly been unfamiliar with deprivation or exploitation prior to their emigration. Indeed, it was the promise of a better life that drew so many poor people to America. Yet, with the exception of the East European Jews and those in several other much smaller groups, most who came—either as temporary sojourners or to settle here permanently—had had little experience with categorical discrimination because of their own cultural distinctiveness, their religious affiliations, beliefs, or practices, or their politics, nor had they had much experience interacting with persons unlike themselves. They quickly learned that in the New World they were different from those in the dominant group and different from other so-called minorities.

The consequences of this were several. Not surprisingly, coping with both phenomena contributed to the strengthening of in-group allegiances as newcomers found themselves increasingly dependent on countrymen who shared their ascribed identities. This led to the development of networks for employment and welfare and for taking collective action against rival groups. It also led to the adoption of community-based political tactics to press for rights, services, and recognition. These developments, in time, would enhance the acceleration of their entry into the wider society as they evolved—psychologically and politically—from being immigrants to becoming American-style ethnics.[9]

While group rights were not to be officially recognized for more than half a century, many had developed skills for engaging in bloc power to ensure the ability of those like themselves to overcome barriers of prejudice and discrimination. Yet it is also true that, despite the fact that they had often faced considerable racist sentiment and blatant discrimination themselves, it was rare for the new ethnics to identify with the African Americans, to see their situations in any sense as analogous. On the contrary, whatever else was going on, part of their general acculturation involved taking on many of the prejudices of those in the dominant society.

In time, overcoming the considerable hostility to their presence, most of those known as "national minorities" did succeed in becoming "ordinary" Americans,[10] and saw themselves as such. So did many others.

Wherever our parents came from, whatever language we spoke at home, we reached for a common overriding identity. Those born abroad, or to immigrants, understood that in part it was an identity given to us by the country. We took it with pleasure, when we sang " . . . land where our fathers died" we knew it was not our fathers we were singing of but it was sure our country. Our teachers knew that. Everybody knew that.[11]

The descendants of the involuntary migrants from Africa who, in

9. See, for example, Alejandro Portes and Ruben Rumbaut, *Immigrant America: A Portrait* (Berkeley: University of California Press, 1990), pp. 94-140 passim.

10. See Stephen Steinberg, *The Ethnic Myth: Race, Ethnicity, and Class in America*, 2d ed. (Boston: Beacon Press, 1989), esp. chap. 2, "The Ethnic Crisis in American Society," pp. 44-74.

11. A. M. Rosenthal, "The Lucky Americans," *New York Times*, 8 Dec. 1992. Copyright © 1992 by The New York Times Company. Reprinted by permission.

many ways, had long been quite ordinary Americans in manners and mores and religious practices were not so lucky. They remained marginalized. This paradoxical reality has not only continued to affect relationships between black and white people—including those now called "white ethnics"—but also those many African Americans have had with other newcomers, including those who, while frequently categorized as racial minorities themselves, were and remain nationality groups, too.

THE IDEA OF PLURALISM

The immigrant-to-ethnic metamorphosis of the newcomers and their politicization, while strengthening communal ties and enhancing leverage, served to many outside their communities as evidence of persisting clannishness, feeding fears of disloyalty or, at the least, conflicting allegiances. Those in positions of power and authority worried aloud about subversion, about the fragmentation of the polity, about the possibility that the "hyphenates" might be responsible for "the disuniting of America." " 'Americanism is a matter of the spirit and of the soul. Our allegiance must be purely to the United States. The one absolutely certain way of bringing this nation to ruin . . . would be to permit it to become a tangle of squabbling nationalities.' "[12]

Theodore Roosevelt and others who agreed with his remarks and his view that " 'there is no room in this country for hyphenated Americanism' "[13] advocated the acceleration of procedures that would discourage any thoughts of separatism while holding out the carrot of full partnership. Integration was to depend on eshewing distinctiveness and fully accepting the ways of the dominant group.

The promoters of such a policy sometimes invoked the image of the melting pot, but savvy listeners would realize that they were less interested in what the new Americans would bring to any new social alloy than in controlling the damage the immigrants might inflict on the body politic. Regardless of the colorful rhetoric, it was forced assimilation rather than fusion that was most favored.

Some of the immigrants and some of their supporters, seeing through the rhetorical legerdemain of what came to be known as Americanization, offered alternatives. Perhaps the most thoughtful and surely the most effective came from a group of liberal and radical intellectuals, a mixed group of old Americans and new ones. The concept of cultural pluralism was to become the watchword of an ideology first formally presented in 1915 by the philosopher Horace Kallen, himself an immigrant from Eastern Europe.[14]

The basic premise was that there is strength in diversity, that being proud of one's past and appreciating where one came from complements rather than compromises membership in an ever more heterogeneous

12. From a speech delivered by Theodore Roosevelt in 1917, as quoted in *Roosevelt in the Kansas City Star*, ed. Ralph Stout (Boston: Houghton, Mifflin, 1921), p. 137.

13. Ibid.
14. Horace Kallen, "Democracy versus the Melting Pot," *Nation*, 18 Feb. 1915, pp. 190-94; ibid., 25 Feb. 1915, pp. 217-20.

society. To Kallen and such allies as Jane Addams, Lillian Wald, Randolph Bourne, and John Dewey, the United States was not a fondue of amalgamation but a symphony of accommodation.[15] Pushing his own metaphor, Kallen saw the orchestra —that is, the society—as consisting of groups of instruments—nationalities—playing their separate parts while together making beautiful music resonant with harmony and good feeling.

Kallen's pluralism was especially appealing to the immigrants from Eastern and Southern Europe. At the time, others, including those in the small Asian communities and the growing Latino ones, seem to have paid it little mind. The same was true of the far larger black community. For good reason. It was heavily biased, "encapsulated," as John Higham aptly put it, "in white ethnocentrism."[16]

While generally sympathetic and frequently in league with supporters of better treatment to those still called Negroes,[17] few of the pluralists had had much to say about the contribution of those from Africa, or, for that matter, from Asia or Latin America, to the society they liked to characterize as "the new America." As Bob Suzuki and Nicholas Appleton point out, when first proposed, "pluralism in the United States was concerned with liberty and equality [of European immigrants] and not with pro-

moting the historic identities of non-English subcultures."[18] The latter was not to come until the last decades of the twentieth century, when, as shall be noted, "multiculturalism" became an alternate shibboleth, a slogan most enthusiastically endorsed by nonwhite Americans and looked upon with considerable suspicion by many others.

The acculturation and acceptance of the "national minorities" to which Raymond Aron referred did occur, but not overnight. It was a slow and uneven process, taking place mainly in the four decades between the mid-1920s and the mid-1960s, a time when immigration from outside was almost at a standstill and debates shifted from the rights of foreigners to the rights of Americans; a time when the society underwent a series of dramatic political and economic reversals as well: boom, bust, war, peace, prosperity, and the wrenching conflicts in Vietnam and the streets of America. Affecting the speed of the integration were a number of cultural, social, and situational factors, many related to these ups and downs.

Despite periodic resurgences of old prejudices and the implementation of new ways of blocking entry to neighborhoods, jobs, and social institutions, and a number of serious interethnic conflicts,[19] white ethnics did begin to move from the margins into the mainstream. Especially after World

15. Kallen, "Democracy versus the Melting Pot," 25 Feb. 1915, p. 220.

16. John Higham, *Send These to Me* (New York: Atheneum, 1975), p. 208.

17. See John Roche, *In Quest for the Dream: The Development of Civil Rights and Human Relations in Modern America* (New York: Macmillan, 1963), pp. 86-87.

18. Nicholas Appleton, *Cultural Pluralism in Education* (New York: Longman, 1983), p. 3.

19. See, for example, Ronald H. Bayor, *Neighbors in Conflict: The Irish, Germans, Jews, and Italians of New York City, 1929-1941* (Baltimore, MD: Johns Hopkins University Press, 1978).

War II, often abetted by such entitle-ments as the G.I. Bill for armed ser-vice veterans, the arrivistes faced a world of expanding opportunities and took advantage of them. While some were left behind, increasing numbers moved to new homes in new neigh-borhoods where they were to enjoy life as proud, patriotic Americans, of-ten defining themselves in class terms rather than strictly ethnic ones.

One result of their "making it" was the loosening of many bonds to old communities. But they were rarely severed completely. Even in what some saw as a "twilight of [white] ethnic-ity,"[20] there was almost always a glow of nostalgia and the retention of sym-bolic ties.[21] Yet, ironically, for many who were also well on the way to what Milton Gordon once called "struc-tural assimilation,"[22] the dying em-bers were to be fanned afresh in a reaction to three trends that occurred in the 1960s: the Black Power or Black Consciousness movement, the renewal of immigration, and the con-tentious debates over the meaning of multiculturalism.

BLACK MIGRANTS

Toward the end of the period of the Great Migration, the sons and daughters of former slaves and their grandchildren began moving north seeking to find acceptance in what, like the immigrants, they, too, saw as a "promised land."[23] It was in the north where those who were in so many ways the least foreign but still the most alienated of all—save, per-haps, for the native peoples—often came face to face with a new problem: ethnic diversity. It was in the cities of the north where the seeds of consid-erable interminority tension so often highlighted in the press today—blacks versus members of the old white ethnic groups, such as the Irish in Boston, Italians in Brooklyn; blacks versus Jews, as in Crown Heights; blacks versus Latinos, as in Miami; blacks versus Asians, as in Los Ange-les—were sown alongside, and, in some instances, in lieu of, more traditional black-white conflict.

In the segregated south, those called Negroes had been well aware that they were a people apart. But their sepa-rateness was largely a harshly en-forced relegation to a fixed subordi-nate status, an ascribed and main-tained marginality based not so much on cultural differences as on far more base assumptions of absolute inferi-ority. Jim Crow laws that emerged in the wake of the brief post-Civil War

20. See Richard D. Alba, *Italian Ameri-cans: Into the Twilight of Ethnicity* (Englewood Cliffs, NJ: Prentice-Hall, 1985).

21. Herbert M. Gans, "Symbolic Ethnicity: The Future of Ethnic Groups and Cultures in America," *Ethnic and Racial Studies*, 2:1 (Jan. 1979). See also Stephen Steinberg, *The Ethnic Myth*, rev. ed. (Boston: Beacon Press, 1989), esp. pp. 44-74 passim.

22. Milton M. Gordon, *Assimilation in American Life* (New York: Oxford University Press, 1964), pp. 80-81.

23. See St. Clair Drake and Horace Cay-ton, *Black Metropolis: A Study of Negro Life in a Northern City* (New York: Harcourt, Brace, 1945); Allan H. Speak, *Black Chicago: The Making of a Negro Ghetto, 1890-1920* (Chicago: University of Chicago Press, 1967); and the much more recent Nicholas Lemann, *The Promised Land: The Great Black Migration and How It Changed America* (New York: Knopf, 1991). See also John H. Bracey, August Meier, and Elliott Rudwick, eds., *The Rise of the Ghetto* (Belmont, CA: Wadsworth, 1971).

period of Reconstruction returned them for many intents and purposes to their preslavery status as America's *Untermenschen*. One result was to institutionalize an apartheid system in which the South would formally remain—at least until the mid-1950s —along with much of the rest of the country, what Pierre van den Berghe once aptly labeled a *"Herrenvolk* democracy."[24]

When the African Americans started to move north, it was a given, a fact of life, that white people, like those they had known back home, no matter how poor, were privileged members of the society, privileged enemies. Thus even the optimism with which they undertook the city-bound movements to New York, Philadelphia, Cleveland, Detroit, and Chicago was always tempered by the realization that northern whites might not be all that different from those in the south. They were more or less an already known entity to be guarded against. The immigrants were something else altogether.[25]

Owing to the precariousness of their economic situation, the African American migrants sought housing in the cheapest parts of town. By the time of their movement, many of the areas were already heavy with the presence of Jews, Italians, Slavs, and the others who looked stranger, sounded stranger, and acted stranger

than the sort of white folks they knew and knew about. In a number of cities, it would not be long before some of those who settled in these mixed communities would have their confusion compounded by the fact that the ghettos that seemed to be serving as way stations for the others were, for them, more characteristic of their original, medieval form, that is, places of confinement.[26]

Recognition of the relativity of their freedom was further aggravated by the belief—which sometimes had a sound basis in truth—that it was the "foreigners" who were most directly in control of their lives. They were frequently the people who employed them, sold to them, rented to them, loaned them money, and in general leap-frogged their way to positions of even greater power and influence in the economic nexus, politically, and in public institutions—as policemen, welfare workers, and school teachers—and, frequently, right out of the neighborhoods.[27]

For many, immersed in their own struggles, the fact that the immigrants around them had had hard lives before, that many of them had also been persecuted and continued to be discriminated against, meant very little, if they were aware of such situations at all. Seen either as agents of The Man or as interlopers, and sometimes as both, the Jews and

24. See Pierre van den Berghe, *Race and Racism* (New York: John Wiley, 1967).

25. For a brief but pointed discussion of this phenomenon, see Gilbert Ofsofsky, *Harlem: The Making of a Ghetto, Negro New York, 1890-1930* (New York: Harper & Row, 1964), esp. chap. 6, "The Other Harlem: Roots of Instability," pp. 81-91.

26. See Stanley Lieberson, *Ethnic Patterns in American Cities* (New York: Free Press of Glencoe, 1963); and Karl E. Taeuber and Alma F. Taeuber, *Negroes in Cities: Residential Segregation and Neighborhood Change* (New York: Atheneum, 1965), esp. pp. 16-19.

27. James Baldwin, "The Harlem Ghetto," in *Notes of a Native Son*, ed. James Baldwin (Boston: Beacon Press, 1955), pp. 57-72.

other white ethnics[28]—and, in time, others, such as Cubans in Miami[29] and Koreans in New York and Los Angeles[30]—were close-at-hand targets for their bitter rage at the "oppressive system," a rage often expressed in what, heard from the mouths of others, would be called "nativist sentiment."

In the 1950s, Ralph Ellison spoke of the black migrants in the northern slums, who "like some tragic people out of mythology . . . aspired to escape from its own unhappy homeland to the apparent peace of a distant mountain; but which, in migrating, made some fatal error of judgment and fell into a great chasm of maze-like passages that promise ever to lead to the mountain but end ever against the wall."[31] He knew who they were but, he argued, others did not see them; they were "invisible."

In the early 1960s, Michael Harrington identified them as part of "the other America."[32]

By the mid-1960s, those in that "other" America, in particular those who were black, were not only known by all but heard by all. The cries for justice, sounded mainly in the southern campaigns led by traditional civil rights leaders, mingled with other cries—for assertiveness, for retribution—as the civil rights movement for inclusion turned into a Black Power revolt and as a spirit of ethnicization spread through the African American communities.

Many white Americans, including numerous children of European immigrants and many others now living at some distance from what Kenneth Clark called "the dark ghettos,"[33] were, by then, firmly imbued with the spirit of Kallenesque pluralism. Yet they were quite unprepared for what blacks—and those in some of the other racial minorities who often used Black Power advocates as their models and frequently adapted the tactics and rhetoric of Black Consciousness to their own conditions—began to demand, and to do, often in the name of cultural recognition. Organized struggles for community control of neighborhoods, requests for assurances of representation in jobs and on campuses, demands for special programs in universities and equal time in the curriculum are examples of the sorts of activities that seemed particularly threatening.[34]

Jules Feiffer captured the essence of the changing mood in a cartoon in which one of his white liberal characters says, "Civil rights used to be

28. See Jim Sleeper, *The Closest of Strangers* (New York: Norton, 1990); Hillel Levine and Lawrence Harmon, *The Death of an American Jewish Community: A Tragedy of Good Intentions* (New York: Free Press, 1992).

29. Raymond Mohl, "On the Edge: Blacks and Hispanics in Metropolitan Miami since 1959," *Florida Historical Quarterly* (July 1990).

30. K. Hugh Kim, "Blacks against Korean Merchants: An Interpretation of Contributory Factors," *Migration World*, 18(5):11-15 (1990); Susumu Awanohara and Shim Jae Hoon, "Melting Pot Boils Over," *Far Eastern Economic Review*, 14 May 1992, pp. 9-10.

31. Ralph Ellison, *Shadow and Act* (New York: New American Library, 1953), p. 285.

32. Michael Harrington, *The Other America* (New York: Macmillan, 1962).

33. Kenneth B. Clark, *Dark Ghetto: Dilemmas of Social Power* (New York: Harper and Row, 1965).

34. See, for example, Diane Ravitch, *The Great School Wars: New York City, 1805-1973: A History of the Public Schools as Battlefields of Social Change* (New York: Basic Books, 1974).

much more tolerable until the Negroes got into it."[35]

Of course, not all blacks in the 1960s were militants, and not all militants were poor, ghetto-dwelling members of what has become known by the controversial term "urban underclass." Nor are they today. There are many, probably the majority, who want to have what so many others simply take for granted; who wish to be judged, in the words of Martin Luther King, Jr., not "by the color of their skin but by the content of their character."[36] Yet it remains a fact of life that the bus drivers, nurses, auto workers, schoolteachers, and social workers, even the lawyers and doctors and professors among them, are, to this day, far from free of color-based prejudice, far from free from distorting assumptions about how they got to where they are—and what they are doing there anyway.[37]

In the eyes of others, and often in their own eyes, even at the dawn of an era when the President's cabinet, for the first time in history, "looks like America," most black Americans still remain a people apart. "Black students at Yale University, black members of the Omaha police force, even black passengers on an airline flight," Andrew Hacker reports, "never cease to be aware of their white surroundings."[38] Rich, poor, well-educated or illiterate, having police records or Ph.D.s, they are reminded of this fact of American life by both blatant and subtle indicators at every turn. It is something Hacker rightly claims that most white Americans, even those intellectually well aware of how black people have suffered due to the inequities imposed on them, simply cannot fathom.[39]

THE NEW IMMIGRATION

In "The Politics of a Multiethnic Society," Nathan Glazer suggested that, in addition to the two paradigms of intergroup relations in the United States—one "Southern," essentially the familiar dichotomous black-white model in which the principal characteristic was the color bar or caste line of privilege; the other "Northern," characterized by a spectrum of competing European groups arranged in a fluid hierarchy[40]—that he and Daniel Patrick Moynihan had specified in the preface to the revised edition of *Beyond the Melting Pot* in 1970, there might well be a third in the offing. With the dramatic changes in patterns of immigration flows, following the passage of the Immigration Reform Act of 1965, he anticipated the development of the new type, a "Western" or "Southwestern" one.

35. The Jules Feiffer cartoon, from Robert Lantz, Candida Donadio Literary Agency, Inc., appears in Peter I. Rose, *They and We*, 2d ed. (New York: Random House, 1974), p. 79.

36. Martin Luther King, Jr., "I Have a Dream," *SCLC Newsletter*, 12:8 (Sept. 1963).

37. See Jack Miles, "Blacks vs. Browns," *Atlantic*, 270(4):41-45, 48, 50-52, 54-68 (Oct. 1992).

38. Andrew Hacker, *Two Nations: Black and White, Separate, Hostile, Unequal* (New York: Scribners, 1992), p. 22.

39. See Martin Kilson, "Realism about the Black Experience," *Dissent*, pp. 519-22 (Fall 1990), a response to Shelby Steele, "The Memory of Enemies: On the Black Experience in America," ibid., pp. 326-32 (Summer 1990).

40. Nathan Glazer, "The Politics of a Multiethnic Society," in *Ethnic Dilemmas, 1964-1982* (Cambridge, MA: Harvard University Press, 1983), pp. 215-336.

It should be noted that at the time the new bill was being debated, those working most diligently for the removal of quota restrictions imposed in the 1920s assumed that the beneficiaries of the lowered barriers would be, in the main, Europeans, as had most immigrants before. Yet one of the unexpected consequences of the 1965 act was the entry of millions of newcomers from Asia and Latin America.

Many who worried about what such changes might portend would agree with Ellis Cose's observation that "Congress had ended up with a most expansive result—one ensuring that an already steady stream of strange people knocking on America's door would swell into a torrent, heightening not only the potential for ethnic enrichment but also for ethnic turmoil."[41]

The last five words highlight an old and familiar problem that, in recent years, has taken on renewed urgency, that is, finding a way to reconcile diversity—the most recent flow of immigrants contains the largest influx of nonwhites of any time since the peak years of the slave trade—with the potential for a renewal of group-based competition so characteristic of the years of the Great Migration and their immediate aftermath.

The recent tensions between new immigrants and old minorities, especially African Americans, in cities across the land are pointed indicators of the sorts of conflicts Cose fears. But there is something more, something suggesting that Glazer was only partially correct. The latest

"newcomers" may be, as he put it, "more distant in culture, language and religion from white Americans, whether of the old or new immigration, than [they] were from each other,"[42] but many of the Asians and some of the Latinos—especially Cubans who, of course, are in the Southeast, not the West—have tended to take a path that seems quite northern in character, reenacting in a variety of instances the strategies and proclivities of the European immigrants. This has included methods of dealing with racism directed against themselves; patterns of intergroup competition in city neighborhoods; differential mobility based on class, contacts, and cultural values; assertions—and reassertions—of historical identities (this time as Chinese, Japanese, Korean, Filipino, Vietnamese Americans); and, in many cases, in attitudes toward and in relationships with blacks.[43] Moreover, many Asians and, again, some Latinos appear to be recapitulating the white ethnics' movements from the peripheries of communities into ever more direct involvement at the centers. But their acculturation as new, clearly hyphenated Americans has not been without difficulty, and it is far from complete. There is resentment on many sides—as there had been for their white ethnic counterparts. The most successful of the new foreigners are particularly threatening to the status quo of both whites and blacks, but especially the blacks,

41. Cose, *Nation of Strangers*, p. 219.

42. Glazer, "Politics of a Multiethnic Society," p. 331.

43. See David Rieff, *Los Angeles: Capital of the Third World* (New York: Simon & Schuster, 1991).

as they—like their earlier counter-parts from Europe—move in, up, and over.

Racial animosity is very sharply felt. Not surprisingly, those caught in its complex web are seeking ways to protect themselves and whatever hard-won gains they have achieved. Intergroup rivalries are nothing new. Once again they are proving to be "both an enduring American phe-nomenon and an invaluable political tool . . . [one that] has more resem-bled a virus that at times lies dor-mant but can suddenly erupt with vengeance—particularly during pe-riods of stress."[44]

Half a year after the worst urban Ameri-can riots of the century, Los Angeles seems to be a city coming apart rather than coming together. Though there are some signs of progress and hope, there are others that the violence and destruc-tion served only to intensify competition and mistrust in this most diverse of major American cities.

Black, Hispanic, Asian and white commu-nities have withdrawn into themselves, more aware than ever of their differences, competing for scarce resources, aid, jobs, and political power.[45]

GOING TO EXTREMES

A decade ago, Milton M. Gordon, the sociologist who had written so insightfully about cultural and struc-tural assimilation, seemed to recon-ceptualize the old idea of pluralism, suggesting that there were, in fact, two kinds, one "liberal"—which

44. Cose, *Nation of Strangers*, p. 219.
45. Seth Mydans, "Separateness Grows in a Scarred Los Angeles," *New York Times*, 15 Nov. 1992. Copyright © 1992 by The New York Times Company. Reprinted by permission.

sounds, to this writer at least, rather conservative—and the other "corpo-rate."

"Those who favor the liberal form," Gordon argued,

. . . emphasize in their arguments the ethical and philosophical value of the idea of individual meritocracy and the notion that current generations should not be expected to pay for the sins of their fathers—or, at least, those who lived here before them, whether genetically related or not. They also point to functional con-siderations such as the possibility that measures such as forced busing and affir-mative action to ensure group quotas will create white backlash and serve as con-tinuing major irritants in the relation-ships between racial and ethnic groups. Those who favor policies which fall, logi-cally, under the rubric of corporate plura-lism emphasize . . . the moral and philo-sophical position which posits group rights as well as individual rights, and the need for major compensatory mea-sures to make up for massive dimensions of racial discrimination in the past.[46]

Gordon predicted that deciding which approach to pluralism to adopt, or which path to follow, would become an issue not only for scholars of American culture but for the soci-ety as a whole. Resolving this "new American dilemma," as he referred to the problem, "will have much to do with determining the nature, shape, and destiny of racial and ethnic rela-tions in America in the twenty-first century."[47] More recently, Arthur M.

46. Milton M. Gordon, "Models of Plural-ism: The New American Dilemma," in *America as a Multicultural Society*, ed. Milton M. Gor-don, *The Annals* of the American Academy of Political and Social Science, 454:187-88 (Mar. 1981).
47. Ibid., p. 188. See also Bart Landry, "The Enduring Dilemma of Race in America," in

Schlesinger, Jr., suggested that the time had already come to make the choice. He posited the dilemma as a challenge to the inclusive trend of American democracy by those fostering an ideology of balkanization, one that clearly plays on the sorts of tensions that have been reappearing on the streets and on the campuses in recent years.

Instead of a transformative nation with an identity all its own, America increasingly sees itself as preservative of old identities. Instead of a nation composed of individuals making their own free choices, America increasingly sees itself as composed of groups more or less indelible in their ethnic character. The national idea had once been *e pluribus unum*. Are we now to belittle the *unum* and glorify *pluribus*? Will the center hold? or will the melting pot yield to the Tower of Babel?[48]

While seeming to alter the basic premises of the old pluralists, especially the core idea that the hyphen connects instead of separates, the polarization that both Gordon and Schlesinger posit is the topic of intense debate. Their distinctions are not only philosophical but strategic, depending, in large part, on the class, status, power, and, especially, the race of the antagonists.

It ought not to be at all surprising that those who have become successful, particularly but not exclusively the old white ethnics, favor what Gordon calls the liberal approach and see

the other one less in terms of enhancing the richness of the society—as many of their own parents and mentors might have argued—than as the vehicle for its disintegration. On the other hand, it is equally understandable that those who are still on the outside—and who have suffered discrimination generally greater than that ever conferred upon the others—want to use collective action to satisfy a desire for acceptance on their own terms. It is something that another pluralist of "The Hyphen-Connects School," W.E.B. Du Bois, said in 1903, before pluralism was an ideology—and before John Dewey's felicitous expression had ever been uttered!

Du Bois's famous statement that "one ever feels his twoness,—an American, a Negro" ends with a desire: "He simply wishes to make it possible for a man to be both a Negro and an American, without being cursed and spit upon."[49]

Horace Kallen once said that "men may change their clothes, their politics, their wives, their religions, their philosophies to a greater or less extent: they cannot change their grandfathers. Jews or Poles or Anglo-Saxons, in order to cease being Jews or Poles or Anglo-Saxons would have to cease to be."[50] The same sentiment is now again being expressed not only by newcomers but also by many spokespersons for those old, very old, Americans—from Africa.

Few engaged in the new movements for group recognition want to

---

America at Century's End, ed. Alan Wolfe (Berkeley: University of California Press, 1991), pp. 185-207 passim.

48. Arthur M. Schlesinger, Jr., *The Disuniting of America: Reflections on a Multicultural Society* (Knoxville, TN: Whittle Communications, 1991), p. 2.

49. W.E.B. Du Bois, *The Souls of Black Folk* (1903), as reprinted in *Three Negro Classics* (New York: Avon Books, 1965), p. 215.

50. Kallen, "Democracy versus the Melting Pot," p. 220.

tear down the foundations of society, but they do favor altering the structures to truly be more inclusive. But their opponents, often using the most extreme examples, claim that the would-be multiculturalists are, in fact, "polarizing particularists" or "subversive separatists." They further argue that the corporate tactics are alienating members of their own groups from still-needed allies while accelerating the disintegration of the United States into a fractured mosaic. If it continues, it is argued, only cohort membership will be the sine qua non of identity and power. *E pluribus plures* (out of many, many)![51]

While concerned about the "centricities" of all who are making demands,[52] there seems to be an underlying motif in the expressions of many who worry about "the cult of ethnicity."[53] Their most strident language is often used in objection to the rise of Black Chauvinism and, as Schlesinger puts it, "the guilt trips laid on by champions of cultures based on despotism, superstition, tribalism, and fanaticism, especially, the Afrocentrists."[54]

It should be noted that, even for opponents of multiculturalism, somehow the demands of Native Americans to recapture their old ways, the assertions of those from Japan and China and India to have their presence acknowledged and to be granted special recognition, even certain cultural proclivities of Mexican Americans once viewed, as were those of Italian Americans and French Canadians, as being too peasantlike seem more tolerable to many white Americans—including the old-fashioned liberals—than the claims of blacks. The old argument that "the Negro has no culture of his own"[55] is now transmuted into one that states that he has no culture worth resurrecting or reasserting: not the African heritage; not that of the diaspora, which, of course, would have to include so much of the music, literature, and icons of the popular culture now regarded here and throughout the world as quintessentially American. The persistence of what George Frederickson has called the peculiarly American "arrogance of race"[56] continues to diminish the significance of Afro-American culture and the significance of those who want to celebrate their own contributions to a society that claims to be one that appreciates those "of every hue and caste."

There are many parallels to what was going on in the waning days of

51. Diane Ravitch, "Multiculturalism: E Pluribus Plures," *American Scholar*, 59(3) (Summer 1990).

52. Ronald Takaki, "Multiculturalism: Battleground or Meeting Ground?" this issue of *The Annals* of the American Academy of Political and Social Science.

53. Schlesinger, *Disuniting of America*, p. 70. See also Dinesh D'Souza, *Illiberal Education: The Politics of Race and Sex on Campus* (New York: Free Press, 1991).

54. Schlesinger, *Disuniting of America*, p. 76.

55. See, for example, Gunnar Myrdal, *An American Dilemma* (New York: Harper & Row, 1944); E. Franklin Frazier, *The Negro in the United States* (New York: Macmillan, 1957), p. 680; Nathan Glazer and Daniel Patrick Moynihan, *Beyond the Melting Pot* (Cambridge: MIT Press, 1963), p. 53.

56. George Frederickson, *The Arrogance of Race: Historical Perspectives on Slavery, Racism and Social Inequality* (Middletown, CT: Wesleyan University Press, 1988).

the last century and what is happening today. But whereas the main fault line in the society, north and south, had long been between whites and nonwhites, the ground now is shifting. In the future, the sharpest divisions may well be between blacks and nonblacks.

Book Department

	PAGE
INTERNATIONAL RELATIONS AND POLITICS	203
AFRICA, ASIA, AND LATIN AMERICA	204
EUROPE	207
UNITED STATES	210
SOCIOLOGY	212
ECONOMICS	213

INTERNATIONAL RELATIONS AND POLITICS

LeBLANC, LAWRENCE J. *The United States and the Genocide Convention.* Pp. xii, 290. Durham, NC: Duke University Press, 1991. $39.95.

The Convention on the Prevention and Punishment of the Crime of Genocide was unanimously adopted by the fledgling United Nations on 9 December 1948. It had been inspired by the Nazi Holocaust, in which 6 million Jews and millions of Poles, Soviet prisoners of war, Gypsies, and others were exterminated between 1939 and 1945. The members of the United Nations—including the United States—sought to establish a benchmark in international law that would deter future genocides and, if deterrence failed, punish the perpetrators.

This book does not focus on the success of the Genocide Convention in accomplishing its goals, which, unfortunately, has been minimal, judging from the number of genocides that have occurred and gone unpunished since the convention went into effect in January 1951. Instead, it presents a detailed analysis of reasons that the United States, among the most enthusiastic early advocates of the convention, failed to ratify it for 35 years. When it finally agreed to ratify, in 1986, the U.S. Senate attached a number of reservations and other statements that signaled serious misgivings about the convention. Many ardent supporters of the convention within both the United States and the international community argued that such senatorial hedging only weakened further what was already a belated U.S. endorsement.

Lawrence LeBlanc, a political scientist at Marquette University, provides a valuable historical account of the actual framing of the convention by examining debates that occurred over such issues as how the crime of genocide should be defined, which types of groups should be included within its protection, and how the punishment provisions of the convention should be implemented. LeBlanc also examines the opponents' arguments against ratification, including the fear that racial discrimination and lynchings in the United States qualify as genocide, and a reluctance to relinquish national sovereignty to an international court of justice. He also considers each of the eight limiting statements attached by the Senate to the convention, identifying the rationales given by those who demanded them as a price for their support for ratification and assessing the impact of each on the value of the convention itself.

This book will be useful for scholars of genocide as well as for those concerned with international law, particularly as it applies to human rights.

ERIC MARKUSEN

Southwest State University
Marshall
Minnesota

AFRICA, ASIA, AND LATIN AMERICA

GUHA, RAMACHANDRA. *The Unquiet Woods: Ecological Change and Peasant Resistance in the Himalaya.* Pp. xx, 214. Berkeley: University of California Press, 1989. $34.95.

The Unquiet Woods by Guha is an exceptional piece of research for it successfully intertwines the cognizance of traditional peasant movements with the newly emerging awareness of the ecological movement. This study differs from most others in the field because Guha does not see the ecological crisis as an unprecedented phenomenon. Therefore, he argues that the modern-day ecological movement is not an aberration. By taking a social-historical look at social uprising in two separate hill communities in northern India, Guha ascertains that the ecological movement is, in fact, a new

reflection of the old peasant resistance. Through a skillfully applied methodology and lucid language, Guha demonstrates that ecological issues are so closely linked with the basic survival issues of village life that the two cannot be separated. At the heart of both movements—peasant and ecological—is the same quest for moral economy. Guha argues that it has been the decadence of the moral economy of provision and the advent of the political cal economy of profit that lie at the root of the present-day ecological movements.

Guha, who has written extensively on forestry and peasant insurgency in colonial and postcolonial India, takes a comparative approach in this book. First, he sets the stage for his analysis by providing excellent images of the region, including social rituals and customs. In brief, the hill society in the precommercial era is depicted as an ideal society. It is prosperous due to its egalitarian structure, social solidarity, and the abundance of natural resources. At this point, Guha's case study of the hill society bifurcates. It offers the reader a rare opportunity to observe ecological uprisings in two different settings within the same region: Tehri Garhwal, an independent kingdom, and Kumaun, a colonial territory. The bifurcation allows Guha to demonstrate that the peasant resistance, even though appearing different on the surface, originates and terminates in the same quest for moral economy. With the introduction of scientific, state-directed forestry in the 1860s, the social fabric of the region changes: fragmentation of the family, erosion of local authority structures, and a crisis of confidence result as the ideals of moral economy turn into the practices of political economy.

Guha also affords us with yet another brilliant case study of the Chipko Andolan, an internationally acclaimed ecological movement. Needless to say, the Chipko case confirms the thesis developed throughout the book; however, it also provides interesting insights into the role of women in peasant protests and ecological movements.

The Unquiet Woods is a pathbreaking contribution to the literature on ecology. This in no way undermines its importance for sociologists and students of peasantry.

RENU KHATOR

University of South Florida
Tampa

HARRIS, RICHARD L. *Marxism, Socialism, and Democracy in Latin America.* Pp. xiii, 234. Boulder, CO: Westview Press, 1992. $44.00. Paperbound, $16.95.

Richard Harris's comparative analysis of the theory and practice of creating a socialist society may appear to have been outdated as a result of recent history. Nonetheless, it still speaks to issues of fundamental importance.

The opening chapters of the book analyze a number of classic Marxist writings in search of guidelines for the transition to a socialist society. While the principal concerns of Marxist theory lie elsewhere, Harris shows that it is possible to derive a number of broad generalizations and a general framework in regard to this process. The remainder of the volume is, on the whole, guided by that framework. Each chapter discusses a major concern and objective of the transition to socialism. It does so using as case material the recent efforts at broad societal transformation in Cuba, Nicaragua, Chile, and Grenada, with some attention to the Soviet Union and China. Harris thus provides a useful blend of theory and practice.

Harris initiates his analysis by arguing strongly for a democratic polity and society with direct participation and deconcentration of power. Related, his lengthiest chapter discusses socialist forms of organization, that is, self-government at the community level and especially worker control in the sphere of production. At the same time, some will see his acceptance of the notion of the dictatorship of the proletariat as compromising democratic practice. Socialist practice and theory are also reviewed and assessed in regard to stages of socialist transformation, expropriation of property, agricultural policy, development of productive forces, moral and material incentives, transformation of consciousness and ideology, and emancipation of women. He urges developing new values and greater attention to gender, racial, and ethnic equality.

The present study will be of interest to anyone concerned with a sympathetic albeit in part critical account of efforts at building socialism, especially in Latin America and the Caribbean. It will also have appeal for its affirmation of the importance of democratic values and procedures and for its stress on the importance of workplace democracy, worker self-management, and participatory forms more generally, as well as for its hostility to statist regimes. These are part of a growing dialogue today among many with concerns quite removed from Marxism or socialism.

In spite of the virtues of Harris's analysis, I believe that it remains at too general and abstract a level. Contemporary societies are characterized by conflicted interests, uneven and insufficient resources, the profound importance of personal worlds, large numbers, a high degree of integration, immense organizational size, and the like. While such circumstances do not prevent increased democratization of society and the workplace, they do raise considerable difficulties and inevitable compromises. Thus what becomes crucial is how such broad concepts are translated into practice; however, this problem receives no mention in the present analysis, in spite of its other strengths.

SANDOR HALEBSKY

Saint Mary's University
Halifax
Nova Scotia
Canada

HAYNES, DOUGLAS E. *Rhetoric and Ritual in Colonial India: The Shaping of a Public Culture in Surat City, 1852-1928.* Pp. xi, 363. Berkeley: University of California Press, 1991. $49.95.

Surat is a city on the west coast of India, north of Bombay. At one time, Surat was the most important port and manufacturing city of the region, but a series of natural disasters and the gradual silting up of the Tapi River meant that Surat lost its importance compared to Bombay. Given increased competition from factory-produced cloth and goods, Surat survived by exploiting niches in the market and specializing in the production of pearl necklaces and fine silk and cotton textiles, which were sold to well-off elites in Bombay and other cities.

Traditional ways of banking and production survived in Surat, at least through the period studied in *Rhetoric and Ritual in Colonial India*. Douglas Haynes describes the ways in which traditional business and political practices changed in relation to the assumptions of British colonial practices. His focus is on how each side influenced the other in the debate over the future of the city and the movement toward self-rule.

Haynes is very harsh on simplistic notions of social change, such as the idea that the British introduced liberal democracy to India over the objections of traditional elites. In reality, the British were hardly models of democracy at home. In India, the British assumed some people were better than others and made the feudal assumption that some people were simply natural leaders. Local elites agreed. Communalist rhetoric was an integral part of the way the British viewed India.

Haynes finds his conclusions "bleak." It can no longer be assumed that tribal and ethnic considerations will disappear as liberal democracy emerges victorious in all parts of the world. In Surat, the British and the Surtis merged their ideas of ruling into what Haynes labels tropical gothic. The merged ideas of ruling became what passed locally as common sense. Neither side was very effective in determining the ultimate values that emerged.

In reading this book, I was struck by how many of the decisions the British had to make in running a city in the late 1800s are exactly the same as those that local leaders face today. The Surtis were famous for resenting taxes of any sort, even for sewers and a new waterworks; the British viewed coming out in favor of dirty water as regressive. The same debate was just held in Durham, North Carolina, involving the corporation of a famous United States senator. Haynes could easily turn his skills to the United States in the 1990s.

This is an important book. In many ways, Haynes's approach could be studied by all of us who are puzzled by why, as communism fails in Eastern Europe, we get communal riots and not liberal democracy. This book deserves to be widely read.

GEORGE H. CONKLIN

North Carolina Central University
Durham

EUROPE

BLACK, CYRIL E., JOHNATHAN E. HELM-REICH, PAUL C. HELMREICH, CHARLES P. ISSAWI, and A. JAMES McADAMS. *Rebirth: A History of Europe since World War II.* Pp. xv, 565. Boulder, CO: Westview Press, 1992. $59.95. Paperbound, $24.95.

The history of Europe from 1945 to 1990 could only be ordered around a single theme, the rebirth of Europe. This rebirth is characterized by the triumph of democracy and economic prosperity in Western Europe and, most recently, the end of the Cold War and the great division between Western and Eastern Europe. This is nominally the main theme of this book, which is well written and supported by helpful bibliographies, 15 maps, and a chronology. However, *Rebirth* does not by the clear use of its dramatic theme or felicity of narrative rise above being a useful, timely, and, for the moment, indispensable text.

Two hurried initial chapters that form the first part of the book offer a brief overview of Europe from the Middle Ages to 1945. The first chapter, carrying the signature of Cyril Black, focuses on the immense power Europe amassed in the course of its modernization to the end of the nineteenth century, while the second chapter focuses on early-twentieth-century Europe in crisis.

The next part of the book looks at Europe and its place in the changing international scene from 1945 to 1990. It offers very useful and perceptive sections on perestroika and the end of the Soviet Union as well as the making of a new Germany and the potential problems of a new order in Eastern Europe. The book contains an outstanding overview of "the miracle year," 1989, and continues with the emergence of antiforeign feelings, skinheads in Germany, the coup against Gorbachev in August 1991, and the independence of the Ukraine and other Soviet republics.

The next section, by far the largest part of the book, shows all too well how this period in institutional complexity and societal development defies a narrative around a commanding theme. It surveys separately Germany, the Soviet Union, Eastern Europe, the United Kingdom, France, Italy and the Vatican, the small states of Western and Northern Europe, and the Iberian and Aegean states. The fourth section of the book provides a thoughtful survey of an emerging new Europe in the wake of its recent and altogether unanticipated historical revolution.

In this text, which is dedicated almost exclusively to diplomatic and political history, there are serious omissions. Among them is a failure to explore the development of new social orders, classes, attitudes, and sensibilities, as well as a near total neglect of the history of ideas and cultures of all sorts, and the interactions of high, commercial, traditional, mass, and national cultures.

This criticism, however, is not meant to detract from the book's usefulness in the areas it does cover. Indeed, it may remain for some time the best text we have of post-World War II Europe, setting the standards for any textbook intended to replace it.

JOE AMATO

Southwest State University
Marshall
Minnesota

BREMENT, MARSHALL. *Reaching out to Moscow: From Confrontation to Cooperation.* Pp. ix, 191. New York: Praeger, 1991. $42.95.

KRIESBERG, LOUIS. *International Conflict Resolution: The U.S.-USSR and Middle East Cases.* Pp. xii, 275. New Haven, CT: Yale University Press, 1992. $35.00.

The pace of change in the former Soviet Union has made writing about this region almost as dangerous as trying to govern it. Marshall Brement's book, *Reaching out to Moscow,* which is based on information prior to August 1991, tends to confirm this point. As a current prescription for change, most of this text is badly out of date. It refers to a country, the USSR, that no longer exists and dwells heavily on a leader, Gorbachev, who is currently not a major force on the international stage. As a result, most of the text is best viewed as recent history and not as current commentary. Even with these weaknesses, however, Brement is still right on target in his chapters on nuclear deterrence, the need to reduce nuclear forces, and the need to restructure and reduce conventional forces. These recommendations, most of which are aimed equally at the United States and the former Soviet Union, address the core of the current discussion about the future of military activities in both countries.

Later discussions in the book about our alliance partners and about the actions of a more unified Europe have also been overwhelmed by recent events, but, again, the core ideas are very useful. In the end, the book seriously underestimates the economic difficulties facing the former Soviet Union, partially because of difficulties that developed since the dissolution of the USSR and partially because the economic problems are too overwhelming to even be addressed in the short space devoted to them.

Louis Kriesberg's book, *International Conflict Resolution,* also suffers from being out of date but in a different way. This interesting volume uses conflicts between the United States and the USSR

and between Israel and Egypt to illustrate the difficult art of international conflict resolution. In the process, it presents a complete view of this difficult area, and it uses these two major conflicts to advantage as each specific point is made. Further, the book incorporates some Persian Gulf war experience in an epilogue to further bolster its points. But the gulf war data appear to end by February 1991, and the rest of the data in the book are for the period 1989 and prior. This means that the reader, with almost two years of more current experience as a guide, generates a number of questions about the claims and descriptions of conflict resolution provided by the book. These confusions ought to have been addressed to make this work complete. Still, this is an important, easy-to-follow book, and it should be a valuable addition to the growing body of literature on this subject.

WILLIAM J. WEIDA

Colorado College
Colorado Springs

HORNE, THOMAS A. *Property Rights and Poverty: Political Argument in Britain, 1605-1834.* Pp. 296. Chapel Hill: University of North Carolina Press, 1990. $34.95.

In *Property Rights and Poverty,* Thomas A. Horne explores the philosophical connection between exclusive (or private) property rights and inclusive (or common) property rights developed in England during the seventeenth, eighteenth, and early nineteenth centuries, a period marked by an intense public debate on the nature and meaning of property rights in British society. Horne argues that while conservative political theorists believed that property systems must be either exclusive or inclusive, liberal political theorists did not. The liberal tradition provides a defense of private ownership of property—private accumulation of wealth—that does not undermine an intellectual basis for aiding the poor. Thus in classical liberalism we find fertile ground for both property systems.

Horne develops this argument by beginning with a fundamental principle of classical liberalism, which holds that it is one's natural right to possess property, that the right of property possession vests in the individual independent of and before society. This tenet unifies the most individualistic, atomistic classical liberals—the libertarians—and the most collectivist, communitarian classical liberals—the socialists—who might disagree on other political issues, such as the issue of limited government.

But is this original property right exclusive or inclusive? Most traditional liberals, Horne argues, saw this fundamental property right as inclusive—"a common inheritance"—based on natural law. Thus it was Adam Smith who wrote that "the earth and the fullness of it belongs to every generation."

Against this intellectual backdrop, classical liberals offered a defense of private property based on several theories, each of which is richly discussed in the book. The most important was the contract theory of property rights, which argues that individuals living in a society have a natural right to agree to arrangements that sanction exclusive property rights in order to mediate conflicts or deal with disincentives and inefficiencies that can arise under a regime of common property rights. Likewise, the labor theory, another natural law theory, protects private property rights on the ground that one must be allowed to keep the fruits of one's labor independent of the consent of others.

Horne argues, however, that the grant of exclusive property rights under each of these theories was not absolute but conditional. "Virtually every defense of the right to exclude written during this period carried with it a self-limiting feature under which exclusion could no longer legitimately occur," Horne writes. For example, recognizing that, in the liberal creed of "life, liberty, and property," property comes last, some liberal theorists argued that individual property rights could be overturned to secure life and liberty within the community. Other liberals argued that exclusive property rights could be rescinded to maintain equality. Still others went so far as to attack the intellectual basis for private property altogether, arguing, for example, that labor was not a legitimate title to private property involving land because land does not result from anyone's labor; land exists independent of human effort.

Classical liberal discussions concerning the meaning of property rights, Horne argues, have less to do with the choice between contraposed property systems—exclusion or inclusion—than with finding ways to allow both property systems to coexist. Horne believes that the liberal welfare state offers the best compromise between exclusive and inclusive property rights. Welfare liberalism simultaneously protects private property (unlike socialism) and social welfare (unlike libertarianism). It tolerates a measure of private ownership of property while at the same time providing a level of property rights to the poor—public education, public housing, income maintenance, and other forms of property transfer. Thus welfare liberalism is the only form of classical liberalism that can facilitate the traditional goals of liberalism: political and economic freedom.

ROY L. BROOKS

University of San Diego
California

UNITED STATES

BOBBITT, PHILIP. *Constitutional Interpretation*. Pp. xx, 228. Cambridge,
MA: Basil Blackwell, 1991. $47.95. Pa-
perbound, $16.95.

After reading in the area of constitutional interpretation, one often finds that
one confronts new wine in old bottles.
While the reader might be prone to respond in such a fashion to Philip Bobbitt's
broad topic, he or she will be happy that
the vintners are at it again, albeit the
bottles seem to have become quite small,
especially for holding such a large har-
vest as "constitutional interpretation."
Lest the reader suggest that I am suspicious of such enterprises, I will recommend a book of the same title that is much
more befitting of its title: *American Constitutional Interpretation* by Walter Mur-
phy, James Fleming, and William Harris.
While Bobbitt's *Constitutional Interpretation* lacks the thorough coverage of this
earlier work, it should be mentioned that
Bobbitt's effort is a continuation of his
examination of constitutional interpretation begun in *Constitutional Fate* (1982).

Bobbitt's examination of the essential
question of constitutional government is
thankfully neither an academic tome of
no consequence nor an ideological pam-
phlet. In this work, he reexamines how
the different modes of constitutional argument he presented earlier support the
exercise of judicial review. The goal is to
look at how we should choose one form of
argument over another, especially when
different modes of constitutional interpretation produce very different substantive outcomes. What constitutes the
criteria for judging the legitimacy of
modes of constitutional interpretation in
actual controversies? Do these criteria
lead to either efficient or equitable constitutional outcomes? Hence this book is not
an overview of all of the issues in constitutional interpretation nor is it a cata-
loguing of every possible response. It is

the presentation of a variety of positions,
but Bobbitt chooses these carefully to
support his argument. This is not meant
as a criticism but only as an explanation
of an arguably misleading title.

The text is well organized, and Bobbitt
discusses well the more recent and major
constitutional theorists. The distinctive
quality of *Constitutional Interpretation* is
that Bobbitt places the descriptions of the
forms of constitutional interpretation
within the context of two major constitutional controversies: the Bork hearings
and the Iran-contra affair. Bobbitt's experience as Associate Counsel to the Senate
Select Iran-Contra Committee shows
through clearly as he examines what constitutes both legitimate and just constitutional interpretation. In so doing, Bobbitt
brings unique practical insights that make
the constitutional issues much more vivid
than traditional examinations of select
cases. There is much of value in this book,
and it will receive notice among practi-
tioners and academics.

JOHN B. GATES

University of California
Davis

COSTAIN, ANNE N. *Inviting Women's
Rebellion: A Political Process Inter-
pretation of the Women's Movement*.
Pp. xx, 188. Baltimore, MD: Johns
Hopkins University Press, 1992.
$28.00.

In order to understand the future
prospects for women's movement politics,
Anne Costain, whose first interviews included in this book were conducted
twenty years ago, tries to evaluate the
political success of second-wave feminism. In so doing, she reviews much of the
national-level movement's history and
how the media covered it, and she pro-
poses a new reading of the relationship
between government and social movements.

Most social scientists who write about social movements see them as outside forces that bring unaddressed social issues into the government's agenda and concerns. Costain's "political process interpretation" of social movements suggests that there is a more complex interaction between social movements and government. Indeed, she suggests that social movements are often inspired, materially aided, and, most important, shaped by governmental agendas. Costain suggests that the women's movement, through its successes and ties with Congress and the executive branch, was directed toward an agenda that emphasized issues of equality—such as equal pay, equal credit opportunities, equal educational opportunities—and ultimately the Equal Rights Amendment. For Costain, women's movement organizations pursued this equality agenda to the relative neglect of other special-needs issues of importance to women, such as reproductive freedom and child care. Then, during the 1980s, when the Republican administrations in Washington were relatively hostile to women's equality, there was no place for feminists to turn. Although the changes wrought by feminism in the last twenty years have changed attitudes and political perceptions permanently, Costain believes that if women's movement organizations had been willing to act more as outsiders and had been less concerned with pure issues of equality, then they might have accomplished more.

Costain's views deserve serious attention, but in the end, part of her argument depends upon how we evaluate some political events of the 1970s. The defeat of a national child care act in 1972 and Jimmy Carter's ambiguity about a pro-choice position may be stronger signals than Costain acknowledges that her alternative, that feminists should have pursued a special-needs agenda, was also doomed to relative failure.

Readers may or may not be persuaded by Costain's political advice. Nevertheless, her book suggests an important new model for understanding social movements and contributes to our rethinking of the place of the women's movement in our recent political history.

JOAN C. TRONTO

Hunter College
New York City

PRATT, ROBERT A. *The Color of Their Skin: Education and Race in Richmond, Virginia, 1954-1989.* Pp. xvii, 134. Charlottesville: University Press of Virginia, 1992. $22.95.

Written some 35 years after the *Brown* decision, *The Color of Their Skin* is an excellent study of white resistance to school desegregation in Richmond, Virginia. White opposition to desegregation was intense and shifted from segregation to desegregation to resegregation.

In contrast to the massive resistance on the state level that resulted in the closing of schools, the schools in Richmond remained open, but segregated. The strategy of the Richmond officials was passive resistance that would avoid blatant defiance of the law, keep the schools open, and minimize integration by admitting token black students, thus maintaining a segregated school system and forestalling integration for nearly two decades.

A Pupil Placement Board was created in 1956 to administer pupil assignment and transfer. Residential patterns and lower academic achievement were the criteria. Residential segregation had confined blacks and their schools to certain areas. Black applicants for white schools were refused on the basis that neighborhood schools were available. Where black and white children lived in the same neighborhood, they were often assigned to different schools, race being the sole criterion.

The first real change in Richmond occurred in 1960 when the board approved the transfer of two black students to a white school. The whites were satisfied that, as a consequence of demographic factors and residential segregation, only a small amount of desegregation would take place, sufficient to satisfy the courts. By the fall of 1963, of an estimated 26,000 blacks in Richmond schools, only 312 attended white schools.

The Supreme Court decision of 1964 and other decisions resulted in a revised freedom-of-choice concept. Residential segregation remained a major obstacle. This was apparent in the 1968 Supreme Court ruling that freedom of choice was unconstitutional so long as it resulted in a dual school system. In accordance with the watershed decision of the Supreme Court, *Swann* v. *Charlotte-Mecklenburg Board of Education*, which approved extensive busing to advance school desegregation, District Court Judge Robert R. Merhige, Jr., stipulated in 1971 that students be assigned so that the ratio of blacks to whites in each school approached that in the school system and, furthermore, that busing be extended to all students within Richmond. The demography of the metropolitan area operated against the busing order, as white emigration to the suburbs resulted in the gradual resegregation of the city schools. Legal action to merge city and country schools was ultimately, in 1973, not upheld by the Supreme Court. All signs were of a growing conservatism in the national government.

The years after the Supreme Court disallowed consolidation have been ones of "transition and adjustment" for the faculty and students of both races. A loss of revenue accompanied white flight and contributed to a decline in educational standards. Lower standards and a lessening of discrimination led to an increase in the number of blacks in both public and private country schools, reflecting class differences between the blacks. Efforts have been made to upgrade the city schools with some success, especially as the result of magnet schools.

With the national government pursuing a more conservative course regarding school desegregation, the focus of the Richmond schools must be on the quality of education, rather than integration, in the hope that good students will attract good students, who will come together as equals and who will come to understand each other's history and culture.

ARNOLD A. SIO

Colgate University
Hamilton
New York

SOCIOLOGY

REINHARZ, SHULAMIT. *Feminist Methods in Social Research.* Pp. vii, 413. New York: Oxford University Press, 1992. $39.95. Paperbound, $19.95.

Feminist Methods in Social Research is an excellent and comprehensive work; thus it is difficult to do it justice in the limited space provided. In order to offer "models to emulate or to modify," to illustrate "how some people have struggled for 'the right to be producers of knowledge without being trapped into the reproductions of patriarchal ways of knowing,' " the book's overarching goal is to answer two major questions: (1) "what is the difference between feminist research methods and other research methods?" (2) "how do feminist research methods differ from one another?"

The introduction to the book is outstanding, setting the background for the issues to be dealt with, articulating the key questions and themes, and giving an explanation of the book's format. A critical point addressed in the introductory chapter is that the author has not imposed a definition of "feminist" or "feminism" but has listened to the diversity of the voices of researchers themselves and used "people's self-definition." Reinharz does, however, provide a definition of the key concept of "feminist research methods," the critical factor being that the person doing the research "had to identify herself [or in a few cases, himself] as a feminist."

Subsequent chapters each present particular research methods used by feminists—interviews, ethnography, survey and other statistical research formats, experimental research, cross-cultural research, oral history, content analysis, case studies, action research, multiple methods research, and original feminist research. Unifying themes appear throughout; these include the use of multiple methods in practice; challenging the status quo; the quest for, and struggle to hear, women's own historically silenced and diverse voices; the importance of women's lives sui generis; exploration of the lived experiences of women's lives in the complexities of social contexts—such as gender together with race and class—which much research has rendered invisible; recognition of the actual connectedness of researcher with the research project; and the reciprocal effects of the research project and the people with whom the project deals on the researcher.

Like the introductory chapter, the final chapter is exemplary. It focuses on ten major themes, arrived at inductively from the preceding chapters, which, according to Reinharz, characterize feminist methodology. This chapter also recognizes the fact that feminist research is a "dialectical process" and that feminist researchers, although trained in traditional academic disciplines and theories, are engaged in active criticism of these

disciplines and theories. This chapter points out the fact that some feminist researchers are struggling to deal with racism and heterosexism; it makes clear "that feminist researchers do not consider feminism to be a method. Rather they consider it to be a perspective on an existing method in a given field of inquiry"; that feminist research values inclusivity over orthodoxy; that feminist research is cross-disciplinary and uses multiple methods; and that feminist research is directly connected to social change.

The first and last chapters could stand by themselves as a valuable commentary on feminist methods in social research. The intervening chapters are a veritable encyclopedia of feminist research, although a bit uneven in coverage: for example, some lack consistent depth in historical background or critical analysis compared to others. This is a book that should be read by every educated individual but especially by all social scientists, by students in all research methods courses, by all social policy planners, makers, and implementers, as it provides a perspective that has been lacking in many scholarly works and in many areas of practice.

M. F. STUCK

State University of New York
Oswego

ECONOMICS

BEST, MICHAEL H. *The New Competition: Institutions of Industrial Restructuring.* Pp. x, 296. Cambridge, MA: Harvard University Press, 1990. No price.

This is an excellently researched and presented book that addresses industrial, competitive, and governmental issues that will be with us for the remainder of this decade and probably longer. The blend of historical, economic, and organizational research, detail, and thoughtful discussion and reflection separates this book from those that can be classified in any one discipline.

The major theme of *The New Competition* is that

the New Competition is the entrepreneurial firm, an enterprise that is organized from top to bottom to pursue continuous improvement in methods, products and processes. The pursuit of continuous improvement is a production-based strategy that has refined the meaning of entrepreneurial activity from its traditional individualist approach to a collectivist concept. The entrepreneurial firm seeks a competitive edge by superior product design, which may or may not lead to lower costs, but it demands organizational flexibility which in turn requires organizational commitments to problem solving, a persistence to detail, and an integration of thinking and doing in work activities (pp. 2-3).

Michael Best states that the New Competition is manifest in interfirm complexes that range from cooperative groups of Italian firms to large Japanese organizational structures that coordinate trading companies, banks, and manufacturing firms. The New Competition includes examples found in Germany, Sweden, South Korea, Taiwan, Hong Kong, Singapore, and the United States.

One dimension of the New Competition is the organization of the firm as "the collective entrepreneur"—as contrasted with the hierarchical structured company —which is strategically oriented on the basis of product innovation, process, and the choice of the terrain on which to compete. The second dimension is the second level of organization of the new competitive firm, which "links micro production units into a production chain extending from the first to the last operational phase in turning raw material and labor into a final product." The New Competition manages interfirm production ar-

rangements through "consultative coordination," or "cooperation amongst mutually interdependent firms each of which specializes in distinct phases of the same production chain."

Ford represented the hierarchical Old Competition's form of organization and rules of competing; Nissan represents the New Competition's form of interfirm organization and competing. "Ford engineers prepared the specifications for component products and sent them out to a list of subcontractors who bid on the basis of price." "Nissan engineers do not prepare the specifications for the part and send them to a list of subcontractors . . . they describe the function of the product and ask a familiar supplier to design it." Ford dictated the design specifications to its suppliers; Nissan engineers interact consultatively with its suppliers through iterative dialogue until a design based on performance, quality, and production characteristics is mutually agreed upon.

A third distinguishing characteristic of the New Competition is the creation of a sector strategy that can originate from private firms. A sector strategy links interfirm practices and extrafirm agencies — such as trade associations, apprenticeship programs, regulatory agencies—to a cooperative alliance around mutually agreed-upon competitive goals and methods of competing. German cartels, financial consortia in Italy, and the postwar Japanese Union of Scientists and Engineers are such interfirm and extrafirm alliances.

Finally, the fourth dimension of the New Competition comprises patterns of cooperative government industrial policy and interfirm relationships. New consortia, buyer-vendor relations, interfirm associations, and industrial policies supported by governments characterize the New Competition. "Without the extrafirm infrastructure, enterprises seeking to become entrepreneurial firms will likely pursue a 'go it alone' strategy and be at a competitive disadvantage in the international arena."

To successfully compete in the New Competition on an international scale, Best argues that the global corporation must combine interfirm cooperation with competition. "The international consortia often involve alliances amongst a number of past (and present) rivals," he notes. Also, the global corporation organized nationally and internationally among industrial sectors learns to "harness the entrepreneurial and 'ownership' energies that decentralization enhances." Increasing independence in the design and production of the work units, and thus decreasing the role and power of top management, gives employees a stake-holding claim within individual business units. This form of empowerment leads to superior competitiveness.

Best also argues that the presence of industrial districts is a key advantage in competing with foreign rivals. He notes, "The informal networks and protean character of such districts makes them ideally suited to design-led, fashion-oriented or service-oriented competitive strategies."

The book is organized into two parts. In the first part, Best makes several conclusions. The first is that the emergence of mass production changed coordination mechanisms. The second conclusion is that "the official [U.S.] policy signalled to enterprises that either market or hierarchical coordination [is] legal but that inter-firm cooperation is subject to criminal offense." The third conclusion is that public policy should administer a paradox: "it should promote both competition and cooperation." This did not and has not happened in the United States.

The last conclusion is that government regulation has been defined by price competition and has inhibited the very features of the New Competition

from taking hold in the United States, namely, "consultative inter-firm relations between large and small firms organized into supplier networks." The post-World War II emergence of Japan and other Asian and European models of successful competitive and cooperative forms of cartels and intrafirm industrial policy examples took the U.S. government and businesses by surprise.

Best points to Schumpeter and Penrose for guidelines into the future. "Schumpeter extends the notion of competition from price to product, process, and organization. Penrose gives us concepts for understanding the uniqueness of every firm and the crucial role of teamwork and cooperation." The Japanese example of industrialization has already demonstrated the success of these perspectives in world markets.

Part 2 of the book describes in detail the differences between U.S. and Japanese production concepts; human resource management in firms; industrial and antitrust policy in Japan; and sector strategies. A surprise for some readers may be the author's explanation of how post-World War II U.S. policy and influence in Japan led to Japan's development of close cooperation between the Ministry of International Trade and Industry and private firms, thus furthering a highly competitive and successful industrial policy that might otherwise not have matured. Best also describes successful cooperative and cartel strategies and industrial policies in Germany and Italy—other international examples of the New Competition.

Best concludes the book with some caveats concerning the New Competition. Examples of some of the controversial themes that call for additional research and observation include "competitiveness and community: convergence or divergence?" "skill-based production versus the 'unmanned factory,'" "worker loyalty: commitment versus regimentation," "partnership versus anonymity in parent-supplier relations," the "stability of industrial districts versus the growth of individual firms," "macroeconomic stability and strategic industrial policymaking," and "economic security and ecological integrity."

This is a very detailed, excellently researched book that is thoughtfully written. It demands the attention of academics and industrial executives.

JOSEPH W. WEISS

Bentley College
Waltham
Massachusetts

ROSNER, DAVID and GERALD MARKOWITZ. *Deadly Dust: Silicosis and the Politics of Occupational Disease in Twentieth Century America.* Pp. xiii, 229. Princeton, NJ: Princeton University Press, 1991. $29.95.

REICH, MICHAEL R. *Toxic Politics: Responding to Chemical Disasters.* Pp. xi, 316. Ithaca, NY: Cornell University Press, 1991. $45.00. Paperbound, $15.95.

Occupational disease and chemical disasters are topics about which it is hard to be dispassionate. No one could read these books without experiencing profound pity for the victims of the events described in the books. Both books describe human suffering of a degree and nature that makes one shudder and reflect on the advantages of an academic life in which physical threats to our health are so much rarer than in mining or many manufacturing industries. At times, these books also arouse anger. Rosner and Markowitz, for example, describe the exposure of workers by Union Carbide and Carbon Company at Gauley Bridge in the 1930s to hazards of silicosis

on such a scale and with such foreknowledge of the risks to the workers that the company's behavior can truly be described as murderous. The company was caught out because the length of time it took for its miners to show signs of silicosis was unusually short due to the massive doses of dust to which they had been exposed. Similarly, Reich describes how officials of the Kanemi corporation allowed the use of what they knew to be contaminated rice oil by consumers to continue, with agonizing consequences for Japanese consumers.

Both these books are reminders of the failings in the tide of conservative thinking about government and the economy, now evidently in retreat. Corporations cannot always be trusted, and Reich shows that the failings of corporations are not limited to any one country or culture. Japanese corporations behaved more dishonorably over contaminated rice oil than did Italian (admittedly Swiss-owned) corporations over the escape of dangerous chemicals at Seveso. Japanese corporations, so often admired for their capacity to regulate themselves and act in a manner consistent with the well-being of Japanese society, proved that they are fully capable of putting short-term interest and profit ahead of the health of consumers. Government, President Reagan used to like to say, is not the answer; it is the problem. These books prove that business can be the problem, not the answer, and our best chance to avoid frightful disasters in the future probably lies in the hands of admittedly imperfect government agencies.

Yet conservatives are on surer ground when they criticize occupational safety and health advocates for viewing problems one-sidedly. Both of these books present occupational hazards and risks to consumers as avoidable problems. A more tragic and more realistic view might be that risk is as unavoidable in industry as it is in most other aspects of life. The authors of these books, in a manner strikingly reminiscent of attitudes on occupational safety and health more common twenty years ago than recently, devote little attention to the benefits as well as the costs that flow from the hazardous activities they describe. There can be little excuse for the behavior of Union Carbide at Gauley Bridge or for the incompetence compounded by dishonesty of the Kanemi corporation. Yet chemicals do bring many advantages to our lives; there are probably always risks associated with their production; and the real issue for most us will therefore be whether the inevitable risks are as low as possible. Only toward the very end of his book and then very briefly does Reich assess whether the disasters he describes are the inevitable but rare cases that represent the limitations inherent in any safety regime, or whether they represent a totally unnecessary and unacceptable level of danger. The reader is left unsure whether there is always the risk of the occasional error or act of dishonesty that results in disasters of the type Reich analyzes or whether we could enjoy the products of the chemical industries while being safer in our homes.

While the two books raise similar concerns, they are very different in character. Rosner and Markowitz, like many historians, proceed without much regard for the contribution that other disciplines can provide to the topic they are studying. The vast political science literature on regulation figures almost not at all in their analysis or bibliography. Nor, *contra* their subtitle, do the authors even begin to analyze "the politics of occupational disease in twentieth century America." Yet, as is so often the case with good historians, a point of general relevance emerges from their story. Rosner and Markowitz remind us that the study of occupational health and disease is not a

pure scientific enterprise in which knowledge accumulates steadily but an uneven process in which the perceptions of medical experts can be shaped more by the general intellectual mood than by scientific knowledge. Concern about silicosis rose and fell not because of increased knowledge about the extent of the disease but because of changes in attitudes toward workers, the poor, and illness more generally.

Reich, in contrast, is fully conversant with a wide range of social science analysis and theory. Indeed, if there is a criticism of him to be made in this regard, it is that he strives too hard to force his cases into a theoretical framework. In particular, he uses the "three faces of power" analysis that Steven Lukes outlined in the 1970s. This approach has enormous methodological problems, which it would take too long to outline here; in particular, it is almost impossible to use the approach with the author specifying externally what the subjects of the study ought to have defined as their interests, rather than accepting what they did define as their interests. Reich, however, has an additional problem in using the three-faces-of-power approach. As formulated by Lukes, or, in the case of the second face of power, by Bachrach and Baratz, the second and third faces of power were meant to explain the quiescence and submission of subjects to power hierarchies. With understandable delays given the technical problems involved, the victims Reich describes were not quiescent. They often received too little help from their governments, or fellow citizens, but they were not the hapless victims of second or third faces of power for long enough to make the use of that framework convincing.

The reader might conclude, therefore, that Rosner and Markowitz might have done well to try to take more account of wider theorizing about regulation and that Reich might have felt less obliged to adopt a theoretical framework that, as often happens, did little to improve his study. Both books, however, are very fine pieces of scholarship. Reich's book in particular is based on extensive research in three countries and mastery of the relevant literatures. Both books also remind us—particularly those of us in safe and comfortable occupations—of the human tragedies that still underlie our industrial civilizations.

GRAHAM K. WILSON

University of Wisconsin
Madison

OTHER BOOKS

ARNOLD, R. DOUGLAS. *The Logic of Congressional Action.* Pp. xi, 282. New Haven, CT: Yale University Press, 1992. $35.00. Paperbound, $15.00.

BARNES, JAMES F. *Gabon: Beyond the Colonial Legacy.* Pp. xii, 163. Boulder, CO: Westview Press, 1992. $38.50.

BIX, HERBERT P. *Peasant Protest in Japan, 1590-1884.* Pp. xxxviii, 296. New Haven, CT: Yale University Press, 1992. $35.00. Paperbound, $16.00.

BLOCK, ALAN A. *The Business of Crime: A Documentary Study of Organized Crime in the American Economy.* Pp. vii, 294. Boulder, CO: Westview Press, 1991. $44.50. Paperbound, $14.95.

CAMP, RODERIC A. *Mexican Political Biographies, 1884-1934.* Pp. xxix, 458. Austin: University of Texas Press, 1991. $75.00.

CRYSTAL, JILL. *Kuwait: The Transformation of an Oil State.* Pp. xii, 194. Boulder, CO: Westview Press, 1992. $37.50.

DAVID, STEVEN R. *Choosing Sides: Alignment and Realignment in the Third World.* Pp. xiii, 247. Baltimore, MD: Johns Hopkins University Press, 1991. No price.

DENBER, RACHEL, ed. *The Soviet Nationality Reader: The Disintegration in Context.* Pp. ix, 635. Boulder, CO: Westview Press, 1992. $52.00. Paperbound, $21.50.

EVENSEN, BRUCE J. *Truman, Palestine, and the Press: Shaping Conventional Wisdom at the Beginning of the Cold War.* Pp. 243. Westport, CT: Greenwood Press, 1992. $45.00.

FISHER, FRANKLIN M. *Econometrics: Essays in Theory and Applications.* Pp. xxiv, 408. Cambridge: MIT Press, 1992. $45.00.

GARFINKLE, ADAM, ed. *The Devil and Uncle Sam.* Pp. ix, 135. New Brunswick, NJ: Transaction, 1992. $24.95.

GEELHOED, E. BRUCE. *Margaret Thatcher: In Victory and Downfall, 1987 and 1990.* Pp. xxxvi, 200. New York: Praeger, 1992. $47.95.

GEYER, FELIX and WALTER R. HEINZ, eds. *Alienation, Society, and the Individual: Continuity and Change in Theory and Research.* Pp. xxxiii, 221. New Brunswick, NJ: Transaction, 1992. $32.95.

GITELMAN, ZVI, ed. *The Quest for Utopia: Jewish Political Ideas and Institutions through the Ages.* Pp. xiii, 162. Armonk, NY: M. E. Sharpe, 1992. $39.95. Paperbound, $14.95.

GOODMAN, ALLAN E. and SANDRA CLEMENS BOGART, eds. *Making Peace: The United States and Conflict Resolution.* Pp. xiii, 132. Boulder, CO: Westview Press, 1991. $39.95. Paperbound, $10.95.

HADDAD, YVONNE YAZBECK, ed. *The Muslims of America.* Pp. x, 249. New York: Oxford University Press, 1991. $39.95.

HELLER, AGNES and FERENC FEHER. *The Grandeur and Twilight of Radical Universalism.* Pp. viii, 579. New Brunswick, NJ: Transaction, 1991. $39.95. Paperbound, $29.95.

HERZOG, LAWRENCE A. *Where North Meets South: Cities, Space, and Politics on the U.S.-Mexico Border.* Pp. xiv, 289. Austin: University of Texas Press, 1990. $24.95. Paperbound, $12.95.

HOLBRAAD, CARSTEN. *Danish Neutrality: A Study in the Foreign Policy of a Small State.* Pp. vi, 190. New York: Oxford University Press, 1991. $48.00.

HUGHES, HELEN, ed. *The Dangers of Export Pessimism: Developing Countries and Industrial Markets.* Pp. xxvii, 446. San Francisco: ICS Press, 1992. Paperbound, no price.

KAHN, JOEL S. and FRANCIS LOH KOK WAH, eds. *Fragmented Vision: Culture and Politics in Contemporary Malaysia.* Pp. vi, 326. Honolulu: University of Hawaii Press, 1992. $35.00.

KESSLEMAN, AMY. *Fleeting Opportunities: Women Shipyard Workers in Portland and Vancouver during World War II and Reconversion*. Pp. xii, 192. Albany: State University of New York Press, 1990. $14.95.

LISOWSKI, JOSEPH, ed. *Environment and Labor in the Caribbean: Caribbean Perspectives*. Vol. 2. Pp. viii, 148. New Brunswick, NJ: Transaction, 1992. Paperbound, $19.95.

MacGREGOR, DAVID. *Hegel, Marx, and the English State*. Pp. x, 345. Boulder, CO: Westview Press, 1992. $44.50.

MARKS, GARY and LARRY DIAMOND, eds. *Reexamining Democracy*. Pp. 365. Newbury Park, CA: Sage, 1992. $45.00.

MATHEW, WILLIAM M., ed. *Agriculture, Geology and Society in Antebellum South Carolina: The Private Diary of Edmund Ruffin, 1843*. Pp. xvi, 368. Athens: University of Georgia Press, 1992. $50.00.

MINGST, KAREN A. *Politics and the African Development Bank*. Pp. xii, 204. Lexington: University Press of Kentucky, 1990. $26.00.

MULLER, STEVEN and GEBHARD SCHWEIGLER, eds. *From Occupation to Cooperation: The United States and United Germany in a Changing World Order*. Pp. 288. New York: Norton, 1992. $24.95.

PEABODY, ROBERT L. and NELSON W. POLSBY. *New Perspectives on the House of Representatives*. 4th ed. Pp. ix, 386. Baltimore, MD: Johns Hopkins University Press, 1992. $55.00. Paperbound, $14.95.

ROGERS, DAVID E. and ELI GINZBERG, eds. *Adolescents at Risk: Medical and Social Perspectives*. Pp. viii, 168. Boulder, CO: Westview Press, 1992. $38.50. Paperbound, $12.00.

ROSENTHAL, MARILYNN and MARCEL FRENKEL, eds. *Health Care Systems and Their Patients: An International Perspective*. Pp. xix, 345. Boulder, CO: Westview Press, 1992. Paperbound, $39.95.

SHKLAR, JUDITH N. *The Faces of Injustice*. Pp. vii, 144. New Haven, CT: Yale University Press, 1992. $22.00. Paperbound, $10.00.

SINOPOLI, RICHARD C. *The Foundations of American Citizenship: Liberalism, the Constitution and Civic Virtue*. Pp. 215. New York: Oxford University Press, 1992. $32.50.

SPARKS, DONALD L. and DECEMBER GREEN. *Namibia: The Nation after Independence*. Pp. xi, 204. Boulder, CO: Westview Press, 1992. $38.00.

SUTTON, JOHN. *Sunk Costs and Market Structure: Price Competition, Advertising, and the Evolution of Concentration*. Pp. xiv, 577. Cambridge: MIT Press, 1991. $39.95.

TRAIN, KENNETH E. *Optimal Regulation: The Economic Theory of Natural Monopoly*. Pp. xiv, 338. Cambridge: MIT Press, 1991. $40.00.

WIENER, JOSHUA M. and JEANNIE ENGEL. *Improving Access to Health Services for Children and Pregnant Women*. Pp. x, 90. Washington, DC: Brookings Institution, 1991. Paperbound, $8.95.

WOLFE, NANCY TRAVIS. *Policing a Socialist Society: The German Democratic Republic*. Pp. xx, 244. Westport, CT: Greenwood Press, 1992. $55.00.

ZUIDERVAART, LAMBERT. *Adorno's Aesthetic Theory: The Redemption of Illusion*. Pp. xxiv, 388. Cambridge: MIT Press, 1991. $37.50.

INDEX

Affirmative action, 45-51, 55, 58-60, 108, 112, 182-85

AGENDA FOR TOMORROW: IMMIGRATION POLICY AND ETHNIC POLICIES, AN, Lawrence H. Fuchs, 171-86

American Immigration Control Foundation, 69

Americanization, 126-29, 143, 192

Anti-Catholicism, 17, 23-24, 66

Anti-Semitism
in France, 103-4
in the United States, 21-24, 26, 46-50, 57-59, 66

Assimilation, 122-36, 192-94
see also Immigrants, adaptation of to the United States

Bach, Robert L., 12

BACH, ROBERT L., Recrafting the Common Good: Immigration and Community, 155-70

Bayor, Ronald H., 11

BAYOR, RONALD H., Historical Encounters: Intergroup Relations in a "Nation of Nations," 14-27

Bilingualism, 163-64

Black Power, 45, 196

Blacks in the United States, 18, 24-26, 42-60, 81, 111-12, 126-36, 142, 144, 147-48, 191-93
Afro-Latinos, 38-39
culture, 201
economic opportunity, 52, 59-60
political collaboration with Jews, 53-56, 58
political participation, 53, 55-56
relations with nonblack immigrants, 194-97
slavery, 31, 44
voluntary black immigrants, 28-41

Bloom, Allan, 111-12

Bryce-Laporte, Roy Simón, 11

BRYCE-LAPORTE, ROY SIMÓN, Voluntary Immigration and Continuing Encounters between Blacks: The Post-Quincentenary Challenge, 28-41

Center for Immigration Studies, 69, 175

Chinese Exclusion Act, 66

Chinese-origin population in the United States, 19

Civil rights
civil rights in France, 97-108
civil rights movement (U.S.), 44-45, 50, 52-53, 59, 99
civil rights in the United States, 99-101

Cuban Loan Program, 85

Cubans in the United States, 19-20, 25-26, 85, 91-96

Cultural pluralism, 129-32, 192-93

Dutch-origin population in the United States, 15-16

Economic restructuring, and relations between immigrants and established residents in the United States, 161-63

English-origin population in the United States, 15-16

Environmentalism, and immigration restriction, 72-73, 175

Faludi, Susan, 118-19

Federation for American Immigration Reform, 68-69, 175

France
civil rights in, 97-108
and the Holocaust, 102
immigrants in, 101-2, 106-7
Jews in, 103-4
North Africans in, 101-3
race and ethnicity in, 97-108
racism, expression of, in, 98, 101, 104-5

Fuchs, Lawrence H., 12

FUCHS, LAWRENCE H., An Agenda for Tomorrow: Immigration Policy and Ethnic Policies, 171-86

Germans in the United States, 20-23

Glazer, Nathan, 12, 197

GLAZER, NATHAN, Is Assimilation Dead? 122-36

Gordon, Milton M., 199-200

Graff, Gerald, 116

Grant, Glen, 12

GRANT, GLEN and DENNIS M. OGAWA, Living Proof: Is Hawaii the Answer? 137-54

Great Depression, 32-33

Haitians in the United States, 81-82, 87, 91-96
Hawaii
  race relations, 137-54
  sugar plantations, 142-46
Hein, Jeremy, 12
HEIN, JEREMY, Rights, Resources, and Membership: Civil Rights Models in France and the United States, 97-108
Hirsch, E. D., 119
HISTORICAL ENCOUNTERS: INTERGROUP RELATIONS IN A "NATION OF NATIONS," Ronald H. Bayor, 14-27

Immigrants
  adaptation of to the United States, 74-96, 158, 180, 193-94
  admission of to the United States, 171-86
  American attitudes toward, 61-73, 156, 174-77, 189-91
  in France, 101-2, 106-7
  interactions of with established residents in the United States, 155-70, 198-99
  languages used by, 163-64, 182, 185
  see also Assimilation
Immigration Act of 1990, 33, 165-66, 172
Immigration Act of 1965, 33, 197-98
Immigration Act of 1924, 32-33
Immigration Reform Act of 1965, see Immigration Act of 1965
Immigration Reform and Control Act of 1986, 33, 69, 165, 172
Irish-origin population in the United States, 18, 20-22
  Irish Catholics, 16-17
  see also Anti-Catholicism
IS ASSIMILATION DEAD? Nathan Glazer, 122-36
Isolationism, 67-68
Italians in the United States, 19-20, 23, 25

Japanese-origin population in the United States, 23
Jews
  in France, 103-4
  political collaboration of with blacks in the United States, 53-56, 58
  in the United States, 20-25, 42-60
  see also Anti-Semitism

Labor market, 83, 85-87
Labor unions, and immigrants, 167
Lewis, Read, 134-35
LIVING PROOF: IS HAWAII THE ANSWER? Glen Grant and Dennis M. Ogawa, 137-54

Mexican-origin population in the United States, 87-89
Miami
  blacks in, 25-26
  Cubans in, 25-26, 91-96
  Haitian immigrant community in, 81-82, 87, 91-96
  Nicaraguans in, 91-96
  West Indians in, 91-96
Morris, Milton D., 11
MORRIS, MILTON D. and GARY E. RUBIN, The Turbulent Friendship: Black-Jewish Relations in the 1990s, 42-60
MULTICULTURALISM: BATTLEGROUND OR MEETING GROUND? Ronald Takaki, 109-21

National Association for the Advancement of White People, 69, 72
National Quota Act of 1924, 67
Nativism, 7, 16, 17, 19-21, 23-24, 26-27, 119-20
Negative Population Growth, 72
NEW SECOND GENERATION: SEGMENTED ASSIMILATION AND ITS VARIANTS, THE, Alejandro Portes and Min Zhou, 74-96
Nicaraguans in the United States, 91-96

"OF EVERY HUE AND CASTE": RACE, IMMIGRATION, AND PERCEPTIONS OF PLURALISM, Peter I. Rose, 187-202
Ogawa, Dennis M., 12
OGAWA, DENNIS M., see GRANT, GLEN, co-author
OLD MINORITIES, NEW IMMIGRANTS: ASPIRATIONS, HOPES, AND FEARS, Rita J. Simon, 61-73

Park, Robert E., 132-33
Pelley, William, 23-24
Population control, and immigration restriction, 69, 72, 175
Population Crisis Committee, 73
Population Environment Balance, 72-73
Portes, Alejandro, 12
PORTES, ALEJANDRO and MIN ZHOU, The New Second Generation: Segmented Assimilation and Its Variants, 74-96
Public schools, control of, 16, 17, 24-25, 45
Punjabi Sikhs in the United States, 89-91
Quota Act of 1921, 67

Race and ethnicity
  in France, 97-108

in the United States, 7-13, 14-27, 28-41, 42-60, 74-96, 109-21, 122-36, 137-54, 187-202
Racism
  in France, 98, 101, 104-5
  in the United States, 16, 26, 50-51, 57-58, 59, 83, 92, 95, 108, 148, 184, 189
Ravitch, Diane, 114
Reagan, Ronald
  and discrimination against minorities, 8-9
  and U.S. immigration policy, 175
RECRAFTING THE COMMON GOOD: IMMIGRATION AND COMMUNITY, Robert L. Bach, 155-70
Refugee Act of 1980, 33, 86, 165-66, 172
Refugees, admission of to the United States, 179
Reverse discrimination, 9
RIGHTS, RESOURCES, AND MEMBERSHIP: CIVIL RIGHTS MODELS IN FRANCE AND THE UNITED STATES, Jeremy Hein, 97-108
Rockford Institute, 69
ROSE, PETER I., "Of Every Hue and Caste": Race, Immigration, and Perceptions of Pluralism, 187-202
ROSE, PETER I., Preface, 7-13
Rubin, Gary E., 11
RUBIN, GARY E., see MORRIS, MILTON D., coauthor

Schlesinger, Arthur, Jr., 114-15, 138, 200
Sierra Club, 73
Simon, Rita J., 11-12
SIMON, RITA J., Old Minorities, New Immigrants: Aspirations, Hopes, and Fears, 61-73

Social sciences, attention to black immigrants, 34-35
Spaniards in the United States, 19-20
State Legalization Impact Assistance Grants, 165-66

Takaki, Ronald, 12
TAKAKI, RONALD, Multiculturalism: Battleground or Meeting Ground? 109-21
TURBULENT FRIENDSHIP: BLACK-JEWISH RELATIONS IN THE 1990s, THE, Milton D. Morris and Gary E. Rubin, 42-60

U.S. Citizens, Inc., 72
University curriculum, and multiculturalism, 109-21

Voluntary organizations, 164-69
VOLUNTARY IMMIGRATION AND CONTINUING ENCOUNTERS BETWEEN BLACKS: THE POST-QUINCENTENARY CHALLENGE, Roy Simón Bryce-Laporte, 28-41

West Indians in the United States, 91-96
World War I, and U.S. ethnic groups, 20, 23
World War II, and U.S. ethnic groups, 22-23

Ybor City, Florida, 19-20

Zero Population Growth, 72, 175
Zhou, Min, 12
ZHOU, MIN, see PORTES, ALEJANDRO, coauthor

The information you need to make intelligent judgments regarding the issues affecting you. . . your work. . . your society. . . and your world. Subscribe to

THE ANNALS

Subscription Order Form

	Individual			**Institution**		
	One Year	Two Years	Three Years	One Year	Two Years	Three Years
Hardcover	❏ $60	❏ $120	❏ $180	❏ $156	❏ $312	❏ $468
Softcover	❏ $42	❏ $84	❏ $126	❏ $132	❏ $264	❏ $396

Name / Institution _____

Address _____

_____

City _____ State _____ Zip _____ Country _____

❏ My check or credit card information is enclosed.   ❏ Bill me.

Charge my: ❏ MasterCard   ❏ Visa   Exp. Date _____

Account # _____ Signature _____

Prices effective through December 31, 1993. Make checks payable to Sage Publications. Institutional checks for personal orders cannot be accepted. In Canada, add 7% GST (#R129786448). On subscriptions outside the United States, add $9 per year for foreign postage. All foreign orders must be paid in U.S. funds.

Ⓢ **SAGE Publications, Inc.** • P.O. Box 5084 • Newbury Park, CA 91359 • (805) 499-0721   **T3627**

THE ANNALS

Gift Order Form

Please send **THE ANNALS** as my gift, preceded by a gift announcement in my name, to:

	Individual			**Institution**		
	One Year	Two Years	Three Years	One Year	Two Years	Three Years
Hardcover	❏ $60	❏ $120	❏ $180	❏ $156	❏ $312	❏ $468
Softcover	❏ $42	❏ $84	❏ $126	❏ $132	❏ $264	❏ $396

My Name _____   Gift To _____

Address _____   Address _____

City _____ State _____   City _____ State _____

Zip _____ Country _____   Zip _____ Country _____

❏ My check or credit card information is enclosed.   ❏ Bill me.

Charge my: ❏ MasterCard   ❏ Visa   Exp. Date _____

Account # _____ Signature _____

Prices effective through December 31, 1993. Make checks payable to Sage Publications. Institutional checks for personal orders cannot be accepted. In Canada, add 7% GST (#R129786448). On subscriptions outside the United States, add $9 per year for foreign postage. All foreign orders must be paid in U.S. funds.

Ⓢ **SAGE Publications, Inc.** • P.O. Box 5084 • Newbury Park, CA 91359 • (805) 499-0721   **T3627**